# CIVIL LIABILITIES IN AMERICAN POLICING

## A TEXT FOR LAW ENFORCEMENT PERSONNEL

# CIVIL LIABILITIES IN AMERICAN POLICING

## A TEXT FOR LAW ENFORCEMENT PERSONNEL

Rolando V. del Carmen

Criminal Justice Center
Sam Houston State University

Brady

A Prentice Hall Division
Englewood Cliffs, New Jersey 07632

Library of Congress Cataloging-in-Publication Data

Del Carmen, Rolando V.
   Civil liabilities in American policing : a text for law
enforcement personnel /Rolando V. del Carmen.
      p.   cm.
   Includes bibliographical references and index.
   ISBN 0-89303-135-6
   1. Police—Malpractice—United States. 2. Law enforcement—United
States. I. Title.
   KF1307.D45  1991
   346.7303′3—dc20                                          90-27580
   [347.30633]                                                  CIP


Aquisitions Editor: Natalie Anderson
Editorial/production supervision: Evalyn Schoppet
Cover design: Ben Santora
Manufacturing buyer: Mary McCartney
Prepress buyer: Ed O'Dougherty

© 1991 by Prentice-Hall, Inc.
A Division of Simon & Schuster
Englewood Cliffs, New Jersey 07632

Printed in the United States of America
10   9   8   7   6   5   4   3   2

ISBN 0-89303-135-6

Prentice-Hall International (UK) Limited, London
Prentice-Hall of Australia Pty. Limited, Sydney
Prentice-Hall Canada Inc., Toronoto
Prentice-Hall Hispanoamericana, S.A., Mexico
Prentice-Hall of India Private Limited, New Delhi
Prentice-Hall of Japan, Inc., Tokyo
Simon & Schuster Asia Pte. Ltd., Singapore
Editora Prentice-Hall do Brasil, Ltda., Rio de Janiero

This book is dedicated to all law enforcement personnel who live under the cloud of lawsuits daily in their difficult work of policing a free and democratic society.

# CONTENTS

# PREFACE

Lawsuits are a way of life in the United States. Court litigation affects just about every phase of American life, including education, business, religion, medicine, the arts, the economy, and corrections, to name just a few. Law enforcement has not been spared; in fact, it has had more than its proper share of liability lawsuits.

Law enforcement officers will continue to be sued by the public in the foreseeable future, primarily because of the nature of their work. Law enforcement involves using force—sometimes deadly force—and making unwelcome decisions that deprive individuals of unfettered choice or unrestrained freedom. A person who, justly or unjustly, feels wronged by the police finds the court an appealing avenue for redress. In a free society, lawsuits are an occupational hazard with which police officers must learn to live and cope.

Law enforcement officers must know the basics of civil liabilities in hopes that such knowledge will minimize the possibility of their being sued or, if sued, of being held liable. It is to that end that this book was written. Gone are the days when "ignorance is bliss," particularly in the area of policing.

The law on civil liabilities is complex and often difficult to master. This text seeks to translate legal concepts into terms that laypersons without any legal background can understand. It is not a book for lawyers. It must be stressed, however, that the book is written for a national audience; therefore, many of the concepts discussed may not apply to particular jurisdictions. The text is written mainly for general informational purposes and is not meant to be a source of legal advice. Such advice must be sought and obtained from agency legal counsels or lawyers in private practice in particular jurisdictions.

This book would not have been possible without the help of individuals with expertise in the field of legal liabilities. The author would like to thank the many reviewers without whose help and critique this book would have been more difficult to write. They are (in no particular order): Steve Rittenmeyer of Western Illinois University, Macomb, Illinois; William C. Collins, Attorney at Law, Olympia, Washington; Richard Becker, North Harris County College, Houston, Texas; Larry Michal Scheck, Assistant Division Head of the Law Enforcement and Security Training Division, Texas A & M University, College Station, Texas; Timothy N. Hunter, Lieutenant, Hollywood Police Department, Hollywood, Florida; Dennis Waller of Kevin Parsons & Associates, Inc., Appleton, Wisconsin; Raymond Beach, Jr.; Emory A. Plitt, Jr., Assistant Attorney General, Department of Public Safety, Baltimore, Maryland; Donna Sheperd, American Police Academy, Washington, D.C.; Norman Raasch, Lakeland Community College, Mentor, Ohio; and Thomas J. Bader, Cleveland Electric Illuminating Company, Cleveland, Ohio.

I would also like to thank my students at the College of Criminal Justice of Sam Houston State University, and the many law enforcement officers with whom I have had the privilege to interact in the various continuing education programs in Texas and other states. From them I have learned a lot.

Rolando V. del Carmen

# WHY KNOW ABOUT CIVIL LIABILITIES?

## INTRODUCTION

A legal wit has said, with a grain of truth, that suing police officials has become a popular sport in the United States. While no comprehensive figures are readily available, it is reported that in one state alone claims amounting to more than $325 million in 1983 were filed against police officers.[1] Multiplying that figure by the number of states in the country gives an indication of the amount of damage claims sought in liability lawsuits against law enforcement officers and agencies that year. Headlines like the following highlight the seriousness of the problem:

MARYLAND TROOPER ORDERED TO PAY INJURED MAN $2 MILLION[2]

NEW ORLEANS AGREES TO PAY $2.8 MILLION TO SETTLE 13 ALLEGED POLICE BRUTALITY SUITS[3]

OVER $100,000 AWARDED TO ARRESTEE KICKED BY OFFICER RESPONDING TO DOMESTIC DISTURBANCE CALL[4]

CASE OF POLICE FAILURE TO HANDLE COMPLAINTS ABOUT VIOLENT HUSBAND SETTLED FOR $1.9 MILLION[5]

USE OF DEADLY FORCE AGAINST NONDANGEROUS FLEEING FELON RESULTS IN $472,000 JUDGMENT[6]

## I. LIABILITY AWARDS

It is reported that in 1982 the average jury award in liability lawsuits filed against cities or city agencies was $230,000. In 1985, that average went up to $2 million. In 1966, only one lawsuit against a city had ever resulted in a jury award exceeding $1 million. By 1983, there were more than 350 such judgments.[7]

Many damage awards are eventually settled for a lower amount because plaintiffs may be unwilling to go through the delay and uncertainty of the appellate process. In a survey of jury awards, the South Carolina Bar Association found that, between 1976 and 1986, in roughly half of the cases where the award was $100,000 or more in that state the parties settled for a lower amount.[8] Another study showed that, between 1982 and 1984, in some California and Illinois counties jury awards to plaintiffs were reduced in about 25 percent of all verdicts won by the plaintiffs. On the average, the awards were cut in half, the larger verdicts getting the biggest cuts.[9] A third study found that of 198 verdicts (including nonpolice cases) totalling $700 million, the amount actually paid to victims was $339 million, a reduction of more than 55 percent.[10] Despite these figures, damage awards can be high in many cases, and the time and effort required can be a drain on an agency's limited resources.

## II. INCREASE IN THE NUMBER OF LAWSUITS

The number of civil liability cases filed against the police continues to grow. An early survey conducted by the International Association of Chiefs of Police showed that the number of civil suits against the police rose from 1,741 in 1967 to 3,894 in 1971. Estimates indicated that by 1975 the number of lawsuits alleging police misconduct exceeded 6,000 a year.[11] The same survey showed that more than 40 percent of the lawsuits filed during the five-year period alleged false arrest, false imprisonment, malicious prosecution, or all three related torts. Twenty-seven percent alleged excessive use of force by officers and another six percent claimed a misuse of firearms. Less than one-fourth of the cases filed went to trial, and out of those fewer than one in five resulted in judgment for the plaintiff.[12]

## III. AREAS OF LITIGATION

A 1986 survey of police chiefs from the 20 largest cities and dozens of other municipalities with populations over 100,000 revealed that most of the police chiefs, their officers, and their agencies have been sued in the past and expect to be sued in the future. The survey revealed that lawsuits were brought most often in the following areas (listed in descending order of importance):[13]

1.  use of force

2.  auto pursuits

3.  arrests/searches

4.  employee drug tests

5.  hiring and promotion

6.  discrimination based on race/sex/age

7.  insurance, risk management

8.  recordkeeping and privacy

9.  jail management

In Houston, Texas, the number of complaints alleging police misconduct soared by 245 percent between 1980 and 1985. In 1980, a total of 432 complaints were brought to the Houston Police Department's internal affairs division; that number increased to 972 in 1985. The most frequent allegations involved misconduct or verbal abuse (340 complaints in 1985), misconduct or improper procedure (314), criminal activity (124), excessive force (174), and harassment (20).[14] Commenting on these numbers, the then Houston Police Chief Lee P. Brown said that the reasons for the rise in complaints were threefold: "No. 1, we have more officers. No. 2, the public has more faith in us [to follow through on investigations]. And No. 3, we have gone through the process of encouraging the reports." Chief Brown added that it was unfair to compare Houston's statistics with those of other cities, because some cities don't log every complaint (such as anonymous phone complaints), whereas Houston keeps an accurate record of each one.[15] This points to a problem in liability cases—the inconclusiveness of complaint figures based on frequency. It may indeed be that some cities are doing a better job of monitoring complaints than others. Whatever the cause, the consensus is that the number of lawsuits is high and that collectively lawsuits have had an impact on police management and practices.

## IV. POLICE WIN MOST LAWSUITS

While it is true that the number of lawsuits is high, cases decided in favor of the police are more numerous than those where liability is imposed, and headlines like the following are more common than those heralding liability:

NO MUNICIPAL LIABILITY FOR INJURY CAUSED BY STUN GUNS WHEN OFFICERS USE THEM IN MANNER INCONSISTENT WITH EXPRESS POLICY[16]

KNOWLEDGE OF SPECIAL DANGER TO WOMAN SHOT BY FORMER BOYFRIEND WAS INSUFFICIENT TO IMPOSE LIABILITY ON OFFICERS AND CITY[17]

CITY NOT LIABLE TO MOTORIST INJURED BY FLEEING SUSPECT'S AUTO: OFFICERS EXERCISED DUE CARE DURING HIGH SPEED PURSUIT[18]

INVESTIGATING AND RESPONDING TO 911 CALL CREATES NO DUTY TO GIVE PROTECTION; NO LIABILITY FOR WOMAN'S ASSAULT AFTER POLICE LEFT HER OUT OF GAS[19]

Not every police officer is sued, and at least one study shows that most lawsuits are decided in favor of the police. Nonetheless, lawsuits can be bothersome and their results unpredictable.

Civil liability lawsuits are not limited to police work. They are brought with increased frequency against private persons, business enterprises, and public officials. In 1986, civil rights actions—one type of lawsuit usually brought against police officers—accounted for 11 percent of private party cases in federal courts. That same year, there were 29,333 prisoner petitions, compared with 19,574 in 1980.[20] Liability awards, in general, have also increased dramatically. In 1970, there were only seven multimillion-dollar damage awards involving private and public persons. In 1984, that figure had gone up to 401.[21] These figures do not include the number of damage awards of less than $1 million or the unknown number of cases that are settled out of court without trial.

## V. FRIVOLOUS LAWSUITS

Despite these figures, only a small number of lawsuits against public officials succeed and most lawsuits never go to trial. For example, in 1979, only 3.5 percent of the thousands of civil rights cases filed by state prisoners went to trial.[22] One reason may be that many lawsuits filed against public officers are based on frivolous or whimsical grounds as in the following examples:

- A convict whose sentence was increased for escaping sued the county and its sheriff, accusing them of negligence in failing to prevent the escape.[23]

- A man sued the state of Pennsylvania for $5 quadrillion, saying that suspension of his driver's license by the Pennsylvania Transportation Department ruined his life and reputation.[24]

- A man sought revocation of the city charter, $15 million, and the right to combat police officers to death.[25]

Cases like the above do not succeed; nonetheless, even if plaintiff's complaint is groundless and absurd, attention must be given to it, because failure to respond or to respond in time leads to judgment for the plaintiff by default. It is important that law enforcement officers be familiar with the basics of legal liabilities if they are to minimize, if not avoid, the hazards of civil liability lawsuits that ensue from their exercise of power and authority. Court intervention leading to accountability has become a part of present-day policing and is a reality to which officers are constantly exposed. Some civil liability lawsuits do succeed and result in huge damage and attorney's fees awards. A good working knowledge of police civil liabilities helps minimize liability exposure and forewarns officers of the legal pitfalls in policing a free and democratic society in which access to a law court is a fundamental right of each citizen.

## SUMMARY

The last two decades have been punctuated by liability lawsuits brought against police. Headlines proclaiming the awarding of damages to plaintiffs as a result of what the police do or fail to do have become common. The number of lawsuits against the police is high, and liability awards are sometimes staggering.

The police are vulnerable to lawsuits in various areas of their work, including the use of force, vehicle pursuits, and arrests. Many lawsuits against the police are frivolous and without basis, and these are often dismissed in court without trial. Although the police win most civil liability lawsuits, such suits nonetheless lead to concerns about legal representation and indemnification. Liability lawsuits have become part of police work, and officers must live with the risk and learn to cope.

## NOTES

1.  *Liability Reporter*, February 1983, at 11.
2.  *Crime Control Digest*, April 14, 1986, at 6.
3.  *Ibid.*, at 2.
4.  *Liability Reporter*, November 1986, at 3.
5.  *Liability Reporter*, September 1987, at 11.
6.  *Liability Reporter*, August 1987, at 6.
7.  H. Cisneros, "High Time for Cities to Fight Back," *The Houston Chronicle*, April 13, 1986, Section 6, at 4.
8.  *Changing Times Magazine*, October 1987, at 12.
9.  *Ibid.*
10. *The Houston Chronicle*, November 1, 1986, at 11.
11. W. Schmidt, "Recent Trends in Police Tort Litigation," *The Urban Lawyer*, Fall 1976, at 682.
12. *Ibid.*
13. C. McCoy, "Police Legal Liability Is Not a Crisis," *Crime Control Digest*, January 19, 1987, at 1.
14. *The Houston Chronicle*, August 8, 1986, at 1.
15. *Ibid.*

16.  *Liability Reporter*, October 1987, at 9.
17.  *Ibid.*, at 12.
18.  *Liability Reporter*, September 1987, at 11.
19.  *Liability Reporter*, July 1987, at 11.
20.  "The Federal Civil Justice System," *Bureau of Justice Statistics*, July 1987, at 4.
21.  "Sky-High Damage Suits," *U.S. News & World Report*, January 27, 1986, at 35.
22.  *Recommended Procedures for Handling Prisoner Civil Rights Cases in the Federal Courts* (The Federal Judicial Center, 1980), at 9–10.
23.  "Everybody Is Suing Everybody," *Changing Times Magazine*, April 1983, at 76.
24.  *The Huntsville Item*, February 16, 1985, at 1.
25.  *Liability Reporter*, June 1987, at 8.

# 2

# THE BIG PICTURE: OVERVIEW OF LEGAL LIABILITIES

Police legal liabilities come from many sources, including state and federal laws, and they carry civil, criminal, and administrative sanctions. For the purpose of an overview, legal liabilities may be categorized as in Table 2.1.

Liability categories differ in the following ways:

- Civil liabilities result in monetary awards for nominal, actual, or punitive damages and/or injunctions.
- Criminal liabilities result in imprisonment, probation, fines, or other forms of criminal sanction.
- Administrative liabilities lead to dismissal, demotion, transfer, reprimand, or other forms of sanction authorized by state law or agency rules or guidelines.

Two points need emphasis. First, the above liabilities apply to all public officers, not just to police officers. Probation and parole officers, jailers, prison officials, and other personnel in the criminal justice system are liable under the above provisions. Second, an officer may be liable under more than one of the above categories based on what essentially may be a single act. For example, an officer unjustifiably uses brutal force on an arrestee, resulting in severe injury. The officer (1) may be liable for conspiracy if he or she acted with another officer to deprive the arrestee of civil rights and (2) may also be liable for beating the arrestee. The officer may be prosecuted criminally and civilly under federal law and then held criminally and civilly liable under state law for the same act. The double jeopardy defense cannot be invoked by the officer, because *double jeopardy applies only in criminal cases when successive prosecu-*

**TABLE 2.1**
**Summary of Police Legal Liabilities**

|  | I. State Law | II. Federal Law |
|---|---|---|
| A. Civil Liabilites | 1. State Tort Law<br>2. State Civil Rights Law<br>3. State Constitutional Claims | 1. Title 42 of U.S. Code, Section 1983: Civil Action for Deprivation of Civil Rights<br>2. Title 42 of U.S. Code, Section 1985: Conspiracy to Interfere with Civil Rights<br>3. Title 42 of U.S. Code, Section 1981: Equal Rights under the Law |
| B. Criminal Liabilites | 1. State Penal Code Provisions Applicable Only to Public Officials<br>2. State Penal Code Provisions Applicable to Everybody, including Public Officials | 1. Title 18 of U.S. Code, Section 242: Criminal Liability for Deprivation of Civil Rights<br>2. Title 18 of U.S. Code, Section 241: Criminal Liability for Conspiracy to Deprive a Person of Rights<br>3. Title 18 of U.S. Code, Section 245: Violation of Federally Protected Activities |
| C. Administrative Liabilites | Agency Rules or Guidelines Applicable to State or Local Agencies | Federal Agency Rules or Guidelines Applicable to Federal Agencies |

tions are made by the same jurisdiction for the same offense. If one case is civil and the other is criminal, or if criminal prosecutions for essentially the same act are made by different jurisdictions (state and federal), the double jeopardy provision of the Constitution does not apply.

## I. UNDER STATE LAW

### A. Civil Liabilities

**1. *State Tort Law.*** This type of liability is discussed in detail in Chapter 3. It is sufficient to state here that a *tort is defined as a private* *wrong, other than a breach of contract, in which the action of one person causes injury to the person or property of another in violation of a legal duty imposed by law.* Torts may be categorized as follows: intentional torts, negligence torts, and other related torts. Each category in turn has subcategories.

**2. *State Civil Rights Law.*** Some states have civil rights laws that are similar in provision to the various federal civil rights laws. They provide civil remedies for violations and are enacted to facilitate implementation of federal civil rights laws on the state level. Reenactment of such laws by a state gives that state authority to monitor and enforce compliance without having to rely on federal agencies, which sometimes do not have enough personnel to implement the laws nationwide. In general, reenactment by a state of federal laws ensures a more effective enforcement of the laws by state authorities. In many cases, federal officials will leave the implementation of reenacted laws to state officials, with minimum federal interference.

### B. Criminal Liabilities

**1. *State Penal Code Provisions Applicable Only to Public Officials.*** Most states have provisions criminalizing acts of public officials that violate the rights or destroy properties of individuals. For example, Section 39.02 of the Texas Penal Code contains a provision on *Official Oppression* stating that a public servant acting under color of his office or employment commits an offense if he

a) intentionally subjects another to mistreatment or to arrest, detention, search, seizure, dispossession, assessment, or lien that he knows is unlawful; or

b) intentionally denies or impedes another in the exercise or enjoyment of any right, privilege, power, or immunity knowing his conduct is unlawful.

Another provision of the Texas Penal Code, Section 39.021, makes violations of the civil rights of a prisoner a criminal act. It provides that a jailer or guard employed at a municipal or county jail by the Texas Department of Corrections or a peace officer commits an offense if he

a) intentionally subjects a person in custody to bodily injury knowing his conduct is unlawful; or

b) willfully denies or impedes a person in custody in the exercise of enjoyment of any right, privilege, or immunity knowing his conduct is unlawful.

**2. State Penal Code Provisions Applicable to Everybody, Including Public Officers.** In addition to specific provisions that are applicable only to public officials, police officers may be liable just like any other person under the other provisions of the state penal code. For example, an officer may be liable for murder, manslaughter, serious physical injury, assault and battery, and other criminal acts committed in line of duty. Again, the double jeopardy prohibition does not apply, because while the prosecutions are by the same jurisdiction, the elements of the criminal acts are different.

### C. Administrative Liabilities

In addition to state, federal, and constitutional laws, police agencies are governed and bound by their own administrative rules and procedures, whether these be in the form of a handbook, a manual, or guidelines. In some states, no rules or laws apply statewide, hence police agencies are on their own and may devise rules and procedures for disciplinary action. These rules and procedures are valid and binding as long as they do not violate an officer's rights under the Constitution, state or federal laws, or court decisions. Agency rules are presumed valid but may be challenged by an officer in court as violative of constitutional or legal rights. For example, an agency rule may prohibit public criticism of agency policy by officers and provide for dismissal without hearing if violated. Such rule may be challenged in court as violative of an officer's constitutional right to freedom of speech (for the cause of dismissal) and due process (for dismissal without a hearing). Whether such legal challenge succeeds or not has not been authoritatively settled by the United States Supreme Court.

## II. UNDER FEDERAL LAW

### A. Civil Liabilities

**1. Title 42 of the U.S. Code, Section 1983: Civil Action for Deprivation of Civil Rights.** This type of liability is discussed in detail in Chapter 4. It is sufficient to state here that a Section 1983 is a civil lawsuit for money damages and/or declaratory relief (as in prison cases), usually filed by the plaintiff in federal court, brought against an officer who has allegedly violated the plaintiff's constitutional rights while acting under color of state law. This is the remedy most often used by plaintiffs (for reasons mentioned in Chapter 4).

**2. Title 42 of the U.S. Code, Section 1985: Conspiracy to Interfere with Civil Rights.** Section 1985 (3) affords a civil remedy against any two or more officers, who

> conspire to deprive a plaintiff of equal protection of the law or equal privileges and immunities under the law, with
>
> a purposeful intent to deny equal protection of the law,
>
> when defendants act under color of state law, and
>
> the acts in furtherance of the conspiracy injure the plaintiff in his person or property, or deprive him of having and exercising a right of privilege of a citizen of the United States.

Section 1985, passed by the United States Congress in 1861, provides for civil damages to be awarded to any individual who can show that two or more officers conspired to deprive him or her of civil rights. An officer may therefore be civilly liable not only for *actually depriving* a person of civil rights (under Section 1983) but also for *conspiring to deprive* that person of civil rights (under Section 1985).

EXAMPLE: Three police officers agree to beat a detainee after booking. These officers may be civilly liable under (1) Section 1983 for *beating* the detainee and therefore depriving him or her of due process rights and under (2) Section 1985 for *conspiring* to beat the detainee.

Section 1983 and Section 1985 are separate, hence violations thereof are punished separately. Under Section 1985, it must be shown that the officers got together and actually agreed to commit the act, although no exact statement of a common goal need be proven. The plaintiff must also be able to prove that the officers intended to deprive him or her of equal protection guaranteed by law. Section 1985, however, is seldom used against public officers, because conspiracy is often difficult to prove except through the testimony of a co-conspirator. Moreover, it is limited to situations in which the objective of the conspiracy is invidious discrimination, which is also hard to prove in court. It is often difficult for a plaintiff to establish that the officer's action was discriminatorily based on sex, race, or national origin.

**3. Title 42 of the U.S. Code, Section 1981: Equal Rights under the Law.** This law provides that

> all persons within the jurisdiction of the United States shall have the same rights in every State and Territory to make and enforce contracts, to sue, be parties, give evidence, and to the full and equal benefit of all laws and proceedings for the security of persons and property as is enjoyed by white citizens, and shall be subject to like punishment, pains, penalties, taxes, licenses, and exactions of every kind, and to no other.

This statute was enacted in 1870, a year earlier than the more popular Section 1983 (otherwise known as the civil rights statute). In one sense its scope is broader than that of Section 1983, because it does not require that the constitutional violation be made under color of state law. Until recently, the plaintiff had to show that he or she was discriminated against because of race, which limited the number of potential plaintiffs. Section 1981 has been widely used in employment and housing discrimination cases, seldom in cases of police action. The courts are in the process of expanding the meaning of this law, so it could be a basis for more extensive litigation in the future.

## B. Criminal Liabilities

1. *Title 18 of the U.S. Code, Section 242: Criminal Liability for Deprivation of Civil Rights.* This law provides that

> whoever, under color of any law, statute, ordinance, regulation, or custom, willfully subjects any inhabitant of any State, Territory, or District to the deprivation of any rights, privileges, or immunities secured or protected by the Constitution or laws of the United States, or to different punishments, pains, or penalties on account of such inhabitant being an alien, or by reason of his color, or race that are prescribed for the punishment of citizens, shall be fined not more than $1,000 or imprisoned not more than one year, or both; and if death results shall be subject to imprisonment for any term of years or for life.

The essential elements of Section 242 are these: (1) The defendant must have been acting under color of law; (2) there must have occurred a deprivation of some right secured by federal laws and the United States Constitution; and (3) the defendant must have specifically intended to deprive the victim of the right. This law provides criminal penalty for the same act for which an officer may be civilly liable under Section 1983. The "color of state law" requirement makes the law applicable primarily to public officials, since private persons do not act under color of state law (with some exceptions, such as when a private person conspires with a police officer to deprive a suspect of constitutional rights).

2. *Title 18 of the U.S. Code, Section 241: Criminal Liability for Conspiracy to Deprive a Person of Rights.* This section provides that

> if two or more persons conspire to injure, oppress, threaten, or intimidate any citizen in the free exercise or enjoyment of any right or privilege secured to him by the Constitution or laws of the United States, or because of his exercise of the same . . . [they shall be guilty of a felony]. . . . They shall be fined not more than $10,000 or imprisoned not more than ten years, or

both; and if death results, they shall be subject to imprisonment for any term of years or for life.

The requirements under this section are as follows: (1) There must be a conspiracy whose purpose is to injure, oppress, threaten, or intimidate; (2) one or more of the intended victims must be a United States citizen; and (3) the conspiracy must be directed at the free exercise or enjoyment by such a citizen of any right or privilege under federal laws or the United States Constitution. Section 241 provides criminal penalty for the same act for which an officer may be civilly liable under Section 1985.

The main distinction between Section 242 and Section 241 is that Section 242 punishes the *act itself,* whereas Section 241 punishes the *conspiracy* to commit the act. Inasmuch as conspiracy, by definition, needs at least two participants, Section 241 cannot be committed by a person acting alone. Moreover, while Section 242 requires the officer to be acting "under the color of law," there is no such requirement under Section 241; hence Section 241 can be committed by a private person. As worded, Section 242 is also broader, in that it punishes violations against an inhabitant of any state or territory of the United States, whereas Section 241 applies only if the victim is a citizen.

**3. *Title 18 of the U.S. Code, Section 245: Federally Protected Activities.*** This section is aimed at private individuals but is also applicable to public officers who forcibly interfere with federally protected activities. The first part of the statute concerns forcible interference with such activities as

- voting or running for an elective office
- participating in government-administered programs
- enjoying the benefits of federal employment
- serving as juror in a federal court
- participating in any program receiving federal financial assistance

Violations of Section 245 carry a fine of not more than $1,000 or imprisonment of not more than one year, or both. Should death result from a violation, imprisonment can be for life. Section 245 is a more recent federal statute, passed in 1968, that seeks to punish private individuals who forcibly interfere with federally protected activities. Therefore, it applies to officers who act in a private capacity.

The second part of Section 245 refers to deprivations of such rights as the right to attend a public school or college; participate in state or locally sponsored programs; serve on a state jury; travel interstate; or use accomodations serving the public, such as eating places, gas stations, and motels. The third part penalizes interference with persons who encourage or give opportunity for others to participate in or enjoy the rights enumerated in the statute.

### C. Administrative Liabilities

Administrative liabilities under federal law apply to federal law enforcement officers. For example, officers of the Federal Bureau of Investigation or the Treasury Department have agency rules that govern their actions. Violations of these rules lead to firing, demotion, or other disciplinary consequences as determined by the agency. As in the case of state agencies, these rules are valid and binding as long as they do not infringe on an officer's rights under the Constitution, state or federal laws, or court decisions. Rules of federal administrative agencies apply only to federal officials; hence state police officers are not governed by federal administrative rules.

### SUMMARY

Legal liabilities of police officers may be classified into two general categories: liabilities under state law and liabilities under federal law. State and federal liabilities may both be subclassified into civil liabilities, criminal liabilities, and administrative liabilities.

Civil liabilities result in monetary award for damages; criminal liabilities result in imprisonment, probation, fine, or other forms of criminal sanction; and administrative liabilities lead to dismissal, demotion, transfer, reprimand, or other forms of sanction authorized by state law or agency regulations.

The above liabilities apply to all public officers, not just to police officers. An officer may be liable under any or all of these laws and rules based on what may be essentially a single act, if all the liability requisites are present.

Criminal liabilities are mentioned briefly in this chapter, while the specifics of administrative liabilities are not discussed at all. The succeeding chapters will discuss various aspects and forms of civil liabilities to the exclusion of criminal and administrative liabilities.

# 3

# CIVIL LIABILITY
# UNDER STATE TORT LAW

This chapter discusses principles under state tort law. The purpose is to familiarize readers with general tort principles and categories of state tort. The principles applicable to specific tort cases (such as false arrest and imprisonment, use of force, search and seizure, negligence, and other types of police conduct) are addressed in detail in Chapters 7–12.

## I. TORT DEFINED

The term *tort* comes from the Latin term *torquere*, which means "to twist, twisted, or wrested aside."[1] Hence a tort is a "twisted" or wrongful act. The act can be described as *tortious*, while the perpetrator is known as a *tortfeasor*.

A tort is defined as a civil wrong, other than a breach of contract, in which the action of one person causes injury to the person or property of another in violation of a legal duty imposed by law. The plaintiff's aim in a tort case is to recover damages from the defendant in an effort to redress an alleged wrong.

State tort law usually represents the accumulation of judicial decisions, and hence it may not be as clear or precise as other remedies established by statute. For example, criminal acts in a state are defined with clarity and precision by that state's penal code. In some states, tort law principles have been codified and enacted into law by the legislature, but that is the exception rather than the rule. Moreover, judicial decisions and legislative acts in some states occasionally add to the category of tortious acts, thus further expanding the scope of tort law.

In most tort lawsuits involving alleged police wrongdoing, the lawsuit is brought against the police officer, the supervisor, and the state or local agency-employer. Tort actions against the federal government are available, but they are usually brought under the Federal Tort Claims Act, which lies beyond the scope of this text.

Tortious acts vary in name and scope from one state to another; nonetheless, general principles are identifiable, and the discussion below concerns these.

## II. KINDS OF STATE TORTS

There are three general categories of state torts, based on a person's conduct or failure to act: (1) intentional tort, (2) negligence tort, and (3) strict liability tort. Of the three, only intentional and negligence torts are used in police cases. Strict liability torts are applicable in activities that are abnormally dangerous such that they cannot be carried out safely even with reasonable care. An example would be operating a nuclear plant; despite safety precautions, risks are a part of the operation. Police work does not fall under strict liability tort; hence that category will not be discussed.

### A. Intentional Torts

*Intentional torts* may be against *person* or *property*. This chapter will not discuss intentional torts against property, focusing instead on torts against persons, because these are the torts to which police officers are often exposed.

*An intentional tort occurs when there is an intention on the part of an officer to bring some physical or mental harm upon another person.* An example is an officer arresting a person without justification or beating a suspect to extract a confession. "Intent" is difficult to define with precision, but in the context of tort, it generally means bringing about some sort of physical or mental effect on another person. That "effect" does not have to be a physical harm. A mental harm suffices.

EXAMPLE: Pointing a loaded gun at a suspect without a justification does not inflict physical harm but it can certainly have a negative mental effect; hence it qualifies as a tortious act.

The problem for the plaintiff in intentional tort cases is that intent is mental and therefore may be difficult for the plaintiff to prove in court. Judges and juries, however, are generally allowed to presume intent from the facts of the case.

EXAMPLE: An officer takes a person to the police station in handcuffs for questioning. When charged with false arrest, the officer denies that he or she intended to place the person under arrest. The judge or jury will most likely reject that defense, because handcuffing a suspect almost always denotes arrest, regardless of what the officer later says. In many cases, denial becomes hard to believe because of what the officer did. In these cases, actions often speak louder than words.

In most states, tort law is a product of common law and judicial decisions. It is therefore more flexible than criminal law and continues to expand. Tortious acts vary greatly from one state to another; only the kinds of tort lawsuit most often brought against police officers are discussed here.

**1. *Excessive Use of Force.*** The police are often charged with "brutality" or using "excessive force." In police work, the improper use of force usually constitutes the tort of battery or assault. *The general rule is that nondeadly force may be used by the police in various situations as long as such force is reasonable.* "Reasonable force," in turn, refers to force that a prudent and cautious man would use if exposed to similar circumstances and that is necessary to achieve legal and proper results. Any force beyond that necessary to achieve legal and proper results is punitive—meaning it punishes rather than controls—and is therefore unreasonable.

EXAMPLE: In one case, the court found that the police used excessive force on a family when responding to a call to settle a neighborhood dispute. The court said that excessive force was used on the father, who was not of great physical strength and who was already being subdued by his brother when the police kicked him in the groin and struck him on the head with a nightstick. It was alleged that the officers kicked the mother on the back and buttocks after she was handcuffed and lying face down in the mud. The son was also injured during the arrest process. The police were held liable for $10,000. Lewis v. Down, 774 F.2d 711 (6th Cir. 1985).

The reasonableness of the use of force, deadly or nondeadly, is determined according to an "objective reasonableness" standard. This means that police behavior "must be judged from the perspective of a reasonable officer on the scene, rather than with the 20/20 vision of hindsight." Graham v. Connor, 45 Crl 3033 (1989).

**2. *False Arrest and False Imprisonment.*** In a tort case for false arrest, the plaintiff alleges that the officer made an "illegal arrest" under state law, which usually means an arrest without probable cause or a valid arrest warrant. False arrest also arises if the officer arrests a person other than the one named in the warrant or if the warrant was issued illegally, as when the magistrate thought there was probable cause when in fact there was none.

An officer is better protected from possible civil liability if the arrest is made with a warrant. The officer making a warrantless arrest bears the burden of proving that the arrest was in fact grounded on probable cause and that an arrest warrant was not necessary because the arrest came under one of the many exceptions to the warrant rule. In contrast, if the arrest is made with a warrant, the presumption is that probable cause exists, as determined by a magistrate, and therefore there is no liability on the part of the officer. Liability arises only if the officer obtained the warrant with malice, knowing that there was no probable cause. Malley v. Briggs, 475 U.S. 335 (1986). Civil liability in arrests with warrant is therefore unlikely unless the officer serves a warrant which he or she knows to be illegal or unconstitutional.

EXAMPLE: Officer M serves an unsigned warrant or a warrant which he or she knows is issued for the wrong person. If sued, Officer M will be liable for false arrest despite the issuance of a warrant.

*False arrest* is different from *false imprisonment*, but in police tort cases one follows the other. This is because arrest denotes some form of confinement, which is also an element of imprisonment. They are similar, in that in both cases the individual is restrained or deprived of freedom without legal justification. They differ, however, in that false arrest leads to false imprisonment but false imprisonment is not necessarily the result of false arrest.

EXAMPLE 1: A suspect is arrested with probable cause (therefore, the arrest is valid) but is detained in jail beyond the legal period allowable without charges being filed (this constitutes false imprisonment).

EXAMPLE 2: An officer makes a warrantless arrest based on what he or she thought was probable cause but later discovers that the person is in fact innocent. In this case, continued imprisonment is false imprisonment even though the arrest was valid.

**3. *Assault and Battery.*** Although sometimes combined into one term, *assault* and *battery* refer to two separate acts. *Assault is the intentional causing of an apprehension of harmful or offensive conduct; it is the attempt or threat, accompanied by the apparent ability, to inflict bodily harm on another person.* An assault is committed if the officer causes another person to think that he or she will be subjected to harmful or offensive contact.

EXAMPLE: If for no justifiable reason, Officer X draws and points a gun at another person, Officer X may be guilty of assault. In many jurisdictions, words alone will not constitute assault. There must be an act to accompany the threatening words.

In contrast, *battery is the intentional, undesired, and unprovoked infliction of a harmful or offensive body contact on another person.* Given this broad definition, the potential for battery exists every time an officer applies force on a suspect or arrestee without justification. The main difference between assault and battery is that assault is generally menacing conduct that results in a person's fear of imminently receiving a battery, while battery involves unlawful, unwarranted, or hostile touching, however slight. In some jurisdictions, assault is attempted battery; therefore the two terms tend to be used together.

**4. *Wrongful Death.*** This tort, usually established by law and found in all states, arises whenever death occurs as a result of an officer's unjustified action. It is brought by the surviving family, relatives, or legal guardian of the estate of the deceased because of the pain, suffering, and actual expenses (such as expenses for the funeral) and for the loss of life to the family or relatives. A wrongful death lawsuit may be filed, for example, when an officer shoots and kills a fleeing suspect, fires shots at a suspect in a shopping center and causes the death of an innocent bystander, or negligently operates a motor vehicle and causes the death of an innocent third party. The possibility of a wrongful death lawsuit arises any time a death caused by the police occurs; however, no liability occurs unless the death was unjustified. Further, the claim must be based on a recognized tort theory.

The use of deadly force is governed by state laws or departmental rules that must be strictly followed. Chapter 7 discusses the specifics of the use of deadly force in police work. The safest rule for purposes of civil liability is that *deadly force may be used only in cases of self-defense or when the life of another person is in danger and the use of deadly force is immediately necessary to protect that life.* Agency rules, however, may give the officer more authority to use deadly force. These rules are to be followed as long as they are constitutional and are in accord with state law.

**5. *Intentional Infliction of Emotional or Mental Distress.*** This is committed when an officer inflicts severe emotional distress on a person through intentional or reckless extreme and outrageous conduct. It is usually filed together with other torts, such as false arrest or assault and battery.

As the term indicates, this tort is vague and therefore may be alleged anytime an officer's conduct is so extreme and outrageous as to cause severe emotional or mental distress. What is extreme and outrageous conduct is difficult to determine; moreover the effect of an act may vary according to the plaintiff's disposition or state of mind. Most state courts have held, however, that rudeness or isolated incidents do not lead to liability. There is a need for the plaintiff to allege and prove some kind of pattern or practice over a period of time. The case law on this tort in police cases is still developing, but the tort has already found acceptance in almost every state.

**6. *Misuse of Legal Procedure.*** This tort includes malicious prosecution and abuse of process.

*Malicious prosecution* requires the following: (1) that the officer instituted a criminal or civil proceeding against the plaintiff; (2) that the proceeding terminated in favor of the plaintiff (who was then the accused or defendant); (3) that the officer had no probable cause; and (4) that the officer was motivated primarily by some purpose other than to bring an alleged offender to justice. False arrest and malicious prosecution may arise out of the same events, but malicious prosecution is based on the improper use of an otherwise valid procedure, while false arrest stems from arrest based on illegal cause or procedure.

*Abuse of process is the improper use by the officer of the legal process for reasons other than that intended by law.* It occurs even if a criminal proceeding is brought with probable cause but the officer uses the various available litigation devices for improper purposes.

EXAMPLE: An officer files a misdemeanor charge against a suspect primarily to intimidate him or her, conviction being only a secondary purpose.

**7. *Invasion of Privacy.*** This occurs in a number of ways, the common element being the violation by the officer of the plaintiff's right to be "let alone." Examples include the unauthorized publication of somebody's picture, the unauthorized obtaining of evidence from a person's home, or the unauthorized publication of the details of a person's private life. The usual defense in these cases is that voluntary consent or authorization was given by the aggrieved party.

**8. *Illegal Electronic Surveillance.*** The Omnibus Crime Control and Safe Streets Act of 1968 prohibits the use of electronic surveillance unless it is authorized by state law and occurs under conditions specified in the federal act. Any form of electronic monitoring by the police that fails to comply with the provisions of federal and state law may lead to liability under state law, particularly if specific penalties are imposed. Violation of wiretap laws may also lead to a separate tort of invasion of privacy and civil rights violations.

**9. *Defamation.*** *Defamation is the publication of any false material injurious to a person's good name or reputation.* Such publication constitutes libel (if printed) or slander (is spoken). To recover damages in a defamation case, the plaintiff must prove (1) that the officer made a false and defamatory statement about the plaintiff, (2) that this was communicated to another person either through writing or speech, (3) that there was fault on the part of the officer, and (4) that harm was inflicted on the plaintiff as a result of what the officer did. Establishing the truth of a statement at issue is an absolute defense in a defamation case.

**10. *Malicious Prosecution.*** *Malicious prosecution is the wrongful prosecution of a person without reason to believe that the person has committed a crime.* In a malicious prosecution action, the plaintiff must prove the following:

1. The officer prosecuted the plaintiff.
2. The case was decided in favor of the plaintiff.
3. The defendant-officer was motivated by malice in prosecuting the plaintiff.
4. There was no reasonable and probable cause for the prosecution.
5. The plaintiff suffered damages.

Police officers are particularly susceptible to charges of malicious prosecution, because they initiate criminal proceedings and are often key witnesses for the prosecution. Should the defendant be acquitted, the door is open to charges of malicious prosecution. Acquittal in a criminal case does not lead, automatically, to civil liability. There is the requirement that the prosecution was motivated by malice and that there was no reasonable or probable cause for the action the officer took. Probable cause, for purposes of a defense in a state malicious prosecution case, can take the form of a mistaken but reasonable belief on the part of the police that the person charged by the police acted unlawfully. That belief, however, must be honest and sincere in addition to being reasonable.

## B. Negligence Tort

As distinguished from an intentional tort, where the officer is assumed to have intended the consequence of the act, a negligence tort often results, not from commission, but from omission.

For purposes of liability under state law, *negligence is the breach of a common law or statutory duty to act reasonably toward those who may foreseeably be harmed by an officer's conduct.* This general definition may be modified or superseded by state law or state court decisions that substitute a different definition in a particular jurisdiction. The usual question to be answered by the judge or jury is, *Would a reasonable person of ordinary prudence in the position of the defendant have behaved the way the defendant did?* Negligence is determined on a case-by-case basis and may vary from one judge or jury to another.

The main difference between an intentional tort and a negligence tort is that in an intentional tort the officer's mental state is important, whereas in a negligence tort the officer's mental state is unimportant or irrelevant. The question to be asked in a negligence tort is whether the officer's conduct created an unreasonable risk for others. In a negligence tort, therefore, the harm done may be unintended but liability ensues because of the officer's failure to exercise due care toward another person. Despite distinctions, however, the boundary line between these two types of tort is not always clear.

Some jurisdictions categorize degrees of negligence as slight or gross. *Slight negligence* means that the officer failed to exercise a great amount of care under the circumstances, thus leading to injury. On the other hand, *gross negligence* means the officer failed to exercise a minimal amount of care. *Black's Law Dictionary* defines gross negligence as "the intentional failure to perform a manifest duty in reckless disregard of the consequences affecting the life or property of another." The distinction between slight and gross negligence is important, because liability often depends on the category of negligence used by the judge or jury. In most cases, gross negligence is required for an officer to be liable.

Negligence tort applies in many aspects of police work but most often in the following instances: provision of medical aid, highway control, use of weapon, operation of motor vehicle, traffic direction for parades and other public events, notification and rectification of dangerous road conditions, and failure to give protection under certain circumstances. Of these, the three most popular negligence torts are negligent operation of motor vehicle, negligent failure to protect, and negligent failure to respond to calls. These are discussed in detail in Chapter 11.

**1. *Negligent Operation of Motor Vehicle.*** Police department manuals often provide guidelines on the proper use of motor vehicles. These guidelines, if valid, constitute the standard by which the actions of police officers are likely to be judged. In some states, departmental policies are admitted in court merely as evidence; in other states, the departmental policy is considered controlling by the courts. In states where departmental policy is considered controlling, any violation thereof becomes a tortious act.

EXAMPLE: Departmental guidelines forbid officers from conducting a high-speed motor vehicle chase in downtown areas at any time. If violated, the officer's conduct may lead to tort liability.

Some states allow tort liability against the police for damage to an innocent third party caused by the car pursued by the police if the behavior of the police was wrongful. Other states, however, prohibit such recovery as a matter of policy.

**2. *Negligent Failure to Protect.*** The police have a general duty to protect the public as a whole and to prevent crime. However, the police in general are not liable for injury to someone whom they fail to protect. Nor is any duty owed by the police to *individuals* to prevent crime. What this means is that the police cannot be held liable if a member of society becomes a victim of crime. The usual exceptions applicable in some states are as follows:

1. if a "special relationship" has been created
2. if the police affirmatively undertake to protect an individual but negligently fail to do so
3. if liability is specified by statute
4. in some cases, if there is foreseeability

These exceptions are discussed in Chapter 11.

The courts are split about whether the police are liable for injuries to third parties caused by drunken drivers who are allowed by the police to drive. Some courts impose liability while others do not. This area of law is fast developing, and changes may be forthcoming in the near future.

**3. *Negligent Failure to Respond to Calls.*** There have been some cases where police officers and departments have been held liable because of negligence in responding to calls. In these cases, however, liability is found only when the department promises to deliver services, then fails to deliver them. For example, if a department assures the public that a 911 call will be responded to by the police in five minutes but the police fail to meet that deadline, a negligence lawsuit might succeed in some jurisdictions.

## III. TYPES OF DAMAGE AWARDS IN STATE TORT ACTIONS

Civil actions under tort law may result in three types of damage awards: nominal, actual, and punitive.

**1. *Nominal (or Token).*** These are acknowledgments by the court that the plaintiff proved his or her allegation but suffered no actual injury. Nominal damages are small monetary amounts, often as little as one dollar, and are therefore not much of a financial concern to the officer.

**2. *Actual (or Compensatory).*** These damages reduce to monetary terms all actual injuries shown by the plaintiff. Consequential damages, such as medical bills and lost wages, are termed special damages and are included in the category of actual damages.

EXAMPLE: A police officer uses excessive force on S during arrest, as a result of which S is hospitalized for a few days and incurs a hospital bill of $500. Actual damages imposed would be $500 plus lost wages, if proved.

**3. *Punitive (or Exemplary).*** These damages are designed to punish or make an example of the wrongdoer and are typically awarded in cases where the officer engaged in reckless or intentional misconduct or acted with callous indifference to the rights of another person. The monetary amount is usually proportional to the gravity of the wrong done, although there is no way to predict the size of jury awards, particularly in sensational cases. Most of the multimillion-dollar damage awards fall in this category. In one case, the court said that punitive damages may be awarded against a public officer when the officer's conduct involves reckless or callous indifference to the plaintiff's constitutional rights as well as when the officer's act was motivated by evil motive or intent. Smith v. Wade, 461 U.S. 30 (1983). In another case, the court ruled that no punitive damages can be awarded against local governments. City of Newport v. Fact Concerts, Inc. 453 U.S. 247 (1981). Individual officers, however, may be held liable for punitive damages.

Punitive damages are a big concern of officers, not only because they may involve huge amounts but, more importantly, because their payment is primarily the responsibility of the officer. Punitive damages are imposed as punishment.

In most states it is against public policy for a government agency to pay punitive damages. Even if damage awards are generally paid by the agency, punitive damages may be excluded because it is against public policy for the agency to mitigate punishment imposed against the officer. Punitive damage awards may also be excluded from professional liability insurance coverage. Some carriers include it; others do not. Most of the time, the officer is on his or her own if assessed with punitive damages. The department may pay punitive damages if it so wishes, but that is optional and may be done only in the absence of a policy prohibiting it.

In the last few years, many states have passed legislation limiting the amount of damage awards a plaintiff can obtain, thus modifying the "deep pocket" approach. Such legislation takes various forms. California, for example, has left the "deep pocket" liability intact for actual damages, such as lost wages, but has eliminated it for "pain and suffering." Texas has placed a ceiling on punitive damages that plaintiffs can receive for certain cases. These changes are part of a nationwide movement toward tort reform, a movement that has had mixed success in various states.

## IV. A WORD OF CAUTION

State tort laws are extremely complex and vary immensely from state to state. They differ in the types of allowable action, the requisites for liability, the degree of fault, the basis for the action, the terms used, when the action can be brought, exceptions to specific actions, and available defenses. The discussion in this chapter, which is simplified and intended merely to illustrate the general principles used in many jurisdictions, represents the tip of the iceberg and is for informational purposes only. It is not meant to be a detailed or authoritative guide to tort law in any specific state or local jurisdiction. State tort law is one area of law where the officer must seek the advice and counsel of a local lawyer if an action is brought.

## SUMMARY

There are two general categories of state torts that occur most often in police cases, namely, intentional torts and negligence torts. An intentional tort occurs when there is an intention on the part of the officer to cause some physical or mental harm to another person. Examples of intentional tort cases include false arrest and false imprisonment, assault and battery, wrongful death, and intentional infliction of emotional distress. Negligence may be defined as the breach of a common law or statutory duty to act reasonably toward those who may foreseeably be harmed by the officer's conduct. Examples of negligence tort cases include negligent operation of a motor vehicle and negligent failure to protect.

Three types of damage awards may be given in state tort cases, namely, nominal, actual, and punitive damages. Nominal damages are acknowledgments by the court that the plaintiff proved his or her allegation but suffered no actual injury, actual damages reduce to monetary terms all actual injuries shown by the plaintiff, while punitive damages punish or make an example of the wrongdoer.

## NOTES

1. *Black's Law Dictionary,* 5th ed. (West Publishing Co., 1979) at 1335. Most legal definitions used in this chapter are taken from this source.

# CASE BRIEF

## LEWIS v. DOWNS
## 774 F.2d 711 (6th Cir. 1985)

### FACTS

Officers Downs and Geil were called to a disturbance. Upon arrival at the scene the officers found the Lewises and neighbors screaming at each other. After numerous attempts to calm Mrs. Lewis, she was placed under arrest. While attempting to affect the arrest, Officer Downs was bitten by the Lewis's dog. After the dog was restrained, Officer Geil arrested Mrs. Lewis. Mrs. Lewis's arm was severely twisted while she was being placed in handcuffs. After Mr. Lewis either slipped or was thrown to the ground, Officer Geil kicked him. In an attempt to prevent the arrest of his mother, Tony Lewis moved towards Officer Downs with a rake. Tony Lewis was placed under arrest. While handcuffing Tony, Officer Geil pulled his hair, twisted his arm, and choked him. Mr. Lewis attempted to intervene. Mr. Lewis's brother prevented this intervention by grabbing him around the waist. While Mr. Lewis was restrained, he was kicked in the groin and hit on the head with a nightstick by Officer Geil. Bleeding profusely, Mr. Lewis was forced to crawl to the gate before the officers called an ambulance for him. While Tony Lewis was being led away, Officer Geil, without justification, struck him in the mouth with a nightstick. Mr. Lewis received a cut on the head and an underlying hematoma, and Tony Lewis received several stitches in his mouth.

Mr. and Mrs. Lewis were charged with several crimes, including disorderly conduct, assault, and battery. They were acquitted on all counts. Tony Lewis was also charged, but the matter was handled by the juvenile courts.

The Lewises subsequently filed suit in the U.S. District Court for the Western District of Tennessee, alleging that the officers had committed assault, battery, malicious prosecution, and false imprisonment, had deprived them of their due process of law pursuant to 42 U.S.C. Section 1983, and had conspired to deprive them of their civil rights under 42 U.S.C. Section 1985. The district court found against the Lewises on all claims except battery and violation of their due process rights under Section 1983. The court awarded compensatory damages and attorney's fees to the Lewises. Additionally, the court found that the officers acted in a "malicious and oppressive manner" and awarded punitive damages to the Lewises.

### ISSUE

Did the degree of force used by Officers Downs and Geil constitute a violation of the constitutional rights of the plaintiff? Yes.

## COURT DECISION

The officers' actions were excessive and violated the constitutional rights of the plaintiffs. The court ruled that the force was malicious and excessive enough to warrant the award of punitive damages.

## CASE SIGNIFICANCE

Pursuant to several previously decided cases, the court in this case developed a test for determining whether a police officer's conduct constitutes constitutional deprivation. The factors are

1. the need for the force
2. the relationship between the need and the amount of force used
3. the motivation of the officer in using the force
4. the circumstances surrounding the use of force

The court also ruled that this test must not subject the officer to unrealistic *post hoc* ("after the event") evaluations and that the court must consider the actions of the police in rapidly developing situations and refrain from indulging in unrealistic second-guessing.

Considering the totality of the force used in the incident, the court reasoned that the officers had acted maliciously and oppressively. The court thus allowed punitive damages to be awarded.

**4** Read This Chapter

# CIVIL LIABILITY UNDER FEDERAL LAW: CIVIL RIGHTS (SECTION 1983) CASES

## INTRODUCTION

This chapter discusses civil rights (also known as Section 1983) cases. It gives the provision of law, discusses the reasons for the law's popularity, provides a historical background, identifies the requirements of a civil rights case and discusses each requirement, looks at attorney's fees, and ends with a section on the applicability of the statute of limitations to civil rights cases.

As stated in Chapter 2, a civil rights case is the remedy plaintiffs most often use against public officials. Such a case seeks damages and/or declaratory or injunctive relief from the defendant and is usually filed in a federal court because the law invoked by the plaintiff is a federal law. Civil rights cases may also be filed in some state courts (under concurrent jurisdiction), but plaintiffs prefer to litigate in federal courts because of advantages to plaintiffs, including more liberal discovery procedures and the tenure enjoyed by federal judges. Among lawyers, the terms *civil rights case* and *Section 1983 case* are used interchangeably and are so used in this chapter.

## I. THE CIVIL RIGHTS LAW

Liability under federal law is based on Title 42 of the United States Code, Section 1983, titled *Civil Action for Deprivation of Rights.* The law provides as follows:

> Every person who, under color of any statute, ordinance, regulation, custom, or usage, of any State or Territory, subjects, or causes to be subjected,

> any citizen of the United States or other persons within the jurisdiction thereof to the deprivation of any rights, privileges, or immunities secured by the Constitution and laws, shall be liable to the party injured in an action at law, suit in equity, or other proper proceeding for redress.

The law itself does not create any substantive right; instead it provides an avenue of redress for violations of constitutional rights and of certain rights protected by federal statutes. It is therefore *procedural* rather than *substantive*. Enacted more than a century ago, the law has gone through periods of nonuse, but because of reinterpretation what was once a forgotten statute has now become a fertile source of litigation.

The law was originally known as Section 1 of the Ku Klux Klan Act of April 20, 1871, enacted by Congress as a means of enforcing the Fourth Amendment guarantee of rights to the newly freed slaves. For a long time, however, the law was given a narrow interpretation by the courts, and hence was seldom used. One writer notes that between 1871 and 1920, only twenty-one cases were decided under Section 1983, and that "an appraisal of the statute's application in 1920 would have revealed little promise that it might develop into an effective bulwark against all invasions of civil liberties."[1]

That restrictive interpretation changed in 1961 in the case of Monroe v. Pape, 365 U.S. 167 (1961). Monroe held that a Section 1983 lawsuit can be brought anytime a constitutional right is violated, whether or not the officer was acting within authorized limits. Plaintiff Monroe filed suit in federal district court against thirteen Chicago police officers and the city of Chicago, alleging that the officers broke into his home without a warrant, routed him and his family from bed, made them stand naked in the living room, and ransacked every room in the house. He further alleged that he was taken to the police station and detained on "open charges" for ten hours and that during that period he was denied the assistance of a lawyer.

The city of Chicago moved to dismiss the complaint on the grounds that the term "under color of law" did not include acts of an official or police officer who can show no authority under state law, state custom, or state usage to do what he or she did. Since what the officers did in this case obviously violated the Constitution and the laws of the state of Illinois and was not authorized by the agency, the city of Chicago could not therefore be liable. The United States Supreme Court disagreed, saying that the phrase "acting under color of law" means the "misuse of power possessed by virtue of state law and made possible only because the wrongdoer is clothed with the authority of state law." This meant that public officials and agencies could be liable even if they acted outside their scope of authority. Prior to this decision, public officials were liable under Section 1983 only if they acted within their scope of authority.

*Monroe* is important for two reasons. First, it paved the way for liability every time an officer commits a job-related act, whether the act is authorized or not. This interpretation has flung the door wide open to liability lawsuits and has led to an avalanche of cases being filed against the police. Second, the court said that municipalities are not "persons" for purposes of Section 1983 and therefore cannot be sued or held liable under that law.

## II. WHY CIVIL RIGHTS LAWSUITS ARE A POPULAR REMEDY

Section 1983 lawsuits are a popular remedy for a number of reasons. First, although Section 1983 may also seek declaratory and injunctive relief, it almost always asks for damages from the defendant. If successful, the lawsuit can bring money to the plaintiff and at the same time cause concern to an officer who may not have the personal resources or the insurance to cover the liability. Second, civil rights lawsuits are usually filed in a federal court, where the procedures for obtaining documents from the defendant (called "discovery") are often more liberal than in state courts. This facilitates access to important agency documents and records needed for trial. Third, civil rights lawsuits, when filed in a federal court, do not have to exhaust state judicial remedies, thus avoiding long delays in state courts. Fourth, and perhaps the most important reason, since 1976 a prevailing plaintiff may now recover attorney's fees under the Attorney's Fees Act. Consequently, lawyers may have become more inclined to accept and file civil rights cases if there is merit in the case, knowing that the defendant police officer or agency may have to pay attorney's fees instead of the indigent plaintiff.

Civil rights lawsuits also continue to be used by plaintiffs despite the availability of criminal sanctions against police officers. One reason is that the two are not mutually exclusive—a civil case can be filed in addition to a criminal case and vice versa. A second reason is that a case filed under Section 1983 is a civil case in which the plaintiff seeks vindication of rights; the plaintiff is therefore in control. Third, significant barriers to the use of criminal sanctions against erring police officers do exist. Among these is the reluctance of some prosecutors to file criminal cases against public officers with whom they work and whose help they sometimes need. Fourth, serious criminal cases in most states must be referred to a grand jury for indictment. Grand juries are not inclined to indict a police officer unless it be shown that the act was a gross and blatant abuse of authority. In many criminal cases involving alleged violation of rights, the evidence may come down to the word of the complainant against the word of the officer. The grand jury may be more disposed to believe the officer's testimony. Lastly, the degree of certainty needed to succeed in civil cases is mere preponderance of evidence, much lower than the guilt-beyond-reasonable-doubt requirement needed to convict criminal defendants.

## III. BASIC REQUIREMENTS OF A CIVIL RIGHTS LAWSUIT

Court decisions indicate that there are two basic requirements of a Section 1983 lawsuit:

1. The defendant must be acting under color of law.
2. There must be a violation of a constitutional or federally protected right.

Both requirements must be present for a lawsuit to succeed; the absence of one means that the lawsuit fails.

EXAMPLE 1: An officer violates another person's rights, but the officer was acting as a private person and not under color of law. The officer is not liable under Section 1983, although liability might ensue under some other law.

EXAMPLE 2: An officer violates a suspect's right established by state law but no constitutional or federally protected right (as when an officer forces a suspect to appear in a police lineup without a lawyer prior to the formal charges—assuming that the presence of a lawyer in these proceedings is guaranteed by state law). Since the officer violated a right established only by state law and did not violate a constitutional right, the officer may not be liable under Section 1983. The officer may be liable, however, under agency rules or state law.

**1. *The defendant must be acting under color of law.*** The phrase "acting under color of law" means *misusing power possessed by virtue of law and made possible only because the officer is clothed with the authority of the state.* The courts have interpreted this phrase broadly to include state law, local law, ordinances, and agency regulations. It excludes, however, actions taken under federal law. Section 1983 does not apply to federal officers, although they may be liable for the same act under a different type of federal processing, which is known as a Bivens-type action because it is authorized by a court decision in Bivens v. Six Unknown Named Federal Agents, 403 U.S. 388 (1971). In contrast, local and state law enforcement officers who exercise public authority generally act under color of law and are therefore liable in a civil rights lawsuit.

Acting under color of law does not mean that the act is in fact authorized by law. It is enough that the act appears to be lawful even if it is not in fact authorized. Hence an officer acts under color of law even if he or she exceeds or misuses lawful authority.

EXAMPLE: An officer arrests a suspect without probable cause or brutalizes a suspect in the course of an arrest. These acts are clearly illegal and exceed the officer's lawful authority; nonetheless they fall under the term "acting under color of law." The terms "acting under color of law" and "acting within the scope of authority" must not be confused. An officer can act under color of law even when acting *outside* the scope of authority, meaning that what the officer did was unauthorized or illegal.

Acting under color of law also includes acts that fall under "pretended" authority.

EXAMPLE: An officer detains a suspect for forty-eight hours without charges, claiming this was authorized by agency rules although knowing it was not. The officer would be liable in a civil rights lawsuit.

Acts of officers while "on duty" clearly fall under color of law. The problem, however, is that while it is usually easy to identify acts that are wholly within color of law, there are some acts in police work that are not as easy to classify.

EXAMPLE 1: P, an officer, works during off-hours as a private security agent in a shopping center. While in that capacity, P shoots and kills a fleeing shoplifter. Was P acting under color of law?

EXAMPLE 2: An officer arrests a felon during off-hours and when not in uniform. Is the officer acting under color of law?

The answer to such questions usually depends on (1) job expectations or (2) the degree of agency involvement as manifested in various ways. Many police departments expect and require officers to respond as officers twenty-four hours a day. For example, an Attorney General opinion in the state of Texas states, "A commissioned peace officer is on duty at all times insofar as he has a duty to prevent any breach of the peace which he observes in his jurisdiction." In a state like Texas, any arrest, search, or other police-related act made on or off duty comes under the requirement of color of law. Some states, however, specifically disclaim liability for what an officer does when off duty. In these states, it is harder to establish that the officer acted under color of law.

Courts have used various "legal handles" to bring what an officer does while off duty under the color-of-law requirement.

EXAMPLE 1: In the case of police officers who "moonlight," courts have held that an officer's being in police uniform while acting as a private security agent, an officer's use of a gun issued by his or her department, and department authorities' knowing that an officer has a second job are all indications that an officer is acting under color of law. In one case, an off-duty officer working as a private security guard identified himself as a police officer when making an arrest and later went to the police station to finish his paperwork and get further information from the police files. The court said that the officer was acting under color of law. Lusby v. TG&Y Stores, 749 F.2d 1423 (10th Cir. 1984).

EXAMPLE 2: An off-duty officer who shot somebody was considered acting under color of law because he had authority to carry the weapon used in the shooting and because the dispute arose out of the performance of police duties. Layne v. Sampley, 627 F.2d 12 (6th Cir. 1980).

EXAMPLE 3: A private physician who treats a state inmate pursuant to a contract with the state prison system acts under the color of law and may be held liable in a civil rights suit.

There are limits, however, to the concept of acting under color of law while an officer is off duty. Here are three examples:

EXAMPLE 1: An off-duty police chief who assaulted his sister-in-law was not considered to have acted under color of law, since what happened was the result of a family and political dispute. The plaintiff was therefore not threatened with arrest. Delcambre v. Delcambre, 635 F. 2d 407 (5th Cir. 1981). Using this rationale, what an officer does as a private person and on his or her own should not fall under color of law even if done during office hours. Suppose Officer P, while on patrol, tries to collect from Officer A, who owes him money. Officer A refuses to pay, whereupon Officer P shoots him. The act should not come under color of law, because what Officer P did arose out of a purely personal matter—even though the shooting took place while both were on duty.

EXAMPLE 2: An off-duty police officer who shot his wife with a police pistol and then committed suicide did not act under color of law. Bonsignore v. City of New York, 683 F.2d 635 (2d Cir. 1982).

EXAMPLE 3: The city of Chicago was not liable for a shooting by an officer during his four-day suspension, even though the suspended officer identified himself as a police officer before shooting and killing a motorist over a dispute. Reason: Suspended officers, unlike off-duty officers, who may be required to enforce laws twenty-four hours a day, are relieved of duty according to the rules of the particular police agency. Bauer v. City of Chicago, 484 N.E.2d 422 (1985).

In these cases, the officers acted as private individuals responding to private and personal concerns, although aided perhaps by access to government-issued weapons. It is sometimes difficult to draw a clear line between what is purely a private act and an act under the color of law when an officer is off duty. Decisions of courts in specific jurisdictions provide the best guide and should be studied. Many court decisions on this issue are inconsistent and difficult to reconcile.

The color-of-law requirement excludes acts of private persons, because such acts are without state authorization. Therefore, if a private person acts purely on his or her own, there is no liability on the part of that private person under Section 1983.

EXAMPLE 1: In one case, a sheriff's wife rode along on a night patrol to keep her husband company. She later fought with two men in the patrol car and was sued under Section 1983. The court held that she was not acting under color of law because the sheriff was out of the car at that time and gave her no instructions. Price v. Baker, 693 F.2d 952 (10th Cir. 1982).

EXAMPLE 2: A Section 1983 case was brought by a university student against a police officer on the grounds that the officer violated the student's Fourth Amendment right by seizing without a warrant a package that had been mailed to the student. The package was in the custody of university employees when the officer took possession of it. The court said that because the university officials had already violated the student's privacy by examining the package and concluding that it contained marijuana, the police officer did not violate the student's Fourth Amendment right by carrying the unopened package away in order to secure a warrant. If there was any violation at all, such was done by private persons, meaning the university officials who examined the package; hence there was no officer liability. The court added that the Fourth Amendment prohibits only governmental action; it does not protect anybody from searches by private persons. Garmon v. Foust, 741 F.2d 1069 (8th Cir. 1984).

The general rule is that only public officers are liable under Section 1983. In the following instances, however, private persons might also be liable:

1.  If a private person conspires or agrees with police officers to commit an act that violates constitutional or federally protected rights. Example: A private person and a police officer agree and conspire to illegally arrest and beat a suspect.

2.  If a private person performs a public function or acts pursuant to a statute. Example: A private person makes a citizen's arrest in accordance with state law or practice authorizing such arrest.

3.  If a private person is under contract with the state to perform a public function. Example: The United States Supreme Court has held that a doctor under contract with a state to provide medical services to inmates at a state prison hospital on a part-time basis acts under color of law when treating a prisoner. West v. Atkins, 108 S. Ct. 2250 (1988).

**2. There must be a violation of a constitutional or of a federally protected right.** The right violated under this requirement must be given by the Constitution or by federal law. Rights given only by state law are not protected under Section 1983.

EXAMPLE: The right of a suspect to have a lawyer present during a lineup prior to being charged with an offense is not given by the Constitution or by federal law; therefore, if an officer fails to inform a suspect of such right, the officer is not liable under Section 1983. If such right is given by state law, its violation may be actionable under state law or agency regulation, not under Section 1983.

Constitutional rights are those given by the United States Constitution, while federally protected rights are those given by the Constitution or by federal law. For example, the right of individuals to see some records kept by the FBI or the police is a right given by federal law and not by the Constitution. Not all violations of rights guaranteed by federal law give rise to Section 1983 cases. Instead, an action can arise only if (1) the federal law demonstrates congressional intent not to foreclose Section 1983 remedies, and (2) the federal law creates rights, privileges, or immunities.

Listed below are the basic constitutional rights most often invoked by plaintiffs in police civil liability cases, together with difficult associated issues.

### FIRST AMENDMENT

Freedom of Religion: May police officers prohibit religious groups (such as the Hare Krishna) from distributing leaflets and soliciting contributions at airports or other public places?

Freedom of Speech: May police officers break up a political rally without a permit in a downtown public area?

Freedom of the Press: May journalists be denied access to certain criminal records?

Freedom of Assembly: May students be prohibited from staging a sit-in in a university building?

Freedom to Petition the Government for Redress of Grievances: May marchers be prohibited from occupying city council chambers to protest an alleged racially repressive ordinance?

### FOURTH AMENDMENT

Right against Unreasonable Arrest: May a suspect be arrested based solely on information from an informant who has a criminal record?

Right against Unreasonable Search and Seizure: May a warrant be issued based on information that is three months old and given to the police by an informant?

### FIFTH AMENDMENT

Right against Self-Incrimination: May the diary of a suspect be confiscated by the police and introduced as evidence in court?

## SIXTH AMENDMENT

Right to Have the Assistance of Counsel: Does a juvenile suspect have a right to counsel during a police lineup?

## EIGHTH AMENDMENT

Prohibition against Cruel and Unusual Punishment: When do jail conditions amount to cruel and unusual punishment and hence violate the rights of detainees or prisoners?

## FOURTEENTH AMENDMENT

Right to Due Process: When is a police lineup so suggestive as to violate a suspect's right to due process?

Right to Equal Protection of the Law: Can male and female suspects be treated differently while in detention?

A violation of any of the above rights leads, if sued and proved, to officer liability. The problem is that it is often difficult for an officer to know the full scope of a person's constitutional rights. For example, the answers to the illustrative issues raised above are not clear; in fact, in some instances court decisions are either nonexistent or in conflict. They may also require a more sophisticated knowledge of the law than a nonlawyer could hope to possess.

The full scope of the constitutional rights, from investigation to incarceration, is detailed in United States Supreme Court and lower court decisions that interpret the above provisions. However, this topic is beyond the coverage of this text and is usually addressed in courses on criminal procedure, constitutional law, or legal aspects of law enforcement.

An officer must be familiar with the provisions of the agency handbook or manual, because it often contains specifics about what the officer can or cannot do. If well drafted and properly reviewed by a competent lawyer, the provisions of the agency handbook will most likely embody the latest court decisions on individual statutory and constitutional rights. Knowledge of and adherence to agency rules protects an officer from liability, because such knowledge and adherence constitute good faith, except when the rules are blatantly unconstitutional. For example, an agency policy that authorizes police officers to keep suspects in jail indefinitely until they cooperate is obviously and blatantly unconstitutional—as every police officer should know. If an officer follows this policy despite knowledge that it is unconstitutional, the good faith defense would not be available to that officer.

## IV.  THE MEANING OF "CLEARLY ESTABLISHED" RIGHTS

What if an officer does something that he or she feels does not violate a constitutional right, but the court, in a Section 1983 case, later says that a constitutional right was in fact violated? Or what if an officer does not know that such a right has in fact been established by a recent court decision? In either or both instances, will the officer be liable?

In Harlow v. Fitzgerald (457 U.S. 800, 1982), the United States Supreme Court said that "government officials performing discretionary functions generally are shielded from liability from civil damages insofar as their conduct *does not violate clearly established statutory or constitutional rights of which a reasonable person would have known"* [emphasis added].

The problem with the "clearly established statutory or constitutional rights" standard enunciated in *Harlow* is that often one is not sure whether a constitutional right has been clearly established. The following statement, however, provides helpful advice:

> It is probably true that a right does not have to be decided by the Supreme Court before it is established, but beyond this there is little on which officials can rely. They should, though, avoid action held unconstitutional by a number of lower federal courts. Where the courts disagree or where there is a paucity of decisions, a right may not be clearly established, but such a conclusion should be made with extreme caution.[2]

Some rights are clearly established and are a matter of common knowledge to the police. For example, police officers know that a suspect cannot be arrested without probable cause (a Fourth Amendment right) or cannot be compelled to appear in a police lineup without a lawyer once formally charged with a crime (a Sixth Amendment right). Many constitutional rights, however, are not that clearly established. In these instances, courts decide on a case-by-case basis. Following are examples of case-by-case determinations based on particular facts.

EXAMPLE 1:  A plaintiff who, when seeking damages from the defendant, asserts that the constitutional issue before the court is of "first impression" in effect loses his or her damage claim, because such claim is an admission that the right asserted has not been clearly established, at least as applied to the case at hand. Davis v. Scherer, 468 U.S. 163 (1984).

EXAMPLE 2:  Defendants who forced a detained suspect to sign a release after the suspect was arrested without probable cause violated clearly established law. Hall v. Ochs, 817 F.2d 920 (1st Cir. 1987).

EXAMPLE 3:  A partial search of the plaintiff, a jail employee, that took place three months after a decision in another circuit limiting the authority to do this did not violate clearly established law. Adrow v. Johnson, 623 F. Supp. 1085 (N.D. Ill. 1985).

The *Harlow* doctrine, stated above, places responsibility on police officers to be familiar with the public's clearly established constitutional rights. That, in turn, requires a good and updated knowledge of all phases of constitutional law related to law enforcement. It is therefore important that police officers be given updated information on recent court decisions interpreting the provisions of the Bill of Rights. Ignorance of recent court decisions may excuse an officer for a while but not after a reasonable period of time. The extent of this "reasonable period of time" is at present left to the judgment of the judge or jury.

## V. RELATED CONSIDERATIONS

In addition to the two basic requirements of a Section 1983 lawsuit, two other requirements are worth knowing:

1.  The defendant in a civil rights case must be a natural person, a local government, a corporate entity, or an association.
2.  The violation must reach the constitutional level.
3.  State officers cannot be sued in their official capacity under Section 1983.

**1. *The defendant must be a natural person, a local government, a corporate entity, or an association.*** This means that states and state agencies cannot be sued unless sovereign immunity is waived by law or judicial decision. State officials, however, can be sued.

EXAMPLE: The state of Texas and any Texas state agency cannot be sued in a civil rights case, but any state officer can be sued in his or her personal capacity if the state official acted outside the scope of official duties. Sovereign immunity, therefore, attaches to the state and not to state officials. Some states, however, have waived sovereign immunity, fully or partially, in Section 1983 cases; hence these states may be sued.

Local governments used to be immune from liability in Section 1983 cases, but that changed in 1978 when, in the case of Monell v. Department of Social Services of the City of New York, 436 U.S. 658 (1978), the United States Supreme Court held that local units of government may be liable if the allegedly unconstitutional action was taken by the officer as part of an official policy or custom. This means that, in addition to local officials, counties, cities, municipalities, and other local government entities may now be held liable.

**2. *The violation must reach the constitutional level.*** Not all violations of rights lead to liability under Section 1983. The violation must be of constitutional proportion. What this means is not exactly clear, except that generally serious violations are actionable under Section 1983 whereas nonserious ones are not. In the words of the Eighth Circuit Court of Appeals,

> Courts cannot prohibit a given condition or type of treatment unless it reaches a level of constitutional abuse. Courts encounter numerous cases in which the acts or conditions under attack are clearly undesirable . . . but the courts are powerless to act because the practices are not so abusive as to violate a constitutional right. Wiltzie v. California Department of Corrections, 406 F.2d 515 (8th Cir. 1968).

Mere words, threats, a push, a shove, temporary inconvenience, or even a single punch in the face does not necessarily constitute a civil rights violation. Nor does Section 1983 apply to cases of false testimony, simple negligence, or name calling. On the other hand, the use of excessive force to compel a suspect to confess constitutes a clear and serious violation of a constitutional right.

**3. *State officers cannot be sued in their official capacity under Section 1983.*** In 1989, the Supreme Court said that state officials cannot be sued in their official capacity for depriving a citizen of constitutional right while acting under the color of law. Will v. Michigan, 45 CrL 3087 (1989). The Court said that based on the language of the statute, a state is not a "person" for purposes of Section 1983 lawsuits and therefore cannot be sued. Given this, a state official cannot be sued in his or her official capacity because such would be equivalent to suing the state. The Will v. Michigan decision is important because although courts have long held that state officials could not be sued in federal court in their official capacity under Section 1983, *Will* is the first case where the Court said that such immunity extends to Section 1983 lawsuits filed in state courts.

## VI. WHO MAY BRING A CIVIL RIGHTS LAWSUIT?

The provision of law states that Section 1983 may be filed by "any citizen of the United States or other persons within the jurisdiction hereof" whose rights have been violated. That clause excludes corporations and business entities, because these are persons only by creation of law. Therefore, Texaco, IBM, or United Airlines cannot file civil rights lawsuits against police officers; neither may a city or a municipal agency bring a civil rights case.

The clause "other persons within the jurisdiction thereof" has been interpreted to include aliens who are legally in the United States. Graham v. Richardson, 403 U.S. 365 (1973). Some courts have held that aliens who are in the United States illegally may also file a civil rights lawsuit if any of the constitutional rights given to illegal aliens (such as the right to due process and equal protection under the Fourteenth Amendment) are violated.

EXAMPLE: A border patrol agent beats up an illegal alien without justification. The illegal alien may bring a civil rights lawsuit against the officer because Section 1983 makes no distinction between legal and illegal aliens, hence giving anybody who is physically within United States territory the right to sue.

## VII. LIABILITY OF FEDERAL GOVERNMENT EMPLOYEES IN CIVIL RIGHTS CASES

Employees of the federal government are not liable under Section 1983 because the term "acting under color of law" in the Section 1983 statute refers to state law, not federal law. Federal employees, however, are suable under Bivens-type actions and the Federal Tort Claims Act (FTCA) for essentially the same rights violations for which state and local officers may be liable under Section 1983. Thus the remedies are different but the results are similar.

A Bivens-type action, sometimes referred to as a constitutional tort, is based on the United States Supreme Court decision in the case of Bivens v. Six Unknown Named Federal Agents, 403 U.S. 388 (1971). In that case, the suspect was manacled, searched, and arrested, and his apartment was ransacked by federal agents in search of evidence of alleged narcotics violation. The arrest and search were conducted without warrant or probable cause and therefore violated the suspect's Fourth Amendment right. Bivens sought damages from the federal agents for mental suffering resulting from the invasion of his privacy. The Supreme Court held for Bivens, stating that his Fourth Amendment right was violated and that such violation by a federal agent acting under color of his authority gave rise to a cause of action for damages. Although the Bivens case involved a search and seizure violation, lower court decisions have extended the ruling to violations of other constitutional rights. Bivens-type actions can be brought only against erring federal government employees; they cannot be brought against the federal government itself, because of sovereign immunity.

In contrast to Bivens-type actions, the FTCA authorizes the filing of lawsuits against the federal government but not against the employee. The lawsuit must be based on some action of an employee acting within the scope of his or her employment. The FTCA therefore represents a partial waiver of sovereign immunity by the federal government. The same factual circumstance can give rise to both Bivens-type and FTCA causes of action, but the difference is that actions under the FTCA cannot be based on a constitutional violation and must be worded in tort terms.

EXAMPLE: The arrest by a federal agent of a suspect without probable cause is a violation of the suspect's Fourth Amendment right, but it is also a false arrest under tort law. Two actions can be combined in one lawsuit: The individual federal officer can be sued in a Bivens-type lawsuit and the federal government can be sued under the FTCA for the same conduct. Both may be liable in the same case but based on two legal theories.

## VIII.   RELATIONSHIP BETWEEN CIVIL RIGHTS AND STATE TORT CASES

In many cases, the same act by the police may be the basis of a Section 1983 lawsuit as well as an action under state tort law. For example, arrest without probable cause may constitute false arrest under state tort law and a violation of the arrested person's Fourth Amendment right under Section 1983. In such cases, a plaintiff may combine his or her claims and sue under multiple legal theories in federal court. Civil rights claims under federal law may usually be brought in state courts as well, but there is disagreement among courts as to whether or not state courts must accept them.

An act of a police officer is a civil rights violation only if it constitutes a violation of a constitutional or a federally guaranteed right. Not all acts fall into this category. For example, the Fifth Circuit Court of Appeals has held that slapping an arrestee is not actionable under Section 1983 because it does not amount to a violation of a constitutional right. Mark v. Caldwell, 754 F.2d 1260 (5th Cir. 1985). This means that a civil rights case against an officer for slapping an arrested person will not succeed, but the officer may be liable under state tort law. Conversely, plaintiffs may use Section 1983 to redress violations of a constitutional right for which there is no counterpart in state tort law.

EXAMPLE: A sheriff may be liable under Section 1983 if conditions in the county jail violate a prisoner's constitutional right against cruel and unusual punishment, but the sheriff cannot be liable under state tort law if such prison conditions do not amount to a violation of a prisoner's right under state tort or any other provision of state law.

## IX.   STATUTE OF LIMITATIONS

A statute of limitations is a law providing that legal action must be filed within a prescribed period of time—otherwise the cause of action lapses and the case can no longer be heard in court. For example, in some jurisdictions tort actions must be brought within two years after the cause of action arises, and the court will dismiss any case not filed within that time.

Section 1983 cases are subject to statutes of limitations, but the United States Supreme Court has decided in effect that these actions are "personal injury" cases and that therefore the statute of limitations for similar personal injury actions in the state in which the cause of action arose should be used. Wilson v. Garcia, 471 U.S. 261 (1985).

EXAMPLE: X alleges that police officers arrested her in Los Angeles, California, without probable cause. Assume that such act is actionable under California tort law as false arrest and under Section 1983 as a violation of X's Fourth Amendment right against unreasonable search and seizure. If the statute of limitations for false arrest in California is one year, the Section 1983 case must also be filed within one year.

The Court decision in *Wilson v. Garcia* led to confusion in some state courts, because a number of states have "personal injury" tort laws and "specific intentional" tort laws with different statutes of limitations. This was cleared up by the Court in 1989 when the Court said that the proper statute-of-limitations period for all civil rights (Section 1983) actions should be determined by the personal injury tort laws in that state, not those statutes on specific intentional tort. Owens v. Okure, 109 S.Ct. 573 (1989).

## SUMMARY

Section 1983 lawsuits (also known as civil rights lawsuits) are the most popular remedy in the arsenal of plaintiff rights. There are a number of reasons for this, including the possibility of obtaining damages and recovering attorney's fees.

The civil rights law giving plaintiffs remedy in federal courts for violations of rights was originally passed in 1871 but was given a narrow interpretation by the courts until 1961. Today a civil rights case may be filed any time an officer acting under color of law violates a constitutional or a federally guaranteed right. The door has been opened wide, resulting in a flood of civil rights cases in federal courts.

States and state agencies are not liable under Section 1983 unless sovereign immunity is waived. State public officers, however, are liable, as are local governments and local public officials. Minor violations of rights, such as mere words, threats, a push, a shove, or a temporary inconvenience, are not actionable; serious violations lead to liability.

Any natural person, including legal or illegal aliens, may bring a civil rights lawsuit. Employees of the federal government are not liable under Section 1983 but may be sued under Bivens-type actions and the Federal Tort Claims Act for essentially the same rights violations for which state and local officers may be liable under Section 1983.

In many cases, the same act by the police may be the basis of a Section 1983 lawsuit and also an action under state tort law. Statutes of limitations apply to Section 1983 cases. The appropriate statute of limitations is that for the equivalent state tort action in the state in which the cause of action arose.

## NOTES

1. Comment, "The Civil Rights Act: Emergence of an Adequate Federal Civil Remedy," 26 *Ind. L.J.* 361 (1951).
2. P. Hardy and J. Weeks, *Personal Liability of Public Officials under Federal Laws* 5 (Institute of Government, University of Georgia, 1980).

## CASE BRIEFS

### HARLOW v. FITZGERALD
### 457 U.S. 800 (1982)

#### FACTS

Bryce Harlow and Alexander Butterfield, senior aides of President Nixon, were accused of violating plaintiff Fitzgerald's constitutional rights by conspiring to have Fitzgerald dismissed as an Air Force official. Fitzgerald claimed that his dismissal was in retaliation for his "blowing the whistle" on the purchasing practices of the Air Force. A district court denied motions by the defendants for a summary judgment, holding that they were not entitled to absolute immunity. A court of appeals denied the appeal. The Supreme Court granted certiorari.

#### ISSUE

What is the scope of immunity available to the senior aides and advisors of the President of the United States in a suit for damages based on their official acts?

#### SUPREME COURT DECISION

Government officials performing discretionary functions are not entitled to absolute immunity but are shielded from liability for civil damages if their conduct does not violate clearly established statutory or constitutional rights of which a reasonable person would have known.

#### CASE SIGNIFICANCE

This case established a new guideline for the "good faith" defense available to government officials in Section 1983 cases. According to the new guideline, an official is deemed to have acted in "good faith" and therefore is not liable if his or her action does not violate clearly established constitutional or statutory rights of which a reasonable person would have known. This guideline applies to civil liability cases involving police officers. Therefore, police officers are not liable in Section 1983 cases if their actions do not violate clearly established constitutional or statutory rights of which a reasonable person would have known.

## MONELL v. DEPARTMENT OF SOCIAL SERVICES OF THE CITY OF NEW YORK et al.
### 436 U.S. 658 (1978)

### FACTS

The petitioners, female employees of the Department of Social Services and the Board of Education, filed suit under 42 U.S.C. Section 1983 against the Department of Social Services, its commissioner, the Board of Education, its chancellor, the city of New York, and the mayor for violation of civil rights pursuant to a policy of requiring pregnant employees to take unpaid leaves of absence before they were medically necessary. The suit sought injunctive relief and backpay for the periods of leave.

Prior to the ruling by the district court, the policy was changed; therefore, the court ruled the issue of injunctive relief moot. The court also decided against the plaintiffs for backpay based on the decision in Monroe v. Pape, 365 U.S. 167, which held that persons sued in their official capacities enjoy the same immunity from civil liability that is granted to municipalities. The Court of Appeals affirmed the decision.

### ISSUE

Can municipalities or local governments be held liable under Section 1983 for monetary damages or declaratory and injunctive relief when an unconstitutional act is the result of a government policy or custom? Yes.

### SUPREME COURT DECISION

Municipalities and other local government units are "persons" that can be sued directly under Section 1983 for monetary damages and declaratory and injunctive relief where an alleged unconstitutional action is the result of a government policy or custom. Government entities, however, cannot be held liable based on respondeat superior. The ruling in Monroe v. Pape, 365 U.S. 167 (1969), is overruled to the extent it holds that local governments are wholly immune from Section 1983 lawsuits.

## CASE SIGNIFICANCE

*Monell* states that local governments may now be sued in a Section 1983 suit, and therefore the governmental immunity enjoyed by the states no longer applies to local governments. Prior to *Monell,* local governments could claim immunity, just as state governments could. Under *Monell,* plaintiffs may sue the city, county, or police agency, which may be held liable if what the officer did was a result of official policy or custom.

### MONROE v. PAPE
### 365 U.S. 167 (1961)

## FACTS

Six black children and their parents brought a Section 1983 action in federal district court against the city of Chicago and thirteen of its police officers for damages for violation of their rights under the Fourteenth Amendment. They alleged that, without warrant, the police officers broke into their home in the early morning, routed them from bed, made them stand naked in the living room, and ransacked every room, emptying drawers and ripping mattress covers; that the father was taken to the police station and detained on "open" charges for ten hours while he was interrogated about a two-day-old murder; that he was not taken before a magistrate, though one was accessible; that he was not permitted to call his family or attorney; and that he was subsequently released without criminal charges being filed against him.

## ISSUE

Were the police officers and the city of Chicago liable under Section 1983 for what was done to the plaintiffs? *Yes.*

## SUPREME COURT DECISION

Police officers acting illegally and outside their scope of authority may be liable under Section 1983 despite the requirement that the officers must have been acting under color of state law. The statutory words "under color of any statute, ordinance, regulation, custom, or usage, of any State or Territory" contained in 42 U.S.C. 1983 do not exclude acts of an official or police officer who can show no authority under state law, custom, or usage to do what he or she did or who even violated the state constitution and laws. The city of Chicago, however, was not held liable, because the Court ruled that Congress did not intend to bring municipal corporations within the ambit of Section 1983 (this ruling was later overturned by the Court).

CASE SIGNIFICANCE

This case virtually opened the floodgates of the courts to civil rights (or Section 1983) litigation. Prior to this, it was difficult to hold public officials liable under Section 1983 because of the requirement that they must have acted under color of state law. Most civil liabilities, however, stem from the abuse of power or authority by the police, and such actions were considered outside the color of state law. *Monell* changed all that. Now police officers can be sued under Section 1983 if what they did arose out of a "misuse of power possessed by virtue of state law and made possible only because the wrongdoer is clothed with the authority of state law." An officer who abuses his or her authority can now be sued under Section 1983 as having acted under color of state law. Under *Monell*, the term "under color of state law" is not synonymous with "acting within the scope of authority." An officer can act *outside* the scope of authority, or even illegally, and still be sued under Section 1983 as having acted under color of state law.

# 5

# LEGAL DEFENSES
# IN CIVIL LIABILITY CASES

## INTRODUCTION

Various legal defenses are available in state tort and Section 1983 cases. Ideally, the best defense is to establish that the officer did not commit the act with which he or she is charged, hence showing the case is without merit or basis. The problem, however, is that views of incidents differ, particularly in the tense and emotional situations in which the police are often involved. What may be a lawful act to an officer may be viewed differently by a suspect or the public. Therefore, an outright denial that the act in question occurred may not be convincing to a judge or jury. An example is the use of nondeadly force by the police. An officer may believe it necessary to use a certain level of force to take a suspect into custody, but the suspect may view the force used as excessive and unnecessary. In these cases, the judge or jury ultimately resolves the issue of whether the use of force was reasonable.

## I. DEFENSES

Many defenses are available to the defendant in civil liability cases. Some of them are substantive, while others are procedural. *Substantive defenses* are those that refute the elements of a Section 1983 suit or a state tort case. For example, one defense in a Section 1983 suit might be that no constitutional right was violated by the police officer or that the arrest of the suspect, in a false arrest state tort case, was justified. *Procedural defenses* are also available, such as challenges based on the requirements for proper filing of the case, the service of process, the statute of limitations, and so on. In certain narrow circumstances, a variety of technical defenses (such as collateral estoppel, res judicata, laches, and the Younger doctrine) can also be used. These defenses, however, are primarily of interest to lawyers and are beyond the scope of this text.

Some liability actions, particularly those under state tort law, have specific defenses. For example, the use of reasonable force is a valid defense in excessive use of force cases, truth in defamation cases, and valid consent in search and seizure cases. Other defenses in state tort are self-defense, defense of others, and public necessity. In negligent tort actions, there are such defenses as contributory negligence, comparative negligence, and assumption of risk.

This chapter focuses on the three legal defenses most often used in police cases: official immunity, good faith, and probable cause.

### A. The Official Immunity Defense

Official immunity is derived from the concept of governmental sovereign immunity, which means that a government is sovereign and therefore cannot be held liable. It differs from governmental immunity, however, in that the main concern is the immunity of the official instead of the agency. The general rule is that in cases where governmental immunity applies, the public official involved in the act is not immune, although the agency might be.

There are two types of governmental immunity: state tort law immunity and civil rights (Section 1983) immunity. State tort law immunity is derived from common law principles and protects officers from liability if sued under state tort law. By contrast, civil rights immunity is derived from the Eleventh Amendment to the Constitution, which provides that "the judicial power of the United States shall not be construed to extend to any suit in law or equity, commenced or prosecuted against one of the United States by citizens of another state or by citizens or subjects of any foreign states." This generally protects the state from liability if sued in federal court.

Only a minority of states maintain sovereign immunity under state tort law. These states have not waived immunity by statute or judicial decision. In these states, the state itself cannot be sued, but a state official can be. In Section 1983 cases, the state cannot be sued because of state immunity under the Eleventh Amendment—unless immunity is waived. Neither can state officials be sued in their official capacity under Section 1983, because such a lawsuit would in effect be a lawsuit against the state. But a state official can be sued in his or her private capacity based on the same act, the difference being that the officer, not the state, will be held liable personally for damages if imposed.

Official immunity is divisible into three types: absolute, quasi-judicial, and qualified (see Table 5.1).

**1. *Absolute Immunity.*** In this type of immunity, there is *no liability for damages at all.* Therefore, a civil liability suit, if brought, is dismissed by the court without going into the merits of the plaintiff's claim. The encouragement of fearless decision making requires the recognition

**TABLE 5.1**
**Guide to Types of Official Immunity**

|  | *Absolute*[a] | *Quasi-Judicial*[b] | *Qualified*[c] |
|---|---|---|---|
| Judges | ✓ | | |
| Legislators | ✓ | | |
| Prosecutors | ✓ | | |
| Parole Board Members | | ✓<br>(If performing a judgelike function) | ✓<br>(If performing other functions) |
| Supervisors (police, probation, parole, prisons) | | | ✓ |
| Law Enforcement Officers | | | ✓ |
| Probation Officers | | ✓<br>(If preparing a pre-sentence report under order of judge) | ✓<br>(If performing other functions) |
| Parole Officers | | | ✓ |
| Prison Guards | | | ✓ |
| State Agencies | ✓<br>(Unless waived by law or court decision) | | |
| Local Agencies | No Immunity | | No Immunity |

[a] Absolute immunity means no liability at all; therefore, a civil liability suit, if brought, is dismissed by the court without going into the merits of plaintiff's claim.

[b] Quasi-judicial immunity means that certain officials are immune if performing judicial-type functions but not when performing other functions connected with their office.

[c] Qualified immunity has two related meanings. Under the first meaning the immunity defense applies only if the official is performing discretionary acts. The second and more popular meaning relates qualified immunity to the good faith defense. Under this concept, a public officer is exempt from liability in Section 1983 cases if the officer did not violate a clearly established constitutional right of which a reasonable person should have known.

of an absolute immunity for some officials. That is the good news. The bad news is that absolute immunity does not apply to police officers. It applies only to judges, prosecutors, and legislators. There is one instance, however, when police officers enjoy absolute immunity from civil liability. In Brisco v. LaHue, 460 U.S. 325 (1983), the Supreme Court held that police officers could not be sued under Section 1983 for giving perjured testimony against a defendant in a state criminal trial. The Court said that under common law, trial participants—including judges, prosecutors, and witnesses—were given absolute immunity for actions connected with the trial process. Therefore, police officers also enjoy absolute immunity when testifying, even if such testimony constitutes perjury. The officer may be criminally prosecuted for perjury, but that is up to the prosecutor to decide.

**2.** *Quasi-Judicial Immunity.* Certain officials have quasi-judicial immunity, which means they are *immune when performing judicial-type functions but not when performing other functions connected with their office.* An example is a probation officer who prepares a pre-sentence investigation report upon order of the judge. Quasi-judicial immunity, however, does not apply to police officers, because they perform functions that are executive, not judicial, in nature. In no instance does a police officer enjoy quasi-judicial immunity.

**3.** *Qualified Immunity.* The qualified immunity doctrine has two related meanings. Under the first meaning, qualified immunity applies in state tort cases only if *the official is performing discretionary acts,* meaning those acts that require personal deliberation and judgment. Police officers are not immune, however, if they perform ministerial acts, meaning those that amount only to the performance of a duty in which the officer has no choice.

EXAMPLE: Officer X handcuffs a suspect upon arrest. Assume that handcuffing a suspect is a matter of discretion according to departmental policy. X is sued for damages by the suspect, claiming that the use of handcuffs by X constituted excessive use of force. X is not liable, because X was exercising discretion given by departmental policy. In contrast, officers are not authorized to beat suspects. Therefore, if Officer X beats a suspect, he or she may be liable, because an officer is prohibited by the Constitution from beating suspects. The duty not to beat a suspect is ministerial, not optional. Note, however, that this type of immunity (based on the performance of a discretionary act) is limited to state tort cases and does not extend to cases brought under Section 1983.

The second and more popular meaning links *qualified immunity to the good faith defense.* In Malley v. Briggs, 475 U.S. 335 (1986), the Supreme Court said that a police officer is not entitled to absolute immunity but only to qualified immunity in a Section 1983 case. In *Malley v. Briggs*, a prominent Rhode Island couple, James and Louisa Briggs, sued a police officer and the state of Rhode Island (later dismissed from the case), alleging that their civil rights were violated when State Trooper Edward Malley obtained a warrant for the couple's arrest based on a telephone conversation intercepted as part of a drug investigation. The affidavit of Officer Malley stated that in this telephone conversation someone indicated that he had been at a party where he smoked marijuana in the presence of "Jimmy Briggs" and had "passed it to Louisa." There was no other evidence against the couple, and criminal charges were later dropped against them because of insufficient evidence. The couple brought a Section 1983 lawsuit for unlawful arrest; the officer asserted that what he did was covered by absolute immunity. The Court unanimously rejected the absolute immunity defense, saying that the officer was entitled only to qualified immunity.

*Malley v. Briggs* is significant in that the Court refused to be swayed by the officer's argument that policy considerations require absolute immunity when a police officer applies for and obtains a warrant. The Court replied that qualified immunity provides sufficient protection for police officers. The Court has made clear that absolute immunity will be available only to judges, prosecutors, and legislators and not to police officers.

*Malley v. Briggs* is also important to police officers because it sets the standard of review courts will use when determining whether or not an officer may be civilly liable when an unlawful warrant is issued based on an officer's affidavit. The standard is as follows: "Whether a reasonably well-trained officer in the petitioner's position would have known that his affidavit failed to establish probable cause and that he should not have applied for the warrant." This standard of liability is the same for arrest and search and seizure warrants.

EXAMPLE: Officer Y knows he does not have enough information derived from personal surveillance of a suspect to be able to establish probable cause. Officer Y then lies in an affidavit, saying that he has information from an unnamed informant implicating the suspect in a crime. If the absence of probable cause is established in a subsequent civil case. Officer Y may be held liable.

**4. *State Immunity Statutes.*** Although most states have abolished the sovereign immunity defense in state tort cases, some states have passed laws providing immunity to state or local law enforcement officers. These laws either exempt officers from liability or authorize the lawsuit against the state instead of the officer in cases where the officer acted within the scope of authority.

EXAMPLE: In one case, a police officer driving to the scene of an accident was found immune from civil suit for a traffic offense under Indiana law because the court said that he was engaged in enforcing the law and was therefore covered by state immunity statute. Weber v. City of Fort Wayne, 511 N.E. 2d 1074 (Ind. Ct. App. 1987).

These immunity laws are valid and therefore protect the officer from liability, but only in state tort cases. Martinez v. California, 444 U.S. 277 (1980). They cannot establish immunity in Section 1983 cases, because such cases are based on federal law, not state statute.

### B. The Good Faith Defense

The good faith defense is perhaps the defense used most often in civil liability cases, although it is not as readily available in state tort lawsuits. While the good faith defense is available to public officials, it is not available to government agencies if the injury can be attributed to agency policy or custom.

In most officers' minds, the term "good faith" is associated with lack of intent to do wrong. This is not the meaning of "good faith" at all. In fact, intent has nothing to do with the good faith defense. Moreover, the good faith defense applies only to damage claims, not to claims for injunctive relief. An officer therefore may have acted in good faith but may still be required to change certain practices that violate plaintiffs' rights.

The current good faith test is this: *Did the official, at the time the act was committed, violate a clearly established statutory or constitutional right of which a reasonable person would have known?* This test was enunciated in Harlow v. Fitzgerald, 457 U.S. 800 (1982), when the Court said,

> We therefore hold that government officials performing discretionary functions generally are shielded from liability for civil damages insofar as their conduct does not violate clearly established statutory or constitutional rights of which a reasonable person would have known . . . . The judge appropriately may determine, not only the currently applicable law, but whether that law was clearly established at the time an action occurred. If the law at that time was not clearly established, an official could not reasonably be expected to anticipate subsequent legal developments, nor could he fairly be said to "know" that the law forbade conduct not previously identified as unlawful.

Although *Harlow* involved the actions of two White House aides under former President Nixon, the Court has said that the *Harlow* standard, which affords immunity from acts that the official could have reasonably believed to be lawful, also applies to police officers who are in performance of their responsibilities. Anderson v. Creighton, 483 U.S. 635 (1987). In *Anderson*, a federal agent and other law enforcement officers made a search without warrant of a home, believing that a bank robber was hiding there. The family that occupied the home then sued for violation of the Fourth Amendment right against unreasonable search and seizure, alleging that the agents' act was unreasonable. On appeal, the Court said that the lower court should have considered not only the general rule about home entries but also the facts known to the agents at the time of entry. According to the Court, the proper inquiry was whether a reasonable law enforcement officer could have concluded that the circumstances surrounding that case added up to probable cause and exigent circumstances that could then justify a warrantless search. If such conclusion is possible, then the good faith defense applies.

The *Harlow* rule may be illustrated as follows: X, a police officer, arrests a suspect, takes her to the police station, and keeps her in jail for two days without filing charges. Assume that this is an accepted practice in the department and that Officer X did not know it was illegal. The suspect challenges the constitutionality of such practice as violative of due process, and the court declares the practice to be unconstitutional. If a Section 1983 case is filed, chances are that X will have a good faith defense, because what he did was not violative of a clearly established statutory or constitutional right of which a reasonable person would have known. If liability exists at all, it will probably be with the agency. In contrast, suppose Officer X knows (as officers are supposed to know) that an arrest cannot be based on a mere hunch but makes an arrest anyway. Then Officer X does not have a good faith defense, because the right not to be arrested except on probable cause *is* a clearly established constitutional right of which a reasonable person would have known.

The *Harlow* test for good faith carries with it good news and bad news. The good news is that not every violation of a constitutional right by the police leads to a civil rights liability. There is a liability only if the official, at the time the act was committed, violated a clearly established statutory or constitutional right of which a reasonable person would have known. The bad news is that police officers have an obligation to know the clearly established constitutionally protected rights of the general public. A violation of these rights leads to civil liability.

Examples of actual cases where the good faith defense succeeded because no clearly established right was violated include the following:

- Police officers on patrol approached the plaintiffs, who were drinking and listening to a car stereo out on the street. Told to quiet down, plaintiffs reacted in a hostile manner, whereupon the officers arrested and detained plaintiffs for forty minutes. The court held that the officers acted in good faith under the circumstances and therefore no liability was imposed under Section 1983. Saldana v. Garza, 684 F.2d 1159 (5th Cir. 1982).

- A sheriff who participated in a mortgage foreclosure sale that was later declared illegal was not liable, because there was no proof or even allegation that he knew or should have known of the illegality. Stafford v. Goff, 609 F. Supp. 820 1 (D. Colo. 1985).

- Officers who strip-searched jail detainees were not held liable, because it was not clearly established at the time of the strip search that such was a violation of the Fourth Amendment right against unreasonable searches and seizures. Kathriner v. City of Overland, 602 F. Supp. 124 (E.D. Mo. 1984).

Examples of cases where the good faith defense was rejected by the courts include these:

- A sheriff retained a suspect in jail for nine months without legal authority and after all the charges had been dismissed. The court ruled that good faith alone was no defense for prolonged retention without the necessary authority. Whirl v. Kern, 407 F.2d 781 (5th Cir. 1969).

- The obtainment and execution of a felony warrant by public officials after knowing that the plaintiff had been granted immunity from prosecution was without probable cause, since there was no reason to believe that plaintiff could actually be convicted. Scannell v. City of Riverside, 199 Ca. Rptr 644 (1984).

- A man was arrested for nonpayment of parking tickets and then was subjected to a strip search and body cavity inspection by the police. The court concluded that the law against strip searches at that time was "clearly established," because the case on strip searches had been decided two years earlier. Walsh v. Franco, 849 F.2d 66 (2nd Cir. 1988).

- In one case, the court concluded that even though there were no decided cases directly on the point, city officials who denied an officer due process rights to a hearing were not entitled to qualified immunity, because the unlawfulness of their conduct should have been clear to them in light of case law or the general subject. Osland v. Bobb, 825 F.2d 1371 (9th Cir. 1987).

The new good faith defense test under *Harlow* has two important implications for police officers and agencies. First, since liability ensues if there is a violation of a statutory or a constitutional right of which a reasonable person would have known, police officers must know the basic constitutional and statutory rights of their constituents. While officers are familiar with these rights from college courses and police academy training, such knowledge needs constant updating, because new court decisions continually occur in criminal procedure and constitutional law. For example, in 1985 the United States Supreme Court decided *Tennessee v.*

Garner, 471 U.S. 1 (1985), an important case on the use of deadly force. That case says that deadly force may be used to apprehend a fleeing suspect only if (1) the suspect threatens the officer with a weapon or (2) there is probable cause to believe that the suspect has committed a crime involving the infliction or threatened infliction of serious physical harm. In addition, the suspect must first be warned, when feasible. The case is clearly important in that any police behavior or departmental policy that goes beyond the limitations prescribed by the Court exposes the officer and the department to civil liability. Any police officer who is not familiar with that case and acts outside its limitations exposes him- or herself to possible liability.

The second important implication of the *Harlow* test is that it places an obligation on police agencies to update their officers' knowledge of new cases and developments that have civil liability implications. This can be done through continuing education programs or an occasional memorandum. Moreover, an agency must update its manual or guidelines to reflect developing case law. It is in the agency's best interest to do this, because chances are that the agency will be included in any lawsuit that alleges failure to train, direct, or supervise. Updating can be done in a number of ways, depending on agency size and resources. What is important is for the agency to realize that this is a responsibility it cannot ignore if it is to minimize the incidence of liability lawsuits.

Courts have said that good faith is an affirmative defense, meaning that it must be raised by the defendant claiming it—otherwise it is deemed waived. Satchell v. Dilworth, 745 F.2d 781 (2d Cir. 1984). Under the affirmative defense concept, the plaintiff has no specific obligation to prove bad faith on the part of the officer. It is enough that the plaintiff proves that the injury resulted from an unconstitutional or illegal act. Once that is established, the officer then has the obligation to prove that the act was done in good faith.

**Instances When the Good Faith Defense Is Likely to Succeed.** Courts and juries vary in their perception of what is meant by "good faith," but chances are that the good faith defense will succeed in the following instances:

1. *The officer acted in accordance with agency rules and regulations.* This is because agency rules and regulations are law as far as the officer is concerned, unless declared otherwise by the courts. In one case the court said that good faith reliance on departmental regulation precludes liability for improper detention. Moore v. Zarra, 700 F.2d 329 (6th Cir. 1983).

2. *The officer acted pursuant to a statute that is reasonably believed to be valid but is later declared unconstitutional.* In Pierson v. Ray, 386

U.S. 547 (1967), the Supreme Court noted that "a police officer is not charged with predicting the course of constitutional law." For example, suppose Officer P arrests D for disorderly conduct. During trial, D challenges the constitutionality of the law because of vagueness. The law is declared unconstitutional by the court. D subsequently brings a tort or Section 1983 lawsuit against Officer P for false arrest. There is no liability, because Officer P had good reasons to assume at the time of the arrest that the law was constitutional.

3. *The officer acted in accordance with orders from a superior that are reasonably believed to be valid.* The reason for this is that the officer is under orders from a superior who supposedly knows what he or she is doing. On the other hand, if the officer acts in compliance with a patently invalid order, the officer may be held liable.

4. *The officer acted in accordance with advice from a legal counsel that is reasonably believed to be valid.* The presumption is that the legal counsel knows what he or she is doing and that the officer should therefore follow that advice.

In the above instances, the officer would have good reasons to believe that what he or she does is valid, because the act is in accordance with agency rules, state law, orders from a superior, or advice from a legal counsel. It is therefore reasonable to assume that the officer could not, at the time the act was committed, reasonably have known that the act was unconstitutional or violative of somebody's rights. The only exception is if the rules of the agency, the orders of the superior, or the advice of the legal counsel is so gross or blatant as to be clearly illegal or unconstitutional.

EXAMPLE 1: An agency rule that allows officers to threaten suspects to obtain a confession is clearly illegal. An officer who acts on the basis of the rule cannot claim the good faith defense.

EXAMPLE 2: An order from a police chief to arrest and detain a suspect without probable cause so as to harass the suspect into cooperating in an investigation is also clearly illegal. An officer who acts on the basis of this order cannot claim the good faith defense.

EXAMPLE 3: A superior officer orders a subordinate to beat a suspect. Again, the good faith defense will not succeed.

In these cases, the officer will not be able to use the good faith defense, because he or she ought to have known that the policy or order is in violation of a clearly established constitutional right.

## C. The Probable Cause Defense

This is a limited defense in that it applies only in state tort law or Section 1983 cases of false arrest, false imprisonment, and illegal searches and seizures. One court has said that for the purpose of a legal defense in Section 1983 cases, probable cause simply means "a reasonable good faith belief in the legality of the action taken." Rodriguez v. Jones, 473 F.2d 599 (5th Cir. 1973). That expectation is lower than the Fourth Amendment concept of probable cause, which is usually defined as "more than bare suspicion; it exists when the facts and circumstances within the officers' knowledge and of which they had reasonably trustworthy information are sufficient in themselves to warrant a man of reasonable caution in the belief that an offense has been or is being committed." Brinegar v. United States, 338 U.S. 160 (1949).

EXAMPLE: An officer makes an arrest that is later determined to be without probable cause. According to the above decision, the officer may be exempt from liability if he or she reasonably and in good faith believed at the time of the arrest that it was legal. Conversely, liability will likely be imposed if the officer either did not honestly believe that there was cause or if such belief was unreasonable.

Probable cause is so strong a defense in arrest and search and seizure cases that some courts have held that if probable cause is present, the officer is not liable even if malice is involved in the officer's act. This is because as long as probable cause is present, the arrest or search is valid regardless of the officer's motives. There are instances, however, when probable cause is not a defense against liability. In particular, it is not a defense (1) if a warrant is defective on its face, as when it is unsigned by a magistrate, or (2) if the officer has no power because the arrest or search took place outside his or her jurisdiction.

## D. The "Acting within the Scope of Employment" Defense

This is a form of defense available to police officers but not to agencies. If sued, an officer can invoke the defense that what he or she did was "within the scope of employment" and that therefore no liability ought to ensue or, if liability exists at all, it should be with the agency that authorized the officer to perform the act. The terms "acting within the scope of employment" and "acting within the scope of authority" are used loosely and interchangeably and may not have much difference in the law. In raising the defense of "acting within the scope of employment," the officer is saying that the act was authorized by the agency rules or regulations and therefore the officer should not be held reasonably liable. The fault, if any, lies with the agency.

An Oregon case sets the following standard for determining whether or not the act was within the "scope of employment." The court said,

> In order to determine whether defendant's actions fall within the scope of his employment, we consider whether the act in question is of a kind he

was hired to perform, whether the act occurred within the authorized time and space and whether the employee was motivated, at least in part, by a purpose to serve the employer. Stanfield v. Laccoarce, 284 Or. 651 (1978).

In a subsequent case, the Fifth Circuit Court of Appeals said that whether a particular act is within the scope of employment is to be decided "on its own particular facts and circumstances by the trier of fact." Jonas v. City of Atlanta, 647 F.2d 580 (5th Cir. 1981).

The term "scope of employment" is usually used in state tort cases. In a Section 1983 case, the "scope of employment" issue is raised in connection with the "acting under color of law" requirement. An officer who acts within the scope of employment is certainly acting under color of law. The term "acting under color of law" is much broader, however, in that it includes acts clearly outside the scope of employment or authority but related to responsibilities to be performed. For example, beating a suspect is an act outside the scope of employment but qualifies as "under color of law."

If the officer acts within the scope of employment and liability is imposed, chances are that the liability will be paid by the agency. The opposite of acting *within* the scope of employment is acting *outside* it. The officer becomes personally liable when acting outside the scope of employment, although the agency may wish to pay for the liability anyway to give the officer support and the benefit of the doubt.

## II. THE WARRANT AS A DEFENSE

Although not an absolute defense, making an arrest or search *based on a warrant* issued by a magistrate constitutes a good faith defense. In such cases, the officer is acting under orders to make the arrest or search. The presence of probable cause has already been determined by the magistrate based on somebody else's affidavit, and the officer's duty is merely to execute the warrant. Should the warrant turn out to be invalid, the officer would not be liable, because the officer is entitled to assume that the warrant is valid. As in the case of the probable cause defense, however, there are exceptions to this rule, notably if the warrant is defective on its face.

The good faith defense using the concept of "clearly established right" applies only if the right violated is in fact a constitutional right or a right given by federal law. The *Harlow* test would not apply if the right violated is given by state law or agency rule. Davis v. Scherer, 468 U.S. 183 (1984). In such cases, the good faith defense is available only if allowed under state law or agency rule.

EXAMPLE: Assume that state law provides that any suspect charged with a misdemeanor must be released on personal recognizance if a resident of the community. An officer who violates that state law (such release not being a constitutional right) cannot claim the good faith defense under *Harlow* unless state law says that the good faith defense is available in such cases.

## III. LEGALITY OF "WE WILL RELEASE IF YOU WILL NOT SUE" ARRANGEMENTS

Some jurisdictions unofficially make use of *quid pro quo* arrangements in which a criminal case against a defendant is dismissed in exchange for the dropping of a civil liability lawsuit against an officer or department. Is this practice legal? The Supreme Court has said yes if the agreement is voluntary but not if the agreement is coerced. What is voluntary or coerced depends on the circumstances surrounding the case. In Town of Newton v. Rumery, 480 U.S. 386 (1987), the plaintiff, whose friend was charged in a sex case, made phone calls to the complaining witness. The witness then accused the plaintiff of threatening her, as a result of which the plaintiff was arrested and charged with witness tampering. Subsequent discussions between the prosecutor and the defense lawyer resulted in an arrangement whereby the prosecutor was to drop the charges and the plaintiff was to refrain from suing for the harm caused by his arrest. The plaintiff violated the agreement by suing. The Court noted that such agreements are suspect because they may not be informed and voluntary. However, it is not inherently coercive to present a defendant with a choice between forcing criminal charges and waiving the right to sue under Section 1983. The possibility of involuntariness alone is no reason to condemn this type of bargain outright. The Court concluded that the agreement was voluntary because (1) the plaintiff was a sophisticated businessman whose attorney fully explained the release agreement, and (2) the prosecutor had a valid reason for making the deal—his wish to spare the victim the embarrassment she would have undergone in a trial. Given these circumstances, the Court concluded that the deal was enforceable. It added that the presumption is that such a deal is valid. In a concurring opinion, Justice O'Connor added that "the greater the crime charged, the greater the coercion."

An example of an invalid arrangement is Hal v. Ochs, 817 F.2d 920 (1st Cir. 1987). In that case, the police illegally arrested a suspect and held him in detention until he signed a release. Detention was continued even after the police had determined that the charges were unfounded. The First Circuit Court of Appeals held that since the plaintiff was detained without probable cause and knew he would not be released until he signed the papers relinquishing his right to a civil lawsuit, such release was coerced and therefore invalid under the *Rumery* principle.

## SUMMARY

Various legal defenses are available in civil liability cases, three of which are discussed in this chapter: official immunity, good faith, and probable cause.

Official immunity is derived from the concept of governmental immunity and is divisible into three types: absolute, quasi-judicial, and qualified. Absolute immunity entails that there is no liability at all; therefore, a civil liability suit, if brought, is dismissed by the court without going into the merits of the plaintiff's claim. Certain officials possess quasi-judicial immunity if performing judicial-type functions but not if performing other functions. Qualified immunity means that a public officer is exempt from liability if the actions taken were reasonable and within the scope of employment.

Police officers enjoy qualified immunity. The United States Supreme Court has unanimously rejected the absolute immunity defense for police officers, saying that officers are entitled only to qualified immunity. The only instance when police officers enjoy absolute immunity is when giving testimony in court against a defendant, in which case the officer enjoys the same absolute immunity given to all trial participants.

The good faith defense, often used by public officers, is based on the principle that there is no liability if the officer did not violate a clearly established constitutional right of which a reasonable person would have known. This places an obligation on police officers to know whether or not what they do is against the law and an obligation on agencies to make sure that their officers are regularly updated on constitutional and legal practices and procedures.

The probable cause defense is based on there being reasonable good faith belief in the legality of the action taken. That expectation is lower than the concept of probable cause under the Fourth Amendment, but it is a strong defense in arrest and search and seizure liability cases.

A warrant is a good defense in civil liability cases, particularly on the issue of probable cause, because a warrant carries the presumption that a magistrate has reviewed the affidavit or complaint and found probable cause. A quid pro quo arrangement, whereby a criminal case against a defendant is dismissed in exchange for dropping a civil liability lawsuit against an officer or department, has been declared constitutional by the Supreme Court as long as the arrangement is voluntary and not coerced.

## CASE BRIEFS

### BRISCOE v. LAHUE
### 460 U.S. 325 (1983)

#### FACTS

Briscoe was convicted of burglary in a state court. He subsequently filed a Section 1983 suit, alleging that Officer LaHue had violated his right to due process by committing perjury in the criminal proceeding leading to his conviction. The district court granted LaHue's motion for summary judgment, and the Seventh Circuit Court of Appeals affirmed the decision.

#### ISSUE

May a police officer be held civilly liable under Section 1983 for giving perjured testimony at defendant's criminal trial? *No.*

#### SUPREME COURT DECISION

Police officers are not liable under Section 1983 for giving perjured testimony at a defendant's criminal trial even if such testimony led to the defendant's conviction.

#### CASE SIGNIFICANCE

The court said that subjecting police officers to civil liability under Section 1983 for their testimony might undermine not only their contribution to the judicial process but also the effective performance of their other public duties. The court said that common law provided absolute immunity from subsequent civil liability to all persons, private citizens, or government officials who were integral parts of the judicial process. When a police officer appeals as a witness, the officer may reasonably be viewed as acting like any witness sworn to tell the truth, in which case the officer is entitled to witness immunity. Nothing in the language of Section 1983 suggests that police officer witnesses belong in a narrow, special category of witnesses lacking protection under damage suits. Not being liable for civil damages does not mean that police officers who lie during trial are not subject to sanctions. Like all other witnesses, police officers may be prosecuted for perjury —should the prosecutor so choose. *Briscoe* simply says that the officer may not be held civilly liable for giving perjured testimony. Criminal prosecution for such testimony is something else.

## MALLEY v. BRIGGS
## 106 S. Ct. 1092 (1986)

### FACTS

On the basis of two monitored telephone calls pursuant to a court-author-ized wiretap, Rhode Island State Trooper Malley prepared felony com-plaints charging Briggs and others with possession of marijuana. The complaints were given to a state judge together with arrest warrants and supporting affidavits. The judge signed the warrants, and the defendants were arrested. The charges, however, were subsequently dropped when the grand jury refused to return an indictment. The defendants then brought action under 42 U.S.C. Section 1983, alleging that Malley, in applying for the arrest warrants, had violated their rights against unreasonable search and seizure. The court, while granting a directed verdict in favor of the officers based on other grounds, stated that a police officer who believes that the facts stated in an affidavit are true and submits them to a neutral magistrate may be entitled to absolute immunity. The court of appeals reversed the de-cision.

### ISSUE

What type of immunity is accorded a defendant police officer in Section 1983 actions when it is alleged that the officer caused the plaintiffs to be un-constitutionally arrested by presenting a judge with a complaint and a sup-porting affidavit that failed to establish probable cause?

### SUPREME COURT DECISION

A police officer is only entitled to qualified immunity, not absolute immu-nity, in Section 1983 cases.

### CASE SIGNIFICANCE

Officer Malley argued that he be given absolute immunity, despite early de-cisions to the contrary, because his function in seeking an arrest warrant was similar to that of a complaining witness. The Supreme Court answered, saying that complaining witnesses were not absolutely immune in common law, adding that in fact the generally accepted rule in 1871, when the civil rights law was passed, was that one who procured the issuance of an arrest warrant by submitting a complaint could be held liable if the complaint was made maliciously and without probable cause. If malice and lack of proba-ble cause are proved, the officer enjoys no absolute immunity. The Court also refused to be swayed by the officer's argument that policy considera-tions require absolute immunity when qualified immunity provides ample protection to all but the plainly incompetent or those who knowingly vio-late the law. The Court considered this protection sufficient, because, under current standards, the officer is not liable anyway if he or she acted in an objectively reasonable manner. *Malley* therefore makes clear that under no circumstances will the Court extend the "absolute immunity" defense (available to judges, prosecutors, legislators, and certain members of the executive branch) to police officers. The only exception occurs when the officer is testifying in a criminal trial. This means that officers enjoy only qualified immunity but that they will not be liable if they act in an objectively reasonable manner.

# 6

# WHO PROVIDES LEGAL REPRESENTATION AND WHO PAYS IF HELD LIABLE?

A police officer facing a liability suit under federal or state law has two immediate concerns: Who will provide legal defense and, if liable, who pays the court-imposed damage fees? These concerns will be discussed in this chapter.

## I. WHO PROVIDES LEGAL REPRESENTATION?

Most state agencies, by law or written policy, provide representation to state law enforcement officers in civil actions. Such representation is usually undertaken by the state attorney general, the legal counsel of the state. Many states have statutes which provide that if a state public officer is sued, the attorney general's office will defend the officer in court, and that if the officer is held liable, the state will pay all or part of the monetary damages imposed, as long as the officer acted within the scope of authority.

The situation is different in local law enforcement agencies. In most counties, cities, towns, and villages, there is no written policy requiring the local agency to defend public officials in liability lawsuits. State legislatures can require local agencies in most states to defend and indemnify public employees who are sued, but legislators are hesitant to do that, because the money used would come from local funds. Legal representation by a local agency is usually informal and decided on a case-by-case basis. This means that the agency is under no legal obligation to provide a lawyer should an officer be sued. Most agencies will likely provide a lawyer, but that is a decision for local policymakers to make as the need arises.

If a local agency provides a lawyer, it will probably be the district attorney, the county attorney, or another lawyer working in some capacity with the local government. In some cases, the officer is allowed to choose a lawyer, with the lawyer's fees being paid by the agency. This is an ideal arrangement but is unpopular with agencies because it costs extra (as opposed to providing an in-house lawyer in the form of a county or district attorney).

If the agency refuses to defend, the officer must provide his or her own lawyer at personal expense. This magnifies the officer's problem and concerns. A suggested approach is this: Make legal representation an obligation of the agency except when the officer acts in gross excess of authority—in which case the officer must provide his or her own lawyer. This policy may be provided for in the agency manual or specifically granted as an employment benefit.

## II. WHO PAYS IF AN OFFICER IS HELD LIABLE?

If an officer is held liable in a lawsuit, who pays for plaintiff's attorney's fees and assessed damages? A majority of states provide some form of indemnification for state employees. The amount varies considerably; some states set no limit, although most states do. If the court awards the plaintiff an amount larger than the maximum allowed by the agency, the employee pays the difference.

Although most state agencies provide some form of payment or indemnification, it does not follow that the agency will automatically pay every time liability is imposed. Most agencies will pay if the officer acted "within the scope of employment." This means that the agency will not indemnify if the officer is grossly, blatantly, or outrageously violative of individual rights or of agency regulations, as determined by the trial court.

By contrast, the degree of indemnification provided by local agencies varies from full indemnification to no indemnification whatsoever. Many states and local agencies will not pay punitive damages (as opposed to token or actual damages) against a public employee, because the imposition of punitive damages usually means that the employee acted outside the scope and course of employment, so that the payment by the agency of punitive damages would be against public policy.

Police officers need to know whether the department will provide legal representation if an officer is sued and whether it will pay if liability is imposed. Ideally, this should be a matter of statute or written official policy. Chances are, however, that only a few departments have explicit and written rules on representation and indemnification.

## III. ATTORNEY'S FEES FOR PLAINTIFFS IN CIVIL RIGHTS CASES: THE ATTORNEY'S FEES AWARDS ACT OF 1976

Although this chapter focuses primarily on the issue of legal representation of defendant police officers, a closely related concern deserves discussion. This is the issue of the possible liability of the defendant police officer for attorney's fees should the officer lose the case.

In 1976, the Congress of the United States passed the Civil Rights Attorney's Fees Awards Act, which allows the court to award attorney's fees to the plaintiff in some types of federal lawsuits, including Section 1983 cases. Section 1988 of that law provides, "In any action or proceeding to enforce a provision of Section 1981, 1983, 1985, and 1986 of 42 U.S. Code . . . or Title VI of the Civil Rights Act of 1964, the Court, in its discretion, may allow the prevailing party, other than the United States, a reasonable attorney's fee as part of the costs." The act allows an award of fees to the prevailing party in a Section 1983 action. The term "prevailing party" has been broadly interpreted by the courts to mean any plaintiff who obtains a favorable result from a lawsuit. Court decisions have allowed attorney's fees in the following cases:

- When the parties reached a voluntary settlement without having tried the case in court. Brown v. Culpepper, 559 F.2d 274 (5th Cir. 1977).

- When a party prevails in a consent decree (where the parties mutually agree on a case settlement). Maher v. Gagne, 448 U.S. 122 (1980).

- Even if damages cannot be awarded because the defendant enjoys absolute immunity (as in the case of a judge). Pulliam v. Allen, 466 U.S. 522 (1984).

- Even if the party does not succeed on all the issues of the case. Attorney's fees, however, are to be awarded only for the work on the successful issues as long as such is unrelated to the other issues. Hensley v. Eckerhart, 461 U.S. 424 (1983). For example, suppose the plaintiff alleges that the arrest by the officer was without probable cause, that the subsequent search was invalid, that the officer used excessive force, and that the plaintiff was forced to give a confession. If the plaintiff proves only one out of the four allegations, perhaps on the issue of use of excessive force, the plaintiff may be considered by the federal court as the prevailing party and entitled to attorney's fees, but only on the issue of the use of excessive force. Fees for filing the three other issues will not be awarded.

- The United States Supreme Court has held that the plaintiff cannot recover attorney's fees for first pursuing administrative remedies prior to filing a civil rights action. The Court stated that the law allows the winner of a civil rights case to recover attorney's fees only for lawyer time that is useful and necessary to advance the civil rights litigation. Time spent by the plaintiff pursuing administrative remedies cannot be considered as preparation for litigation, because a Section 1983 lawsuit does not require that administrative remedies be exhausted before action can be filed. Webb v. Dyer County Board of Ed., 471 U.S. 234 (1985).

- The employer government agency or the unit employing the officer can be ordered to pay the plaintiff's attorney's fees even if the agency was not named as a defendant in the case. Hutto v. Finney, 437 U.S. 678 (1978).

The amount of attorney's fees awarded a prevailing plaintiff is calculated on the following basis: the reasonable hours expended on the litigation multiplied by the reasonable hourly rate for attorneys and professionals in that geographic area. That amount, known as *lodestar*, can be increased or decreased depending on the nature of the legal issues involved, the difficulty of the litigation, and the quality of the representation. The fees are not based on the amount of damages recovered, which has lead to some interesting results:

- Attorney's fees totalling $12,500 were awarded in a civil rights case where plaintiff won $1.00. Nephew v. City of Aurora, 42 CrL 2133 (10th Cir. 1987).
- Legal fees totalling $8,675 were awarded for a $2.00 jury verdict. Branscome v. Longobardo, U.S.D.C. No. 83–2272 AWT (C.D. Cal. 1985).
- Fifty-five thousand dollars in attorney's fees were awarded in a $7,500 judgment. Cool v. Police Department of the City of Yonkers, 620 F. Supp. 954 (D.C.N.Y. 1985).
- Attorneys got nearly $129,000 in fees for winning a $30,000 judgment in an unconstitutional strip search case. Tikalsky v. City of Chicago, 585 F. Supp. 813 (N.D. Ill. 1984).

Most attorney's fees awards tend to be proportionate to the amount of damages recovered; nonetheless, the lodestar method allows for imbalanced results. Many civil rights cases do not result in attorney's fees awards, because in a majority of cases the plaintiff does not prevail.

Note that attorney's fees awards are available in Section 1983 cases because these involve federal law. They are not available in state tort cases unless specifically provided for in state law.

## IV.  ATTORNEY'S FEES FOR DEFENDANTS

Prevailing defendants, such as an officer or agency, may also be awarded attorney's fees, but not on the same basis as prevailing plaintiffs. In order to be awarded attorney's fees, a defendant in a Section 1983 case must show that the plaintiff's suit was frivolous, unreasonable, or groundless. This may be difficult to establish, particularly if the alleged violation in fact took place but was perceived differently by the plaintiff and the defendant. For example, the force used in subduing a suspect may be reasonable to the officer but might be perceived differently by the suspect. Nonetheless, attorney's fees have sometimes been given to defendants as in the following cases:

- The plaintiffs had to pay the defendant's attorney's fees after refusing settlement. Crossonoa v. Marcoccio, 108 F.R.D. 433 (D.R.I. 1985).
- Failure to follow pleading requirements resulted in the lawyers being held personally responsible for the defendants' fees and costs. Stewart v. City of Chicago, 622 F. Supp. 35 (D.C. Ill. 1985).
- $10,000 in defense attorney's fees awarded when officer successfully defends himself against unproven claims of illegal patdown search. Waddell v. Brandon, 528 F. Supp. 1097 (W.D. Okla. 1981).

The attorney's fees law favors plaintiffs, but that is in line with the purpose of Congress, which was to remove economic barriers to obtaining competent counsel for plaintiffs in the litigation of meritorious civil rights claims. Nonetheless, some awards to defendants have been given. For example, in one case, the court awarded $9,815.98 to the defendants (the county, the county police commissioner, and thirty police officers) for unnecessary costs incurred in defending a civil rights case alleging police brutality. Mercy v. County of Suffolk, 748 F.2d 52 (2nd Cir. 1984). In another case, the court awarded $25,860 in attorney's fees and $3,434 in other legal expenses to defendant police officers when the plaintiff failed to prove that the police unjustly assaulted him and inflicted severe injuries. Kappenberger v. Oates, 663 F. Supp. 991 (S.D.N.Y. 1987). No definite figures are available, but a review of civil rights cases indicates that awards of attorney's fees to prevailing plaintiffs are far more prevalent than similar awards to defendants.

## V.  LIABILITY INSURANCE

If police officers in many departments are not assured of legal representation or indemnification, is professional liability insurance to be considered? As the number of lawsuits against public officials increases, liability insurance becomes more attractive. There is, however, the question of who pays the insurance premium. Ideally, the premium should be paid by the agency, but the agency may reject this alternative because of cost. Most liability insurance does not cover punitive damages unless otherwise specified in the contract. In some jurisdictions, liability insurance coverage is the subject of a collective bargaining agreement. A growing number of local governments are "going bare" and resorting to pooling resources for self-insurance in view of the huge increases in insurance premiums in the past few years. In this arrangement, several local governments agree not to obtain liability insurance for their officers but will pool their resources to pay for damages should any of the local agencies be held liable. A great majority of police agencies in the country do not have professional liability insurance and are therefore pooling resources or going bare.

Insurance is sometimes rejected by agencies and officers on the grounds that it may encourage the filing of lawsuits. It is also feared that the amount of damages awarded tends to be larger if the judge or jury knows that the costs will be paid by an insurance company rather than by an individual or a governmental unit. In most jurisdictions, however, insurance ownership or governmental indemnification cannot be mentioned during the trial or hearing. In addition, if insurance coverage is available, the public might well be better served, in that officers will perform their duties more effectively if they are not concerned with personal liability for acts performed in good faith and within the scope of duties. It must be noted, though, that in some states the purchase of liability insurance by the municipality might be held to waive sovereign immunity under state law. Valdez v. City and County of Denver, 764 P.2d 393 (Colo. App. 1988).

In light of such considerations, insurance purchase by police officers is a viable option for protecting police officers. In jurisdictions where either state legal representation or indemnification is uncertain, insurance companies may provide both legal counsel and damage compensation. Insurance policies may, however, limit coverage to acts performed within the scope of employment and may require a demonstration of good faith. In jurisdictions that do not currently provide for paid insurance, officers might wish to work for the modification of statutes and policies so that insurance for agency employees can be obtained. If this is not possible, self-insurance by the officer should be considered.

## SUMMARY

Most state agencies, by law or written policy, provide legal representation to police officers facing civil action, and most also pay for liability, if any is imposed, as long as the officers acted within the scope of employment. Most local agencies, on the other hand, do not have a written policy requiring the provision of legal representation or indemnification. Most will probably defend and indemnify in case of liability, but the policy is usually unwritten and discretionary.

In 1976, Congress passed a law providing for the payment of attorney's fees to prevailing plaintiffs in civil rights lawsuits. The amount is based on the reasonable hourly rates for lawyers in that area. Attorney's fees may also be awarded to defendants, but only if the plaintiff's lawsuit is found to be frivolous, unreasonable, or groundless. While attorney's fees to plaintiffs are usually awarded in successful cases, awarding similar fees to the defendant's lawyers is the exception rather than the rule.

Professional liability insurance needs to be considered by those working in an agency where legal representation and indemnification are not provided or are uncertain. Payment of the premiums should be discussed with the agency. In some cases, the officers may have to pay the premiums on their own.

## CASE BRIEFS

### HUTTO v. FINNEY,
### 437 U.S. 678 (1978)

#### FACTS

Prisoners brought a Section 1983 action against the Arkansas Prison System, alleging a violation of their constitutional rights under the Eighth and Fourteenth Amendments. The district court entered a series of detailed remedial orders. One of the orders challenged by the state of Arkansas on appeal was the award of attorney's fees to be paid out of the Department of Corrections funds based on the district court's finding that state officials acted in bad faith in failing to remedy the violations.

#### ISSUE

Did the award of attorney's fees to be paid from the funds of the Arkansas Department of Corrections violate the Eleventh Amendment guarantee of immunity for the states? *No.*

#### SUPREME COURT DECISION

The fact that neither the state nor the Department of Corrections was expressly named as a defendant in this case did not preclude the district court from awarding attorney's fees to be paid by the state, since, although the Eleventh Amendment prevented the claimants from suing the state by name, their lawsuit against prison officials was, for all practical purposes, brought against the state. There was no indication that the claimants acted in bad faith and therefore it was held the award of attorney's fees by the district court, to be paid out of the funds of a state agency (in particular, the Department of Corrections), was proper.

## CASE SIGNIFICANCE

This case states that governmental agencies as employers are not exempt from paying attorney's fees under the state's Eleventh Amendment immunity. The Supreme Court said that the legislative history of Section 1983 makes it clear that "Congress, when it passed the Act, intended to exercise its power to set aside the States' immunity . . . and to authorize capacities." Although this case involved corrections officials, the principle enunciated by the Court should apply to police agencies as well. This means that a state police agency may be ordered by the federal district court judge to pay the plaintiff's attorney's fees if officials are sued in their official capacities even if the agency was not expressly named as a defendant. State immunity under the Eleventh Amendment is no defense.

## MERCY v. COUNTY OF SUFFOLK
### 748 F.2d 52 (1984)

## FACTS

The plaintiffs filed a Section 1983 suit in federal court against the county, the county police commissioner, and some thirty police officers, claiming acts of police brutality. The case was tried and the defendants won. The court awarded the defendants costs in the amount of $9,875.98. The plaintiffs appealed this award of costs, as well as some other issues.

## ISSUE

Was the award by the court of costs to the county, the county police commissioner, and the police officers proper in this case? Yes.

## COURT DECISION

The award of costs to the defendants in this case was proper and did not constitute an abuse of court discretion. The award was therefore upheld by the court of appeals.

## CASE SIGNIFICANCE

Courts usually award attorney's fees to a prevailing plaintiff in a Section 1983 lawsuit if the plaintiff prevails in at least one of the allegations in the complaint. This case turns the tables on plaintiffs, in that it awards costs to the county and its public officials after verdicts in their favor. Although court costs were at issue in this case and not attorney's fees, there have been cases where both court costs and attorney's fees have been awarded to winning defendants. Plaintiffs challenged the award of costs in this case on the grounds that the suit they brought against the county and the officers "conferred important benefits on the public by informing the public that there is police brutality in Suffolk County, that the award of costs imposes an economic hardship on plaintiffs, and that such an award will deter future claimants from instituting meritorious litigation." The court rejected that claim, saying instead that "we think the exposure to liability for normal court costs will more likely discourage the bringing of frivolous claims than the bringing of meritorious claims." The court hinted that the award would have been rejected had there been abuse of discretion on the part of the trial court. Finding no such abuse here, the court upheld the award.

# 7

# LIABILITY FOR USE OF FORCE: NONDEADLY AND DEADLY

## INTRODUCTION

The law concerning the use of force can be confusing unless studied in a proper legal framework. There are two kinds of force in police work: non-deadly force and deadly force. *Nondeadly force* is defined as force that, when used, is not likely to result in or produce serious bodily injury or death. By contrast, *deadly force* is defined as force that, when used, would lead a reasonable police officer to conclude that it poses a high risk of death or serious injury to its human target.

The use of force has serious implications for police supervisors and departments, because use-of-force lawsuits often include supervisors and the department as defendants. Supervisory and departmental liability, if imposed, is generally based on one of three theories. The first is supervisory negligence. Under this theory, plaintiffs claim that what the officer did could be linked to the supervisor's negligent failure to train, negligent failure to direct, negligent supervision, negligent assignment, negligent entrustment, negligent hiring, or negligent retention.

EXAMPLE: A rookie police officer fatally shoots a fleeing shoplifter. In including the supervisor and the department as defendants, the plaintiff will probably allege that the officer was not properly trained in the use of firearms and was not given proper directives as to when deadly force could be used. In practice, the plaintiff will likely claim all seven traditional areas of supervisory negligence, discussed in Chapter 8, as the basis for liability.

Secondly, supervisory and departmental liability can arise from the existence of written policies on the use of force that are unconstitutional.

EXAMPLE: A departmental policy that authorizes an officer to shoot a fleeing and unarmed misdemeanant leads to liability, because the policy violates a suspect's constitutional rights.

Thirdly, supervisory and departmental liability can arise from customs and practices in the department that are violative of constitutional rights but have been unstopped or tolerated.

EXAMPLE: A department's practice of allowing officers to carry "throw-down" guns so as to establish self-defense in fatal shooting of suspects can, if established, lead to departmental liability. In one case, the court held that inadequate training of deputies or ratification of unconstitutional conduct could lead to liability on the part of the sheriff and the county. Marchese v. Lucas, 758 F.2d 181 (8th Cir. 1985).

The use of force by the police is actionable under state tort law, Section 1983, or both. Most plaintiffs allege violations of both laws in the same complaint, particularly in use-of-deadly-force cases. In most jurisdictions, a complaint containing both types of law may be heard either in a state or federal court. Liability under state tort law is governed by state statutes (for example, the wrongful death statutes found in all states) and court decisions, whereas liability under Section 1983 comes under federal law and federal court decisions.

Since a Section 1983 action succeeds only if there is a violation of a constitutional right or of a right given by federal law, the plaintiff would likely allege that the use of excessive or deadly force violates such constitutional rights as the prohibition against illegal seizure (Fourth Amendment) and the right to due process (Fifth and Fourteenth Amendments) and constitutes cruel and unusual punishment (Eighth Amendment).

EXAMPLE: Suspect X is beaten by the police. X brings a state tort and a Section 1983 lawsuit in a state or federal court. The state tort action will likely allege that the use of excessive force violates rights given under state statutes or court decisions. The Section 1983 allegation might claim that the use of excessive force by the police denied due process, in that a person cannot be subjected to punishment without having been given the opportunity to be heard.

Failure to recover in one cause of action does not mean that the other cause of action also fails; conversely, success in one does not mean success in the other. Though alleged in the same complaint, each cause of action can have different results, because they are based on different laws. Therefore, a plaintiff who fails to recover damages under Section 1983 may collect damages under state tort, and vice versa. The two types of damage claims may usually be filed by the plaintiff in a state or federal court.

## I. NONDEADLY FORCE

Instances of lawsuits against police officers for use of nondeadly force are varied and the damages imposed can be high—as exemplified in the following headlines from the *Liability Reporter:*

$3.4 MILLION COMPENSATORY DAMAGES AWARDED FOR BEATING BY OFFICERS; PO-LICE CHIEF AND MAJOR LIABLE FOR $819,983 PUNITIVE DAMAGES FOR "DELIBER-ATE INDIFFERENCE," INADEQUATE TRAINING.[1]

CITY HELD LIABLE FOR $500,000 IN OFFICER'S BEATING OF SUSPECT DESPITE OF-FICER BEING HELD NOT LIABLE IN SEPARATE LAWSUIT[2]

JURY AWARDS $8 MILLION TO SHEEP RANCHING FAMILY HELD AT GUNPOINT BY OF-FICERS DURING DRUG RAID ON WRONG PREMISES[3]

JURY AWARDS $900,000 TO ARRESTEE WHO CLAIMED POLICE BEAT HIM WHEN HE ASKED TO SEE THEIR IDENTIFICATION[4]

### A. General Rule and Definition in State Tort Cases

The general rule in state tort cases is that nondeadly force may be used as long as it constitutes reasonable force. Reasonable force, in turn, is defined as force that a prudent and cautious person would use if exposed to similar circumstances and is limited to the amount of force that is necessary to achieve valid and proper results. Anything beyond what is necessary to achieve valid and proper results is punitive and therefore unreasonable.

EXAMPLE: The police arrest a suspect who kicks, uses fists, and refuses to be handcuffed. The police may use as much force as is necessary to bring that person under control. Suppose, however, that after subduing him, the police beat him. Such use of force is unreasonable, because the suspect was already under control and the force used was therefore punitive.

It may be best to think of nondeadly force as either *reasonable* or *punitive*. In any areas of police work, the use of reasonable force is legal, whereas the use of punitive force is always illegal and exposes the officer and the department to civil liability.

The problem, however, is that the term *reasonable force* is subjective, and thus what is deemed to be reasonable force depends on the circumstances in each case and the perception of the judge or jury. The officer, therefore, needs to take careful note of the circumstances that led him or her to use a certain level of force. These can be explained during the trial, hopefully to the satisfaction of the judge or jury. Most states allow the use of nondeadly force under a myriad of circumstances. Following are the most common: *when NC law allows Force*

1. overcoming an offender's resistance to a lawful arrest
2. preventing escape
3. retaking a suspect after escape
4. protecting persons and property from harm
5. protecting the officer from bodily injury

Different circumstances justify the use of varying degrees of force. For example, an arrest made by three or more officers of a single suspect in a crowded street during noontime calls for a different amount of force than an arrest of a dangerous suspect (through prior police information) in the suspect's apartment in the evening. Both situations are governed by the same rule—the use of reasonable force under the circumstances—but the circumstances are different.

### B. Assault and Battery Cases

Most lawsuits against the police alleging use of excessive nondeadly force are in the form of assault and battery allegations. These are usually tort cases brought under state law in which the plaintiffs seek damages from the police officers and other defendants for violations of rights.

**1. *Assault.*** Although sometimes combined into one term, *assault* and *battery* refer to two separate acts. Assault is usually defined as the intentional causing of an apprehension of harmful or offensive conduct; it is an attempt or threat accompanied by the ability to inflict bodily harm on another person. An assault is committed if the officer causes another person to think that he or she will be subjected to harmful or offensive contact. For example, for no justifiable reason, Officer X draws his gun and points it at another person. This constitutes assault, because the act is intentional and caused an apprehension of harmful or offensive conduct. In many jurisdictions, words alone do not constitute assault. There must be an act to accompany the threatening words.

**2. *Battery.*** Battery is the intentional infliction of harmful or offensive body contact. Given this broad definition, the potential for battery exists every time an officer uses force on a suspect or arrestee. The main difference between assault and battery is that assault is generally menacing conduct that results in a person's fear of imminently receiving battery, whereas battery involves unlawful, unwarranted, or hostile touching—however slight. In some jurisdictions, assault is attempted battery.

The police may use reasonable force when making an arrest, but unreasonable force constitutes battery. If the arrest by the police is improper or invalid, the handling and handcuffing of the arrestee constitutes a technical battery. Budgar v. State, 414 N.Y.S. 2d 463 (1979).

In one case, the court found that the police had used excessive force on a family when responding to a call to settle a neighborhood dispute, and they were made to pay $10,000. The court said that excessive force was used on the father, who was not of great physical strength and who was already being subdued by his brother when the police kicked him in the groin and struck him on the head with a nightstick. It was alleged that the officers kicked the mother on the back and buttocks after she was handcuffed and lying face down in the mud. The son was also injured during the arrest process. Lewis v. Downs, 774 F.2d 711 (6th Cir. 1985). In another case, the evidence clearly showed that the plaintiff had been repeatedly and severely hit, at times with a nightstick, and had been slammed against the trunk of the car. The amount of force used was considered excessive; hence damages were awarded. Bustamente v. City of Tucson, 701 P.2d 861 (Ariz. App. 1985).

**3. *Defense.*** The obvious defense in assault and battery cases is that the use or threat of the use of force by the police was reasonable under the circumstances. The use of reasonable force includes self-defense by the police and the defense of others, concepts that are usually associated with the use of deadly force but are also applicable in nondeadly force situations. The defense of reasonableness is available not only when an officer is actually attacked but also when the officer reasonably thinks that he or she is in imminent danger of an attack. In other words, perception rather than reality is the test for a valid defense, as long as the perception is reasonable.

**4. *Burden of Proof.*** In assault and battery cases against the police, most courts have held that the burden of proving that excessive force was used lies with the plaintiff. Once that is established during the trial, however, the burden shifts to the defendant officer to prove that such use of force was justified—if that be the defense. This means that the officer must prove that under the circumstances the amount of force used was reasonable. In contrast, a California appeals court has taken a different course. In one case involving battery, it required the police to bear the burden of proving that the force used was reasonable. Valdez v. Abney, 227 Cal. Rptr. 707 (1986). The court added that, "the officer is not entitled to a presumption, a battery is justified simply because of his or her official position." The California decision is the exception rather than the rule. As noted above, the burden of proof usually lies with the plaintiff, and failure to prove the allegation results in the dismissal of the case.


## II. DEADLY FORCE

The use of deadly force by the police has resulted in considerable litigation, as these headlines indicate:

> MUGGER SHOT BY POLICE FLEEING FROM THE SCENE OF THE ROBBERY AWARDED $4.3 MILLION FOR SHOOTING WHICH PARALYZED HIM[5]

> JURY AWARDS $7.6 MILLION TO TWO MEN MISTAKENLY SHOT AT, BEATEN AND CHARGED WITH ATTEMPTED MURDER[6]

> FEDERAL APPEALS COURT UPHOLDS $5.1 MILLION AWARD FOR SHOOTING BY PLAIN-CLOTHES OFFICERS THAT LEFT PLAINTIFF PARAPLEGIC[7]

> $5 MILLION AWARD TO FAMILY OF MAN SHOT AND KILLED BY OFFICER[8]

The rules on the use of deadly force are often more precise, strict, and limiting. *Deadly force is defined as force that, when used, would lead a reasonable police officer objectively to conclude that it poses a high risk of death or serious injury to its human target.* Firearms are good examples of instruments of deadly force; so are long knives, daggers, and lead pipes. A nightstick may be considered an instrument of deadly force, depending on how it is used. An arm or fist may be a deadly weapon and its use likely to produce death or serious injury. For example, the fist of a professional heavyweight boxer is a deadly weapon, whereas the fist of a ten-year-old boy would be considered nondeadly.

Police officers are different from other public officials in that in some instances they are allowed to use deadly force. The authority to use such force is necessary in police work, but it also carries serious obligations and the potential for high-profile liability lawsuits. A potential lawsuit exists every time a police officer uses a gun. Liability may arise under *intentional tort* (specifically the use of excessive force and wrongful death) or *negligence tort* (when negligence in the handling of firearms results in injury to a suspect or a third party). Liability may also arise under Section 1983, because a plaintiff can allege that the use of deadly force by the police under the circumstances constituted a violation of due process rights. Police officers are advised to observe utmost care when using deadly force and must strictly abide by prescribed departmental rules.

Although variations exist from state to state and according to departmental regulations, the general rules are summarized in the discussion below.

## A. In Misdemeanor Cases

The safest advice for police officers is not to use deadly force in misdemeanor cases. The only exception is if deadly force is necessary for self-defense or defense of the life of a third person. The use of deadly force in misdemeanor cases always raises questions of disproportionality, because the designation of the offense as a misdemeanor signifies that society does not consider the act serious in that jurisdiction. If the act is not considered serious, using deadly force is a disproportionate sanction to be used to prevent possible escape.

EXAMPLE: A police officer is serving an arrest warrant for petty theft. The suspect runs away upon seeing the police. If the officer uses deadly force to prevent the escape, the officer will be held civilly liable.

## B. In Felony Cases

**1. *General Rule.*** The safest rule is to use deadly force only when the life of the officer or another person is in danger and the use of such force is immediately necessary to preserve that life. In all other cases— such as resistance to arrest or escape from custody—the use of deadly force poses great liability risks for the police officer and must be regarded only as a last resort. If authorized, however, by state law or departmental policy, then the use of deadly force in instances other than self-defense or defense of third persons is valid, as long as it is not so disproportionate to the severity of the offense committed as to constitute cruel and unusual punishment. For example, a state law or departmental policy that allows the use of deadly force to prevent the escape of a dangerous murder suspect will likely be constitutional because of the seriousness of the crime of murder. On the other hand, if the crime was shoplifting, serious constitutional questions would arise from the use of deadly force because of its disproportionality to the nature of the offense.

**2. Tennessee v. Garner: *The Leading Case on the Use of Deadly Force to Prevent Escape of Fleeing Felons.*** Until 1985, there were no guidelines from the United States Supreme Court on the use of deadly force by police officers. The limits for such use were set instead by state law or departmental rules. That changed in 1985, when the Court decided Tennessee v. Garner, 471 U.S. 1 (1985), setting guidelines for the use of deadly force to prevent escape of fleeing felons.

In *Garner*, two Memphis police officers one evening answered a "prowler inside call." Upon arriving at the scene, they saw a woman standing on her porch and gesturing toward the adjacent house. The woman said she had heard glass shattering and was certain that someone was breaking in. One police officer radioed the dispatcher to say that they were on the scene, while the other officer went behind the neighboring house. The officer heard a door slam and saw someone run across the backyard. The fifteen-year-old suspect, Edward Garner, stopped at a six-foot-high chain-link fence at the edge of the yard. With the aid of a flashlight, the officer saw Garner's face and hands. He saw no sign of a weapon and admitted later that he was reasonably sure Garner was unarmed. While Garner was crouched at the base of the fence, the officer called out, "Police, halt," and took a few steps toward him. Garner then began to climb over the fence. The officer shot him. Garner died; ten dollars and a purse taken from the house were found on his body.

In using deadly force to prevent the escape, the officer was acting upon the authority of a Tennessee statute and pursuant to police department policy. The Tennessee statute provided that "if after notice of the intention to arrest the defendant, he either flees or forcibly resists, the officer may use all the necessary means to effect the arrest." The police department policy was slightly more restrictive but still allowed the use of deadly force in cases of burglary even if there was no danger to the officer.

The Court concluded that the "facts, as found, did not justify the use of deadly force" under the circumstances and therefore remanded the case for further proceedings on the issue of liability.

*Garner* set the following guideline on the use of deadly force to prevent escape:

*Know*

> Where the officer has probable cause to believe that the suspect poses a threat of serious physical harm, either to the officer or to others, it is not constitutionally unreasonable to prevent escape by using deadly force.

Worded affirmatively, it is constitutionally reasonable for an officer to use deadly force to prevent escape when the officer has probable cause to believe that the suspect poses a threat of serious physical harm, either to the officer or to others.

The Court then added,

*Know*

> if the suspect threatens the officer with a weapon <u>or there is probable cause to believe that he has committed a crime involving the infliction or threatened infliction of serious physical harm</u>, deadly force may be used if necessary to prevent escape, and if, where feasible, some warning has been given.

According to one writer, three elements may be deduced from the above quotation that should offer some guidance in assessing situations to determine whether the officer's belief that a suspect is dangerous is in fact justified:[9]

1.  The suspect threatens the officer with a weapon.
2.  The officer has probable cause to believe that the suspect has com-

*injury*

*and if possible give warning.*

mitted a crime involving the infliction or threatened infliction of serious physical harm.

3. The officer has given some warning, if feasible.

The writer goes on to say that either (1) or (2) above would satisfy the requirement of dangerousness but that (3) applies to both (1) and (2), meaning that some warning must be given, if feasible, in either instance.

EXAMPLE 1: Officer Y tries to arrest suspect A, who is sought for murder. Suspect A threatens to shoot the officer so he can escape. Officer Y may then use deadly force to repel that threat and to prevent escape.

EXAMPLE 2: Officer Z has probable cause to believe that suspect B has just killed his wife with a knife. Officer Z tries to arrest B, but B tries to escape. Officer Z may use deadly force to prevent the escape.

In both examples, the officer must give some warning, if feasible, that deadly force is about to be used. This can take the form of such statements as, "Put that knife down or I'll shoot," or "Halt, or I'll shoot." If the suspect heeds the warning, the necessity to use force then ceases.

The Supreme Court, in *Garner*, also concluded that the use of deadly force to prevent the escape of an apparently unarmed suspected felon was constitutionally unreasonable. The Court emphasized that "where the suspect poses no immediate threat to the officer and no threat to others, the harm resulting from failing to apprehend him does not justify the use of deadly force," adding that "a police officer may not seize an unarmed nondangerous suspect by shooting him dead."

The *Garner* decision rendered unconstitutional the then existing "fleeing felon" statutes in nearly half of the states insofar as those statutes allowed the police to use deadly force to prevent the escape of a fleeing felon regardless of circumstances. Fleeing felon statutes are constitutional only if they comport with the requirements set by the Court in *Garner*. The Court based its decision on the Fourth Amendment, saying that "there can be no question that apprehension by the use of deadly force is a seizure subject to the reasonable requirement of the Fourth Amendment." It follows that if an arrest of a suspect with the use of nondeadly force is governed by the Fourth Amendment, the use of deadly force to make an arrest should also be so governed.

### 3. *Unaddressed Issues in* Garner

a. *Must the police actually be threatened before deadly force can be used to prevent escape?* This was not directly answered in *Garner*, but the Tenth Circuit Court of Appeals has said that where a suspect has placed an officer in a dangerous, life-threatening situation, there is no requirement that the suspect actually be armed. It is enough that the officer have a *reasonable belief* that it is so. In cases where the suspect is fleeing after committing an inherently violent crime, the court also said that there is no requirement that the suspect actually be armed. It is enough that the officer have a *reasonable belief* that it is so. In cases where the suspect is fleeing after committing an inherently violent crime, the court also said that there is no requirement that the officer's life actually be threatened by the suspect. Instead, the officer is allowed to infer that the suspect is inherently dangerous by the violent nature of the crime. Ryder v. City of Topeka, 814 F.2d 1412 (10th Cir. 1987).

In another case, the police shot and killed an armed suspect who was positioned in front of a residential home with a rifle. The estate of the deceased brought action against the police, alleging violation of civil rights. The court rejected the plaintiff's claim, stating that since the suspect was armed and the police had a good faith and reasonable belief that such action was necessary, liability did not ensue. Ealey v. City of Detroit, 375 N.W. 2d 435 (MI 1985).

All of the above cases indicate that the police need not be "actually threatened" before deadly force can be used to prevent escape. What is needed is an objective reasonable belief on the part of the officers that they are in a life-threatening situation.

**b.** *Does* **Garner** *allow the use of deadly force by the police to prevent the escape of a felon who committed an offense involving the use or threat of physical violence but who is not armed and does not pose a present threat to the officer or to others at the time he or she attempts to escape?* Suppose X shoots and kills a pedestrian, escapes in a car, and is being chased by the police. In the course of the chase, the police see X throw the gun away. Will the police be justified in using deadly force to prevent the escape? Although *Garner* can be interpreted to mean that deadly force should not be used merely to prevent escape by a fleeing felon, the language of the decision is not all that clear. A safe interpretation of *Garner* would be that deadly force ought not to be used in these instances. However, if a police officer reasonably believes that a threat to his or her life still exists, the situation is importantly different.

**c.** *Must a police officer fire warning shots before aiming at a fleeing suspect?* This question was not addressed in *Garner*. Although the Court said that the officer must give some warning, if feasible, warning shots were not specified. The current practice is that the firing of warning shots is governed by state law or departmental policy. Some jurisdictions require warning shots; others prohibit them. *Garner* set no constitutional rule one way or the other; hence state law or local policy prevails.

**d.** *May the police use deadly force to prevent escape in cases where there are multiple felony suspects but only one is armed?*[10] Suppose A and B rob a 7-Eleven outlet, but only A carries a gun while B acts as the lookout. Will the police be justified in using deadly force to prevent the escape of B, the unarmed suspect? Lower courts have not adequately addressed the issue, but a reasonable interpretation of *Garner* would suggest that deadly force may be used only on the armed suspect.

**e.** *If the use of deadly force is justified, is there a limit to the type or degree of force that is applied?*[11] Does it make any difference, for example, whether a .22-caliber pistol or a double-barrel shotgun was used? How about the firing of multiple shots at a suspect when a single shot would have sufficed? The assumption behind these questions is that there are varying levels of the use of deadly force and that the level of deadly force to be used should be dictated by circumstances. Most lower courts have refused to accept the concept or address further the issue of the proper level of deadly force to be used. The courts are less concerned about the type or degree of force applied than they are with whether such use is justified.

**f.** *When does* **Garner** *take effect?* *Garner* was decided in 1985. The Court's decision applies prospectively, that is, to incidents that happened after the decision was made public. Suppose an officer is uninformed about the decision and shoots a fleeing felon three years after the *Garner* decision. Would qualified immunity (i.e., the good faith defense) apply?

This was partially answered in a subsequent case in the Sixth Circuit Court of Appeals, the same circuit involved in *Garner.* In Robinson v. Bibb, 840 F.2d 349 (6th Cir. 1988), a police officer saw a man dismantling the officer's car. The officer identified himself, whereupon the man began to run away. The officer fired a warning shot and then another shot that killed the fleeing felon. The shooting took place four days after the United States Supreme Court's decision in *Garner.* When sued in a Section 1983 case, the officer claimed qualified immunity, saying that he was unaware of the *Garner* decision when the shooting took place and therefore was entitled to the good faith defense. He maintained that four days did not constitute sufficient time for the average police officer to have known about the Court's decision. On appeal, the Sixth Circuit rejected the officer's claim, saying that although the United States Supreme Court decided *Garner* only four days before the shooting, it itself had decided *Garner* two years earlier, its decision having been merely upheld on appeal by the Supreme Court. The Sixth Circuit then stated that given the two-year time period, a reasonable police officer should have known that the fleeing felon could not be shot unless he was perceived to pose a threat to the pursuing officer or to others during the flight.

The above case fails to give definitive guidelines as to when *Garner* takes effect. It does state, however, that two years is sufficient time for an officer to become aware of a court of appeals decision and therefore to be bound by it. The decision also underscores the fact that a lower court decision has the force of law and is binding on police officers, pending appeal. Although *Garner* did not state a definitive date when it is to take effect, there is no question that at this time, years after the case was decided, the decision has become binding on police officers and that any reasonable police officer should be aware of the civil liability implications of the decision. In fact, the *Garner* rule should by now be incorporated in the use-of-deadly-force policy of every police department in the country.

### C. The "Sudden Emergency" Doctrine[12]

According to this doctrine, a sudden emergency lowers the standard of care for the use of a weapon unless the officer created the emergency. For example, in one case, an officer who had been shot during a robbery of a bar and who returned the fire from the floor where he had fallen was not liable when one of four bullets killed the plaintiff, who was more than a hundred feet away. The jury concluded that this was an emergency situation with "no time for thought," since a sudden decision was necessary; hence no liability. Scott v. City of Opa Locka, 311 So. 2d 825 (Fla. Dist. Ct. App. 1975).

By contrast, the sudden emergency doctrine was rejected in a case where there was a failure to use signals or to warn that officers were present. The court concluded that inadequate supervision at the scene led to a shoot-out and that therefore the shooting of the plaintiff who had called the officers was unjustified. The emergency in this case was of the officers' creation; hence the sudden emergency doctrine did not apply. London v. Ryan, 349 So. 2d 1334 (La. App. 1977). In another case, a police officer testified that he shot the suspect because he thought the suspect had grabbed his partner's gun and posed a threat to their lives. Witnesses said that the officers beat the man on the head as they talked to him in the squad car. The trial court found both officers liable. On appeal, the Eleventh Circuit affirmed the liabilities, saying that "a moment of legitimate fear should not preclude liability for a harm which largely resulted from his own improper use of his official power." Gilmere v. City of Atlanta, 737 F.2d 894 (11th Cir. 1984).

### D. What Governs the Use of Deadly Force?

Numerous cases of legal liability resulting in multimillion-dollar damage awards arise from the use of nondeadly or deadly force. Officers must therefore exercise utmost caution. The use of force, nondeadly or deadly, is governed by the following:

1.  the United States Constitution, particularly the Fourth Amendment prohibition against unreasonable searches and seizures, and the due process clause

2. state law, usually the penal code or the code of criminal procedure, which defines when an officer may or may not legally use force
3. judicial decisions, including cases decided by federal courts (e.g., *Garner*) and state courts
4. departmental or agency rules or guidelines, which can be more limiting but not more permissive than state law or court decisions

Officers must be familiar with all of the above, but particularly with departmental rules on the use of force. Those rules are often more limiting than state law and are binding on the officer, regardless of what state law or court decisions say.

EXAMPLE: Assume that the law of the state of Illinois provides that deadly force may be used to prevent the escape of a jail inmate. If the policy of the Chicago Police Department, however, limits the use of deadly force only to cases of self-defense by the police and therefore precludes the use of deadly force to prevent jail escapes, that departmental policy must be followed. Violation of that policy can mean administrative sanctions by the department even if the act is allowed by state law and court decisions.

### E. Wrongful Death Lawsuits

This tort, usually established by law, arises whenever death occurs as a result of an officer's action or inaction, be it in felony of misdemeanor cases. It is brought by the surviving family, relatives, or legal guardian of the estate of the deceased for pain, suffering, and actual expenses (such as expenses for the funeral and hospitalization) and for the loss of life to the family or relatives. Examples include shooting and killing a fleeing suspect, firing shots at a suspect in a shopping center that result in the death of an innocent bystander, or using a chokehold that results in the death of the arrestee. In some states, a death resulting from a police officer's use of deadly force comes under the tort of misuse of weapons. An officer has a duty to use not merely ordinary care but a high degree of care in handling weapons, otherwise he or she becomes liable for wrongful death.

### F. The Need for a Policy on the Use of Deadly Force

Police use of deadly force is an emotional issue in police departments and in the community. The police are allowed to use deadly force in their work, but such use must be sparing and limited, otherwise serious legal consequences follow. In the words of one observer, "Probably the most volatile issue that creates friction between the police and the minority community today is that of police use of deadly force. To correct this problem, police departments must develop firearms policies that restrict the use of deadly force and place a high value on human life."[13]

Police departments would be wise to follow this advice (in fact, an overwhelming majority of large police departments already have). Deadly force policy must comply with the United States Constitution and state law, but it must also take into account that deadly force is sometimes needed to protect the public as well as police officers themselves.

To minimize civil liability lawsuits, several big city departments have employed a number of techniques designed to properly structure the use of deadly force. Among the many techniques used, the following show promise:[14]

- policies narrowing officer shooting discretion
- violence-reduction training to help officers abide by a "shoot only as a last resort" policy
- use of modern communications equipment and interagency cooperative arrangements that enable officers to summon whatever assistance they need
- protective equipment, such as lightweight, soft body armor suitable for routine wear and "less lethal weapons," including TASERs (electronic dart guns), stun guns (compact cattle prods), rubber bullets, and other similar devices
- strong personnel policies, supervision of line officers, and fair but firm accountability up the chain of command for inappropriate officer aggressiveness and for deficient firearms training, procedures, and practices
- counseling for officers who desire help in dealing with job and other stresses and with postshooting trauma
- "cultural awareness" training to sensitize officers to ethnic, religious, or other traits that might have a bearing on the officer's appraisal of a suspect's dangerousness and on the officer's ability to reduce it
- departmental reward systems that honor both an officer's decisiveness in using deadly force when necessary and his or her ability to resolve situations by less violent means when that option is available

As one writer says,

> A police officer, unlike the vast majority of other public servants in our society, has the legal authority to take a life. But also unlike his fellow servants, the police officer is daily asked to put his own life at risk in attempting to enforce our laws and protect our lives and property. The au-

thority to use deadly force within the constitutional framework is not a luxury... it is a responsibility.[15]

## III. DEFENSES OF SUPERVISORS AND AGENCIES IN USE-OF-FORCE CASES

Supervisors and agencies are wide open to liability in use-of-force cases. In most lawsuits alleging improper use of force, supervisors and agencies are made parties-defendant in addition to the allegedly erring officer. This is particularly true in use-of-deadly-force cases, where the injury can be serious, if not fatal. The "deep pockets" theory encourages the inclusion of multiple defendants in such lawsuits. Plaintiffs usually allege that supervisors and agencies should be held liable based on the general concept of supervisory liability, meaning that the injury can be linked to negligent failure to train, negligent supervision, negligent failure to direct, negligent hiring, negligent retention, negligent entrustment, or negligent assignment. Note, however, that the concept of *respondeat superior* (literally, "let the master answer") does not apply to Section 1983 cases.

One writer has identified the following defenses that may be used by agencies and supervisors in improper force claim cases:[16]

1. There were policies and procedures on use of force and the actions complained of were in violation of the policies.
2. There is no pattern of use of force which violates policies.
3. The officer successfully completed training in the use of force.
4. There is nothing in the officer's record which could have alerted the supervisors about the officer's potential to improperly use force.

## IV. TEST TO DETERMINE CIVIL LIABILITY UNDER SECTION 1983 IN EXCESSIVE-USE-OF-FORCE CASES: *GRAHAM v. CONNOR*

Since the police can be held liable for excessive use of force, nondeadly or deadly, what test will the courts use to determine whether the use of force amounts to a violation of a constitutional right so that the officer can then be held civilly liable under Section 1983? In a case decided in 1989, the Supreme Court said that allegations that law enforcement officers used excessive force in arrests, investigative stops, or other forms of seizure must be analyzed and judged under the Fourth Amendment "objective reasonableness" standard rather than under the "substantive due process" clause of the Fourteenth Amendment. Graham v. Connor, 45 Crl. 3033 (1989).

The facts of *Graham* are as follows: Graham, a diabetic, asked a friend to drive him to a convenience store to buy orange juice to counteract the onset of an insulin reaction. Upon arrival at the store, Graham saw a lot of people ahead of him, so he asked his friend to drive him to another friend's house. Connor, a police officer, saw Graham enter and leave the store hastily. Suspicious, Connor stopped the car and ordered Graham and his friend to wait while he ascertained what happened in the store. Back-up police arrived, handcuffed Graham, and ignored explanations about his diabetic condition. A scuffle ensued and Graham sustained multiple injuries. Graham was released when the officer learned that nothing happened in the store. He later sued, alleging excessive use of force by the police.

*Graham* now sets the legal standard by which allegations of excessive use of force by police officers are determined for civil liability purposes, that standard being "objective reasonableness" under the Fourth Amendment. In a case decided earlier (Johnson v. Glick, 481 F.2d 1028, 2nd Cir. 1973), the court of appeals had enumerated four factors that courts were to use in determining constitutional violations in use-of-force cases. This earlier test required consideration by the court of whether the officer acted in "good faith" or "maliciously and sadistically for the very purpose of causing harm." This substantive due process standard was hard on the police, because it allowed the jury or judge, in the comfort of the courtroom and with sufficient time for deliberation, to evaluate the conduct of an officer who had to make split-second life or death decisions. Nonetheless, a vast majority of lower federal courts applied this test to all excessive force claims against law enforcement and prison officials filed under Section 1983.

All that has changed. Under the *Graham* test, the reasonableness of a particular use of force by the police, deadly or nondeadly, "must be judged from the *perspective of a reasonable officer on the scene*, rather than with the 20/20 vision of hindsight [emphasis added]." The Court added that whether the conduct of an officer is reasonable in an excessive use of force case is determined by asking the following question: "*Are the officers' actions 'objectively reasonable' in light of the facts and circumstances confronting them, without regard to their underlying intent or motivation?*"

The Court did not specify factors that might lead to a finding of objective reasonableness by a judge or jury. All it said was that this should be judged from the perspective of a reasonable officer on the scene. Although a new standard has thus been set, the standard still leaves room for subjectivity, because even reasonable officers can differ as to what action ought to have been taken under the circumstances.

Under this new test, the officer's motivation, therefore, becomes unimportant. Said the Court in *Graham*, "An officer's evil intentions will not make a Fourth Amendment violation out of an objectively reasonable use of force; nor will an officer's good intentions make an objectively un-reasonable use of force constitutional." In sum, if the officer's conduct is objectively reasonable (judged from the perspective of a reasonable of-ficer on the scene), there is no excessive-use-of-force violation, even if the officer had bad motives or evil intent. Conversely, if the officer's con-duct is objectively unreasonable (judged again from the perspective of a reasonable officer on the scene), there is a Fourth Amendment violation, even if the officer's motives were good or pure. Motives, under the *Graham* test, are irrelevant. In short, good motives will not justify the use of unreasonable force; conversely, bad motives do not lead to liability as long as the use of force is objectively reasonable.

Note that the *Graham* test discussed above applies only to Section 1983 cases—a required element of which is a violation of a constitutional right. It does not apply to cases brought under state tort law, such cases being governed by the standards set under state law.

## V.  IS *TENNESSEE v. GARNER* CONSISTENT WITH *GRAHAM v. CONNOR?* YES.

Earlier in this chapter, the case of *Tennessee v. Garner* on the use of deadly force to prevent the escape of a fleeing felon was discussed. Is there any relationship between *Garner* and *Graham*? Are the two consis-tent or inconsistent? The answer is that the two cases are consistent and reconcilable. *Garner* applies to the use of deadly force in fleeing-felon cases, whereas *Graham* applies to all types of excessive-use-of-force cases, deadly or nondeadly, and should be considered to supply the gen-eral rule. *Garner* has a specific application—determining liability in escape attempt cases.

## SUMMARY

There are two kinds of force used in police work: nondeadly force and deadly force. Most lawsuits against the police alleging use of excessive force fall under assault and battery. The main difference between the two is that assault is generally menacing conduct that causes a person to fear imminent battery, whereas battery involves unlawful, unwarranted, or hostile touching. The burden of proof rests with the plaintiff, but once es-tablished, the burden shifts to the defendant officer to prove that such use of force was justified.

Deadly force is force that, when used, would lead a reasonable po-lice officer objectively to conclude that it poses a high risk of death or se-rious injury to its human target. The case of *Tennessee v. Garner* defines the proper use of deadly force to prevent escape. The Supreme Court said that it is constitutionally reasonable for an officer to use deadly force to prevent escape when the officer has probable cause to believe that the suspect poses a threat of serious physical harm either to the officer or to others. Moreover, deadly force may be used if the officer has probable cause to believe that the suspect has committed a crime involving the infliction or threatened infliction of serious physical harm. In both cases, some warning must be given, if feasible. The use of deadly force is governed by the United States Constitution, state law, judicial decisions, and departmental or agency rules or guidelines. To avoid or minimize lawsuits stemming from the use of deadly force, police departments are urged to develop firearms policies that restrict the use of deadly force and still protect the safety of officers. Careful training on the use of deadly force is also a must.

To determine whether or not the use of force amounts to a violation of a constitutional right under Section 1983, the following question needs to be asked: Are the officers' actions "objectively reasonable" in light of the facts and circumstances confronting them, without regard to their underlying intent or motivation. Under this new test, the officers' motivations are unimportant.

## NOTES

1. *Liability Reporter* July 1989, at 1.
2. *Liability Reporter* May 1988, at 1.
3. *Liability Reporter* April 1988, at 3.
4. *Liability Reporter* April 1988, at 1.
5. *Liability Reporter* April 1990, at 57.
6. *Liability Reporter* May 1990, at 68.
7. *Liability Reporter* November 1989, at 167.
8. *Liability Reporter* August 1989, at 119.
9. J. C. Hall, "Police Use of Deadly Force to Arrest: A Constitutional Standard" (Part II), *FBI Law Enforcement Bulletin*, July 1988, at 23.
10. Americans for Effective Law Enforcement, *Legal Defense Manual*, Brief No. 85-4, at 13.
11. Hall, "Police Use of Deadly Force to Arrest," at 27–28.
12. See I. Silver, *Police Civil Liability* (Matthew Bender, 1988), at 5–19.
13. L. Brown and H. Locke, "The Police and the Community," in R. Staufenberger, ed., *Progress in Policing: Six Essays on Change* (Ballinger Publishing Company, 1980), at 101.
14. W. Geller, "Deadly Force," in *Crime File Study Guide* (National Institute of Justice, NCJ 97218), at 3.
15. Hall, "Police Use of Deadly Force to Arrest," at 29.
16. See W. Collins, *Correctional Law: 1986* (Author), at 105.

## CASE BRIEFS

### TENNESSEE v. GARNER
### 53 U.S.L.W. 4410 (1985)

#### FACTS

Memphis police officers Hymon and Wright were dispatched to answer a "prowler inside call." Upon arriving at the scene they saw a woman standing on her porch and gesturing toward the adjacent house. She told them that she had heard glass breaking and that someone was breaking in next door. While Wright radioed the dispatcher to say that they were on the scene, Hymon went behind the adjacent house. He heard a door slam and saw someone run across the backyard. The fleeing suspect, fifteen-year-old Edward Garner, stopped at a six-foot-high chain-link fence at the edge of the yard. He saw no sign of a weapon, and, though not certain, was "reasonably sure" that Garner was unarmed. While Garner was crouched at the base of the fence, Hymon called out "Police, halt" and took a few steps toward him. Garner then began to climb over the fence. Convinced that if Garner made it over the fence he would elude capture, Hymon shot him. Garner was taken by ambulance to a hospital, where he died. Ten dollars and a purse taken from the house were found on his body.

In using deadly force to prevent the escape, Hymon was acting under the authority of a Tennessee statute and pursuant to police department policy. That statute provides that "if after notice of the intention to arrest the defendant, he either flees or forcibly resists, the officer may use all the necessary means to effect the arrest." The department policy was slightly more restrictive than the statute but still allowed the use of deadly force in cases of burglary.

#### ISSUE

Is the use of deadly force to prevent the escape of an apparently unarmed suspected felon constitutional? *No.*

#### SUPREME COURT DECISION

The use of deadly force to prevent the escape of any felony suspect, whatever the circumstances, is constitutionally unreasonable. When the suspect poses no immediate threat to the officer and no threat to others, the use of deadly force is unjustified.

#### CASE SIGNIFICANCE

This case clarifies the extent to which the police can use deadly force to prevent the escape of an unarmed felon. The Court made it clear that deadly force may be used only if the officer has probable cause to believe that the suspect poses a threat of serious physical harm, either to the officer or to others. In addition, when feasible, the suspect must first be warned. The decision renders unconstitutional existing laws in nearly half of the states that impose no restrictions on the use by police officers of deadly force to prevent the escape of a person suspected of a felony.

State laws and departmental rules can set narrower limits on the use of force (e.g., there might be a rule that deadly force cannot be used at all except in self-defense, even when a suspected felon attempts to escape from the custody of a police officer), but broader limits are unconstitutional. The Court based its decision on the Fourth Amendment, saying that "there can be no question that apprehension by the use of deadly force is a seizure subject to the reasonableness requirement of the Fourth Amendment."

### RYDER v. CITY OF TOPEKA
### 814 F.2d 1412 (10 Cir. 1987)

#### FACTS

Candi Ryder, a juvenile, was shot by a police detective while she fled from the scene of a robbery. She brought a Section 1983 action against the police officer. The district court entered judgment on the jury verdict in favor of the police officer and denied a motion for a new trial. Candi Ryder appealed.

#### ISSUES

(1) Did the lower court err when it denied Ryder's motion for judgment notwithstanding the verdict? and (2) Did the misconduct of the defendant's counsel in failing to produce on time a statement of the defective warrant justify a reversal and remand for a new trial?

#### COURT DECISION

The court found (1) that the jury could have found that "the use of deadly force was justified by the officer's need to protect himself and to prevent escape," and therefore did not reverse the jury's finding; and (2) that the plaintiff was not prejudiced by defense counsel's failure to produce on time a statement by the officer that he knew the name of one suspect and that she was a juvenile.

#### CASE SIGNIFICANCE

For the purpose of this chapter on the use of force, the significance of the Ryder case lies in the Tenth Circuit's decision that in cases where the suspect is fleeing after committing an inherently violent crime, there is no requirement that the officer's life be actually threatened by the suspect before deadly force can be used. Instead, the officer is allowed to infer that the suspect is inherently dangerous because of the violent nature of the crime. In the case, the court said that the "police officer who had been told that participants in the robbery would be armed, and who was chasing a suspect who was about to turn into a darkened alley in a residential area could be found to have believed that he was in an ambush situation where his life was in danger. . . ." According to the court, this justified the use of deadly force against the suspect.

# 8

# LIABILITY FOR FALSE ARREST AND FALSE IMPRISONMENT

## INTRODUCTION

Police officers are often sued for false arrest and false imprisonment. The following headlines from the *Liability Reporter* indicate the types of false arrest and false imprisonment cases brought against the police:

JURY AWARDS $132,500 IN DAMAGES AGAINST CITY AND OFFICERS FOR WRONGFUL ARREST AND INDIFFERENCE TO MEDICAL NEEDS RESULTING IN PARTIAL LOSS OF VISION[1]

DIABETIC MAN MISTAKENLY ARRESTED WHEN HE CALLED FOR AMBULANCE AWARDED $950,000 FOR RESULTING AMPUTATED LEG[2]

NO LIABILITY FOR ESTABLISHING ALLEGED "QUOTA" ARREST POLICY IN ABSENCE OF EVIDENCE THAT OFFICERS WERE ENCOURAGED TO MAKE ARRESTS WITHOUT PROBABLE CAUSE[3]

NO LIABILITY FOR MISTAKING DIABETIC AS BEING DRUNK[4]

MAN ARRESTED WHEN COMPUTER MISTAKENLY SHOWED LICENSE PLATE TO BE STOLEN WAS NOT FALSELY IMPRISONED[5]

False arrest and false imprisonment can lead to civil liability under state tort law or Section 1983. Most state penal codes define false arrest and imprisonment, such definition being almost synonymous with false arrest under state tort law. By contrast, false arrest under Section 1983 means that a person has been illegally seized and deprived of due process. This chapter focuses on false arrest violations under Section 1983 and therefore discusses when a valid arrest can be made in compliance with the requirements of the Fourth Amendment and due process.

## I. ARREST DEFINED

*An arrest is defined as the taking of a person into custody against his or her will for the purpose of criminal prosecution or interrogation.*[6] An arrest deprives a person of liberty by legal authority. Mere words alone do not constitute an arrest. There must be some kind of restraint. A person's liberty must be restricted by law enforcement officers to the extent that the person is not free to leave at will. Not all contacts between police officers and citizens amount to a seizure or an arrest. In the words of the Supreme Court, "a person is 'seized' only when, by means of physical force or a show of authority, his freedom of movement is restrained." United States v. Mendenhall, 446 U.S. 544 (1980). Arrest is a form of seizure and comes under the Fourth Amendment prohibition against illegal searches and seizures; hence false arrest is actionable both under state tort law and Section 1983.

The validity of an arrest is determined primarily by federal constitutional standards, particularly the requirement that every arrest must be based on probable cause. Probable cause is defined as more than bare suspicion; it exists when the "facts and circumstances within the officers' knowledge and of which they have reasonably trustworthy information are sufficient in themselves to warrant a man of reasonable caution in the belief that an offense has been or is being committed." Brinegar v. United States, 338 U.S. 1960 (1949). For practical purposes, probable cause exists when the police have trustworthy evidence sufficient to make "a reasonable man" think that it is more likely than not that the proposed arrest is justified. Probable cause in police work is generally established in three ways: (1) through the officer's own knowledge of facts and circumstances; (2) through information given by an informant or any third party; and (3) through information plus corroboration.

An arrest, with or without a warrant, is not valid unless there is probable cause, as determined by federal constitutional standards. State laws or agency practices that are inconsistent with federal standards are invalid and unconstitutional.

EXAMPLE: A police department authorizes officers to make an arrest based on reasonable suspicion, a lower degree of certainty than probable cause, if the arrest is made in the evening. Such a practice is invalid, because an arrest at any time during the day or night must, according to constitutional standards, be based only on probable cause.

## II. WHEN IS THERE AN ARREST?

Four elements must be present for an arrest to take place: (1) intention to arrest, (2) authority to arrest, (3) seizure and detention, and (4) the individual's understanding that he or she is being arrested.[7]

## A. Intention to Arrest

Without the requisite intent, there is no arrest, even if a person is temporarily stopped or inconvenienced. No arrest occurs when an officer stops a motorist for the issuance of a ticket, asks a motorist to step out of the car, stops a motorist to check his or her driver's license, or stops a person to warn of possible danger. In these cases, there may be temporary deprivation of liberty or a certain amount of inconvenience, but there is no intent on the part of the officer to take the person into custody; therefore, there is no arrest.

If it is not clear from the officer's act whether there was intent to arrest or not, the United States Supreme Court has said that "a policeman's unarticulated plan has no bearing on the question whether a suspect is 'in custody' at a particular time; the only relevant inquiry is how a reasonable man in the suspect's position would have understood the situation." Berkemer v. McCarty, 468 U.S. 420 (1984). In unclear cases, therefore, the perception of the detained person rather than the officer's intent becomes the determining factor. The general rule is that a person has been arrested if, under the totality of the surrounding circumstances, a reasonable person would not believe him- or herself free to go. This is ultimately a question for a judge or jury to decide.

## B. Arrest Authority

Authority to restrain distinguishes arrest from deprivations of liberty (such as kidnapping or illegal detention) committed by private individuals. When there is proper authorization, the arrest is valid; conversely, when proper authorization is lacking, the arrest is invalid. Invalid arrest can arise in the following cases: (1) when the police officer mistakenly thinks he or she has authority to arrest when he or she in fact does not, and (2) when the officer knows that he or she is not authorized to make the arrest but does so anyway.

Whether or not a police officer has arrest authority when off duty varies in practice from state to state. Some states authorize police officers to make an arrest anytime they witness a criminal act. In these states, the officer is in effect on duty twenty-four hours a day, seven days a week, for purposes of making an arrest, whether in uniform or not. Other states limit the grant of arrest power only to times when the officer is strictly on duty. Arrest authority is, therefore, defined by law or regulations of the state and police agency.

## C. Seizure and Detention

Restraint of the subject may be either actual or constructive. *Actual seizure* is accomplished by taking the person into custody with the use of hands or firearms (denoting use of force without touching the individual) or by merely touching the individual without the use of force. *Constructive seizure* is accomplished without any physical touching, grabbing, holding, or use of force. It occurs when the individual peacefully submits to the officer's will and control.

Mere words alone do not constitute an arrest. The fact that a police officer tells a person, "You are under arrest," is not sufficient. The required restraint must be accompanied by actual seizure or peaceful submission to the officer's will and control.

EXAMPLE: Officer P tells a suspect that she is under arrest. The suspect disregards what Officer P says and walks away. Seizure has not been effected, because there was no peaceful submission to the officer's will and control. In this case, the officer needs to actually seize the suspect to place her under control. On the other hand, if after being told that she is under arrest, the suspect says, "I'll go with you to the police station," then seizure will have been effected, even though the officer has not seized the suspect in a physical way.

### D. The Arrestee's Understanding

The fact that he or she is being arrested may be conveyed to the arrestee through words or actions. In most cases the police officer says, "You are under arrest," thereby conveying the intention through words. Similarly, some actions strongly imply that a person is being taken into custody, even though the officer makes no statement. Examples include when a suspected burglar is subdued by the police and taken to a squad car or when a person is handcuffed to be taken to the police station. The element of understanding is not required for an arrest in the following instances: (1) if the suspect is drunk or under the influence of drugs and does not understand what is going on, (2) if the suspect is insane, and (3) if the suspect is unconscious.

### III. FALSE ARREST

False arrest is defined as "a tort consisting of restraint imposed on a person's liberty, without proper legal authority."[8] The terms "false arrest" and "illegal arrest" are often used interchangeably in law enforcement.

In a tort case for false arrest, the plaintiff alleges that the officer made an illegal arrest, usually an arrest without probable cause. A claim of false arrest can also arise if the officer fails to arrest the "right" person, the person named in the warrant.[9] An officer who makes a warrantless arrest bears the burden of proving that the arrest was in fact based on probable cause and that an arrest warrant was not necessary because the arrest came under one of the exceptions to the warrant rule.

If the arrest is made with a warrant, the presumption is that probable cause exists, except if the officer obtained the warrant with malice,
knowing that there was no probable cause. Malley v. Briggs, 475 U.S. 335
(1986). Civil liability for false arrest in arrests with warrant is, therefore,
unlikely unless (1) the officer serves a warrant that he or she knows to be
illegal or unconstitutional, (2) an otherwise valid warrant is executed
negligently, or (3) a "reasonable" police officer would have applied for a
warrant. It is therefore better for the officer to make an arrest based on a
warrant whenever possible.

The order to arrest a suspect or defendant must emanate from a duly
authorized person; otherwise the arrest is invalid and actionable. In one
case, a certain Delmar Dennis was stopped by a deputy sheriff, served
with summons to appear in court on a child support case, and placed
under arrest. Dennis asked whether he could be arrested on the basis of a
civil summons. He was told by the deputy that he had no choice in the
matter. Dennis was driven to jail, where he was detained for three and a
half hours. He subsequently filed a lawsuit against the sheriff and the
deputy, alleging illegal arrest and detention.

At the trial, the deputy testified that an attorney for Dennis's former
wife had brought the summons to the sheriff's office and told the deputy,
"Go out and get Delmar Dennis, he is supposed to be coming to town, we
have got a paper for him." The deputy took this to mean that he was to
bring Dennis to jail. The deputy further admitted that he would arrest
anyone in the county based upon papers given him by an attorney. The
trial court held the deputy liable ($6,000 in compensatory damages,
$10,000 in punitive damages, and $10,555 in attorney's fees). On appeal,
the appellate court upheld the liability, saying that a reasonable police officer would not have arrested Dennis based on an attorney's directions to
"go out and get him." Dennis v. Warren, 779 F.2d 245 (5th Cir. 1985).[10]


## IV. FALSE IMPRISONMENT

False imprisonment is defined as "a misdemeanor of knowingly restraining another unlawfully so as to interfere substantially with his liberty."[11]
False imprisonment is a separate tort from false arrest, but in police tort
cases the two are almost the same in that arrest necessarily means confinement, which is an element of imprisonment.[12] In both cases, the individual is restrained or deprived of freedom without legal justification.
The cases differ, however, in that false arrest almost always leads to false
imprisonment, but false imprisonment is not necessarily the result of
false arrest. For example, a suspect could be arrested with probable cause
(a valid arrest) but be detained in jail for five days without the filing of
charges (false imprisonment).

False imprisonment happens in a number of ways. First, if an officer makes an arrest based on probable cause but later discovers that the person arrested is innocent, then continued imprisonment is false imprisonment even though the arrest was valid. Second, false imprisonment also takes place if a suspect's bail hearing is illegally denied or delayed. Jurisdictions differ as to the length of time a suspect can be detained after a valid warrantless arrest without formal charges being filed. Most jurisdictions set a maximum of twenty-four hours, but at least one federal court of appeals has said that a period of up to seventy-two hours is permissible. Williams v. Ward, 845 F.2d 374 (2d Cir. 1988). Third, false imprisonment can be the result of officer negligence, as when a prisoner is kept in jail after he or she is ordered released by the judge. Fourth, false imprisonment takes place if there is unreasonable or unnecessary delay in bringing an arrested suspect before a magistrate. What is unreasonable or unnecessary delay cannot be stated with certainty in terms of hours; moreover, the delay becomes reasonable if there is a valid reason for it. Fifth, false imprisonment takes place when there is an illegal arrest and the person arrested is detained for any period of time.

Like many tortious acts, false arrest and false imprisonment are also punishable under the state penal code. This means that in addition to civil liability in the form of damages, the officer, if found guilty in a separate criminal proceeding, may receive criminal sanctions. There is no double jeopardy, because one proceeding is civil and the other criminal.

## V. TYPES OF AUTHORIZED ARREST

There are two types of authorized arrest: arrest with a warrant and arrest without a warrant. The Supreme Court has repeatedly expressed a preference for arrests with a warrant. In one case, it said, "Law enforcement officers may find it wise to seek arrest warrants where practicable to do so, and their judgements about probable cause may be more readily accepted where backed by a warrant issued by a magistrate." United States v. Watson, 423 U.S. 411 (1976).

Police officers are strongly advised to obtain a warrant, whenever feasible, because of the following two advantages:

**1. *Having a warrant is generally a valid defense in civil liability cases.*** In one case, a sheriff was sued for executing an arrest warrant issued by a justice of the peace that was valid on its face. The person arrested was tried and sentenced to a year and a day in jail for "violation of a peace bond." He then sued the justice of the peace and the sheriff because he was arrested and convicted of a nonexistent crime. The court said that the sheriff was protected by qualified immunity and not liable because the arrest warrant he served was valid and regular. Turner v. Raynes, 611 F.2d 92 (5th Cir. 1980).

The only situation in which having a warrant will not be a defense is where the warrant was served despite its being clearly invalid due to mistakes the officer should have discovered, such as the absence of a signature or the failure to specify the place to be searched or persons or things to be seized.

EXAMPLE: Officer P serves an unsigned warrant or a warrant that Officer P knows is issued for the wrong person. In either case, he may be liable for false arrest despite the issuance of the warrant.

**2. *A warrant carries the presumption that probable cause exists.*** This is because the affidavit or complaint that led to the issuance of the warrant had been reviewed by the magistrate, who presumably found probable cause to justify its issuance. This presumption of warrant validity may be overcome by the accused in court, but the burden of proof is on the accused to establish that in fact no probable cause existed when the magistrate issued the warrant, which is usually difficult to do.

## A. Arrest with Warrant

An arrest warrant is defined as a "writ or precept issued by a magistrate, justice, or other competent authority, addressed to a sheriff, constable, or other officer, requiring him to arrest the body of a person therein named, and bring him before the magistrate or court to answer, or to be examined, concerning some offense which he is charged with having committed."[13] To minimize civil liability, police officers must pay particular attention to four considerations: (1) the *issuance* of the warrant, (2) the *contents* of the warrant, (3) the *service* of the warrant, and (4) the *announcement* requirement.

**1. *Issuance of the Warrant.*** To secure the issuance of a warrant, a complaint (filed by the offended party or by the police officer) must be filed before a magistrate showing probable cause for arresting the accused. It must set forth facts showing that an offense has been committed and that the accused is responsible for it. If it appears to the magistrate from the complaint and accompanying documents or testimony that probable cause exists for the charges made against the accused, the magistrate issues an arrest warrant.

**2. *Contents of the Warrant.*** The warrant must describe the offense charged and contain the name of the accused or, if unknown, some description by which the accused can be identified with reasonable certainty. Thus, a John Doe warrant (defined as one in which only the name "John Doe" appears because the real name of the suspect is not known to the police) is valid only if it contains a description of the accused by which he or she can be identified with reasonable certainty. A John Doe warrant without such a description is invalid, since it could be used by the police to arrest almost anyone and therefore lends itself to abuse.

**3. *Service of the Warrant.*** An arrest warrant is directed to, and may be executed by, any peace officer in the jurisdiction. In some states, a properly designated private person can also serve a warrant.

**a) *Service within State.*** Inside the state of issuance, a warrant issued in one county or judicial district may be served by peace officers of any county or district in which the accused is found. Some states have statutes giving local peace officers statewide power of arrest, thereby allowing peace officers of the county or district where the warrant was issued to make the arrest anywhere in the state.

**b) *Service outside State.*** A warrant has no authority beyond the territorial limits of the state in which it is issued. For example, an arrest in Illinois cannot be made on the basis of a warrant issued in Wisconsin. There is a "hot pursuit" exception: Most states today have adopted a uniform act authorizing peace officers from one state who enter another in fresh pursuit to arrest the suspect for a felony committed in the first state.

**c) *Time of Arrest.*** In general, felony arrests may be made at any time, day or night, but misdemeanor arrests are usually made during daylight hours. In some states, an arrest for any crime—felony or misdemeanor—can be made at any hour of the day or night.

The arresting officer need not have the arrest warrant in his or her possession at the time of the arrest as long as it is shown to the accused after the arrest, if so requested. An arrest warrant should be executed without unreasonable delay, but it usually does not expire until executed or withdrawn. In this, arrest warrants differ from search and seizure warrants, which must be executed within a specified number of days, after which they are no longer valid.

**4. *Announcement Requirement.*** Many jurisdictions require that a police officer making an arrest or executing a search warrant announce his or her purpose and authority before breaking into a residence. The idea is to allow voluntary compliance with the request for entry and thereby avoid violence. Breaking into the premises without first complying with the announcement requirement may or may not invalidate the entry, depending upon the law or court decisions in that jurisdiction.

There is, however, no constitutional requirement that an announcement be made before entry.

As a general rule, an officer may not break into or force entry into private premises without prior self-identification and after being refused admittance. Forced entry includes not only the use of actual force but also the opening of locked doors with a passkey or the opening of a closed but unlocked door. Exceptions to the announcement requirement, in states where it is required, usually are governed by state law, court decisions, and agency regulations, and hence may vary from state to state. Many of these exceptions come under the general heading of "exigent circumstances," meaning emergency circumstances that would justify doing away with the announcement requirement.

## B. Arrest without Warrant

Although arrest warrants are preferred by the courts and desirable for purposes of police protection from civil liability lawsuits, they are in fact seldom used in police work and are not constitutionally required, except in routine home arrests.[14] About 95 percent of all arrests are made without a warrant. Police officers in all states have a general power to arrest without a warrant. Laws vary from state to state, but the following provisions on warrantless arrests are typical.

### 1. *Arrests by Police for Felonies*

**a)** *General Rule.* A police officer has the power to arrest a person who has actually committed a felony in the presence of the officer. The authority is based on common-law principles, which have since been enacted into state statutes. For example, while on patrol an officer sees a robbery being committed. He or she can make the arrest without a warrant. The term *in the presence of* a police officer refers to knowledge gained firsthand by the officer as a result of using any of his or her five senses: sight, hearing, smell, touch, and taste. Therefore, the police may make a warrantless arrest if probable cause is established by such means as these:

*Sight.* The officer sees X stab Y or sees S break into a residence.

*Hearing.* The officer hears a shot or a cry for help from inside an apartment.

*Smell.* The officer smells gasoline, gunpowder, gas fumes, or marijuana.

*Touch.* The officer examines door or windows in the dark or touches the car muffler to determine if the car has just been used.

*Taste.* The officer tastes a white substance to identify it as sugar, salt, or illegal drugs.

**b)** *Arrests for Felonies in Public Places: No Warrant Required.* The police are not required to obtain an arrest warrant before arresting a person in a public place even if there was time and opportunity to do so. United States v. Watson, 423 U.S. 411 (1976).

**c)** *Arrests for Felonies in Homes: Warrant Required.* Police officers must have an arrest warrant to enter a person's home to arrest him or her if circumstances allow them time to obtain a warrant. The reason is that entry into a private home is an extreme intrusion, and an entry for making an arrest is nearly as intrusive as an entry for a search. There is an exception if exigent circumstances or consent justify a warrantless arrest.

### 2. *Arrests by Police for Misdemeanors*

**a)** *General Rule.* The general rule is that police officers have the power to arrest without a warrant for a misdemeanor but only if the offense is actually committed or attempted in their presence. The police cannot make an arrest if the misdemeanor was merely reported to them by a third party. What the officer does in these cases is to secure an arrest warrant or have the complaining party file a complaint, which can lead to the issuance of a warrant or summons. This rule has its origin in common law. The problem, however, is that this rule is subject to so many exceptions that it has become practically meaningless in many states. These are some of the common exceptions:

- The misdemeanant will flee if not immediately arrested.
- The misdemeanant will conceal or destroy evidence if not immediately arrested.
- The case involves a traffic accident.
- The officer has probable cause to believe that a misdemeanor is being committed, although not in his or her presence.

**b)** *Home Entry.* In the case of a minor offense, a warrantless entry into a home to make an arrest will not be justified. For example, in one case, an officer suspected a person of driving while intoxicated, a nonjailable offense in the state. The officer went to the suspect's home to make an arrest before the alcohol could dissipate. The court said that the officer could not enter the home without a warrant or consent. Given the state's relatively tolerant view of this offense, an interest in preserving the evidence cannot overcome the strong presumption against warrantless invasion of homes.[15] Thus, in determining whether there are exigent circumstances to justify entry into a home without a warrant, a court must consider the seriousness of the offense. Welsh v. Wisconsin, 104 S.Ct. 2091 (1984). Note, however, that home entry without a warrant in felony or misdemeanor cases is justified if there is valid consent.

## VI. ARREST VERSUS DETENTION

It does not matter whether an act is termed an "arrest" or a mere "detention" under state law. What is important is that when a person is taken into custody against his or her will for purposes of criminal prosecution or interrogation, there is an arrest under the Fourth Amendment, regardless of what state law says. For example, state law provides that a police officer may detain a suspect for four hours in the police station for questioning without that suspect being considered arrested. If the suspect is in fact detained in the police station against his or her will, that person has been arrested under the United States Constitution and is therefore entitled to all the rights given to suspects who are under arrest.

In contrast, no arrest or seizure occurs when an officer simply approaches a person in a public place and asks if he or she is willing to answer questions—as long as the person is not involuntarily detained. The question, however, is, *How long* can the suspect be detained and *how intrusive* must the investigation be before the "stop" becomes an "arrest" requiring probable cause? The answer depends on (1) the reasonableness of the detention, and (2) the reasonableness of the intrusion. The detention must be no longer than that required by the circumstances and the intrusion must be the "least intrusive means," that is, it must not be more than is required to verify or dispel the officer's suspicions.

## VII. ARREST VERSUS "STOP AND FRISK"

A legal issue in policing is whether a police officer may stop a person in a public place (or in an automobile), question the person about his or her identity and activities at the time, and frisk the person for dangerous (and perhaps illegally possessed) weapons.[16] An officer must know when to arrest and when merely to "stop and frisk," because circumstances that justify only a stop and frisk can lead to civil liability if the officer instead mistakenly makes an arrest.

Several states have passed stop-and-frisk laws that allow an officer to stop a person in a public place and demand the person's name and address and an explanation of his or her actions if the officer has "reasonable suspicion" (a degree of certainty lower than probable cause) that the person has committed or is about to commit a felony. Other states, and some federal courts, have upheld such practices in judicial decisions even without statutory authorization. Underlying both statutory and judicial approval of stopping and frisking is the notion that this practice does not constitute an arrest and hence can be justified on less than probable cause.

Stop and frisk can be distinguished from arrest as follows:[17]

|  | STOP AND FRISK | ARREST |
|---|---|---|
| 1. Degree of certainty | Reasonable suspicion (about 20% certainty) | Probable cause (more than 50% certainty) |
| 2. Scope | Very limited—only pat-down for weapons | Full body search |
| 3. Purpose | Stop—to prevent criminal activity Frisk—to protect officer and others | To take person into custody |
| 4. Warrant | Not needed | May or may not be needed |

Although a stop and frisk is not an arrest, what the officer discovers while stopping or frisking the suspect (based on reasonable suspicion) may establish probable cause to make an arrest. For example, Officer P stops a suspect and subsequently frisks him. In the course of the pat-down, Officer P touches something that feels like a weapon. If it is in fact a prohibited weapon, Officer P may confiscate it and immediately place the suspect under arrest. Once placed under arrest, the suspect may then be searched in full, and any contraband found on the suspect may also be confiscated. In this case, the original stop based on reasonable suspicion could not justify an arrest, but once the prohibited weapon was discovered as a result of the frisk, then probable cause for arrest ensued.

## VIII. THE "PROBABLE CAUSE" DEFENSE

Probable cause is a defense often used in cases of false arrest, false imprisonment, and illegal searches and seizures, whether the lawsuit be under state tort law or Section 1983. In this defense, it is claimed that probable cause was present during the arrest, whether the arrest was with or without a warrant, and that therefore the arrest was valid. One court has said that for the purposes of a legal defense in Section 1983 cases, probable cause simply means "a reasonable good faith belief in the legality of the action taken." Rodriguez v. Jones, 473 F.2d 599 (5th Cir. 1973). That expectation is lower than the Fourth Amendment's definition of probable cause, which is that it exists when "the facts and circumstances within the officers' knowledge and of which they had reasonably trustworthy information are sufficient in themselves to warrant a man of reasonable caution in the belief that an offense has been or is being committed." Brinegar v. United States, 338 U.S. 160 (1949). For example, an officer makes an arrest that is later determined to be without probable cause. According to the above Fifth Circuit decision, the officer may be exempt from liability if he or she reasonably and in good faith believed at the time of the arrest that it was legal. Liability will likely be imposed either if the officer did not honestly believe that he or she had such a cause or if his or her belief was unreasonable.

An officer who arrests a suspect with probable cause is not liable for false arrest even if the suspect is later proved innocent. Neither does liability exist if the arrest is made by virtue of a law that is declared unconstitutional. In the words of the Supreme Court, "We agree that a police officer is not charged with predicting the future course of constitutional law." Pierson v. Ray, 386 U.S. 547 (1967).

EXAMPLE: The police arrest picketers in a local shopping mall in accordance with a municipal ordinance that prohibits picketing in places of business. The picketers are later released and the cases against them dismissed because the ordinance is declared unconstitutional by the court as violative of the freedom of speech. The police are not liable for false arrest or false imprisonment.

The fact that the arrested person is not prosecuted or is prosecuted for a different crime does not make the arrest illegal. What is important is that there be a valid justification for the arrest and detention at the time the officer acted. On the other hand, many courts have decided that a criminal conviction of the suspect defeats a false arrest action and is conclusive evidence that probable cause existed at the time of arrest.

EXAMPLE: In one case, the plaintiff distributed advertising bulletins in a building owned by the defendant. The plaintiff admitted that he had noticed that entry into the building was prohibited. He was arrested and charged with criminal trespass. The court held that even though the arrest of the plaintiff was unreasonable, his action for false arrest could not succeed because he actually committed the crime for which he was arrested. Rains v. Corrigan Properties, Inc. 600 S.W.2d 895 (Tex. Civ. App. 1980).[18]

## IX. POLICE ARE NOT ENTITLED TO ABSOLUTE IMMUNITY WHEN FILING A COMPLAINT THAT RESULTS IN THE ISSUANCE OF AN ARREST WARRANT

The United States Supreme Court has said that a police officer, when applying for an arrest warrant, is entitled only to qualified immunity, not absolute immunity, in Section 1983 cases.[19] The possibility exists that the officer could be held liable. Malley v. Briggs, 475 U.S. 335 (1986).

In *Malley v. Briggs*, State Trooper Malley prepared felony complaints charging Briggs and others with possession of marijuana based on two monitored telephone calls pursuant to a court-authorized wiretap. The complaints were given to a state judge together with arrest warrants and supporting affidavits. The judge signed the warrants and the defendants were arrested. The charges, however, were subsequently dropped when the grand jury refused to return an indictment. The defendants then brought a Section 1983 lawsuit alleging that Malley, in applying for the arrest warrants, had violated their rights against unreasonable search and seizure. Officer Malley argued that he was entitled to absolute immunity because his function in seeking an arrest warrant was similar to that of a complaining witness. The trial court ruled that the officer was entitled to absolute immunity, but the court of appeals reversed that decision. On appeal, the Supreme Court upheld the court of appeals decision, saying that a police officer is not entitled to absolute immunity but only to qualified immunity when filing complaints that result in the issuance of an arrest warrant.

Despite that, however, the Court set a difficult standard for plaintiffs to meet if they seek to hold a police officer liable for preparing a complaint or affidavit that results in the issuance of a warrant that does not lead to prosecution. Said the Court, "Only where the warrant application is so lacking in indicia of probable cause as to render official belief in its existence unreasonable . . . will the shield of [qualified] immunity be lost." This implies that a police officer will be liable for swearing out an arrest warrant when there is no probable cause and the officer knowingly violates the law, the officer is plainly incompetent, or no reasonably competent officer would have concluded that a warrant should issue.[20]

One court has said that if an officer knows or should have known that the affidavit that was the basis for the arrest warrant fails to establish a probable cause, then qualified immunity is lost and the officer may be held liable for having acted in bad faith. Garmon v. Lumpkin County, Ga., 878 F.2d 406 (11th Cir. 1989).

Although *Malley* did not extend the absolute immunity defense (available to judges, prosecutors, and legislators) to police officers, there is one instance when police officers enjoy absolute immunity from civil liability. In Briscoe v. LaHue, 460 U.S. 325 (1983), the United States Supreme Court held that police officers could not be sued under Section 1983 for giving perjured testimony against a defendant in a state criminal trial. The Court said that under common law, trial participants, including judges, prosecutors, and witnesses, were given absolute immunity from civil liability for actions connected with the trial process. Therefore, police officers enjoy absolute immunity when testifying, even if such testimony is false. An officer may be criminally prosecuted for perjury, but that is a decision to be made by the prosecutor.[21]

Giving false testimony in a trial is different, however, from procuring false testimony against a suspect. In one case, the Ninth Circuit affirmed an award of $2 million in compensatory damages, $40,000 each in punitive damages, and $117,000 in attorney's fees against two police officers who *procured false testimony* in a murder trial. In that case, two men were arrested and charged by the police with a brutal murder. Both suspects were convicted, but one of the convictions was reversed on appeal for insufficient evidence. The acquitted suspect later brought a Section 1983 lawsuit, charging that the police officers had conspired to deny him a fair trial by tampering with witnesses and knowingly presenting false evidence and perjured testimony to the jury. One witness stated during the Section 1983 trial that he was intimidated by some officers into testifying falsely in the criminal trial and that in fact he had not seen the plaintiff at a bar near the scene of the murder. The jury found for the plaintiff and imposed stiff monetary damages against the police officers. Venegas v. Wagner, 831 F.2d 1514 (9th Cir. 1987).

Taken together, the Briscoe and Venegas cases hold that although police officers enjoy absolute immunity from a Section 1983 lawsuit when testifying, even if their testimony is false, liability arises under Section 1983 if the police procure false testimony against a suspect.

## SUMMARY

Arrest is defined as the taking of a person into custody against that person's will for the purpose of criminal prosecution or interrogation. An arrest takes place if four elements are present: (1) intention to arrest, (2) arrest authority, (3) seizure and detention, and (4) the arrestee's understanding that he or she is being arrested.

False arrest is defined as an intentional tort that consists of the unlawful restraint or deprivation of a person's liberty; it is an arrest without proper legal authority. False imprisonment is an intentional tort that involves the unlawful restraint of the physical liberty of one person by another. In both false arrest and false imprisonment, the individual is restrained or deprived of freedom without legal justification. However, whereas false arrest almost always leads to false imprisonment, false imprisonment is not necessarily the result of false arrest.

There are two types of authorized arrest: arrest with a warrant and arrest without a warrant. In arrests with warrant, the officer needs to pay attention to four considerations: (1) the issuance of a warrant, (2) the contents of a warrant, (3) the service of the warrant, and (4) the announcement requirement. In arrests without warrant, the police make the initial determination of probable cause. It is advantageous for the police to make arrests with a warrant, because in these cases liability is minimized since there is a presumption that probable cause was present, as determined by a magistrate.

Probable cause is a defense often used in cases of false arrest and false imprisonment. For purposes of a legal defense, at least in Section 1983 cases, probable cause simply means "a reasonable good faith belief in the legality of the action taken." The Supreme Court has decided that the police are not entitled to absolute immunity when they file a complaint that results in the issuance of an arrest warrant. All they are entitled to is qualified immunity.

## NOTES

1. *Liability Reporter*, September 1987, at 5.
2. *Liability Reporter*, February 1989, at 22.
3. *Liability Reporter*, February 1988, at 3.
4. *Liability Reporter*, January 1987, at 5.
5. *Liability Reporter*, February 1987, at 5.
6. This discussion of arrest is largely taken, with modification, from R. V. del Carmen, *Criminal Procedure for Law Enforcement Personnel* (Brooks/Cole Publishing Company, 1987), chap. 5.
7. *Ibid.*, at 96–98.
8. *The Law Dictionary* (Anderson Publishing Company, 1986), at 138.
9. Portions of this discussion of false arrest and false imprisonment are taken from del Carmen, *Criminal Procedure for Law Enforcement Personnel*, chap. 15, at 401–402.
10. Crane, "Legal Issues," at 2.
11. *The Law Dictionary*, at 138.
12. See I. Silver, *Police Civil Liability* (Matthew Bender, 1988), at 4–3.
13. del Carmen, *Criminal Procedure for Law Enforcement Personnel*, at 98.
14. Portions of this discussion are taken from del Carmen, *Criminal Procedure for Law Enforcement Personnel*, at 103–105.
15. *Ibid.*, at 105.
16. *Ibid.*, at 119.
17. *Ibid.*, at 124.

18.  Silver, *Police Civil Liability*, at 4–37.
19.  Portions of this discussion are taken from del Carmen, *Criminal Procedure for Law Enforcement Personnel*, at 427–428.
20.  *Liability Reporter*, September 1986, at 4.
21.  del Carmen, *Criminal Procedure for Law Enforcement Personnel*, at 412.

## CASE BRIEFS

### DENNIS v. WARREN
### 779 F.2d 245 (1985)

#### FACTS

Delmar Dennis, a Tennessee resident traveling through Mississippi, was arrested and jailed based on a civil summons regarding a child support matter. Jerry Bustin, an attorney representing Dennis's former wife, had brought the summons to the sheriff's office. The officer testified that Bustin gave him the papers and urged him to "go out and get Delmar Dennis, he is supposed to be coming to town, we have got a paper for him." The officer (a deputy sheriff) further testified that it was generally understood that if someone brought legal papers to the sheriff's office and said, "Go out and get him," that meant that the person was to be brought to jail. The officer admitted that he arrested Dennis because the lawyer told him to. As a result, Dennis brought a civil rights lawsuit against the sheriff and deputy sheriff, alleging illegal arrest and detention. The trial court awarded $6,000 compensatory damages and $10,000 punitive damages in favor of the plaintiff.

#### ISSUES

(1) Were the arrest and detention illegal and actionable under Section 1983? (2) Were the officers entitled to qualified immunity? (3) Were the damages awarded excessive?

#### COURT DECISION

The court held that (1) the arrest and detention constituted a violation of the plaintiff's constitutional rights against unreasonable search and seizure, (2) the deputy sheriff was not shielded from liability for civil damages, and the sheriff was liable for damages under Mississippi law providing for liability of sheriffs for acts of their deputies, and (3) the damages awarded in this case were not excessive.

#### CASE SIGNIFICANCE

The arrest by an officer of a person based on an attorney's direction to "go out and get him" is unlawful and therefore constitutes false arrest, because a reasonable police officer would not arrest a defendant based only on an attorney's directions. The deputy sheriff who made the arrest did so without an arrest warrant. He acted by virtue of civil summons, which he knew could not authorize lawful arrest. Moreover, he failed to release the plaintiff even after he realized his mistake. This case makes clear that no private person, not even a lawyer, can order somebody's arrest unless there is legal justification for doing that. False arrest leads to liability under Section 1983 and not just under state tort. If a person is arrested by mistake, that person must be released as soon as the mistake is discovered. The case underscores the need for police officers to know when an arrest can and cannot be made. Lack of knowledge concerning valid arrests can lead to civil liability under Section 1983.

## RODRIGUEZ v. JONES
### 473 F.2d 599 (1973)

### FACTS

Four days after three deputy sheriffs were shot, a tip from a reliable informant caused the police to believe that the suspects were in Rodriguez's house. Based on their belief, which was mistaken, the police made a forcible entry into the house. Upon returning pistol fire, the police shot and wounded Rodriguez and his wife. Rodriguez filed suit in United States District Court seeking damages from the officers for violation of his Section 1983 rights. The district court found for the defendants.

### ISSUES

(1) Was the forcible entry into plaintiff's house unreasonable and in violation of his constitutional rights? (2) Were the defendants excused from a state law requiring announcement of the purpose and authority of the entry because of the circumstances? (3) Are the appellants entitled to damages pursuant to the search?

### COURT DECISION

The plaintiffs were not entitled to recover damages under Section 1983. The court said that the "law officers in forcibly entering plaintiffs' premises and in exchanging gunfire with the husband-plaintiff were mistaken in the belief that murder suspects were on the premises but were acting under circumstances which would have justified reasonable men in such belief."

### CASE SIGNIFICANCE

This case reiterates the principle that good faith and reasonable belief in the validity of the arrest or search are valid defenses against civil liability. Reasonable belief is equated in this case with the concept of probable cause. Quoting an earlier United States Supreme Court case, the Fifth Circuit said,

"We hold that it is a defense to allege and prove good faith and reasonable belief in the validity of the arrest and search and in the necessity for carrying out the arrest and search in the way the arrest was made and the search was conducted. We think, as a matter of constitutional law and as a matter of common sense, a law enforcement officer is entitled to this protection."

## VENEGAS v. WAGNER
### 831 F.2d 1514 (1987)

### FACTS

Juan Venegas and Lawrence Reyes were arrested by the police for murder. Both were later charged with and convicted of first-degree murder. Venegas's conviction was reversed by the California Supreme Court on appeal; that of Reyes was affirmed. Venegas then filed a Section 1983 suit against the police officers, alleging that they conspired to deny him a fair trial by tampering with witnesses and knowingly presenting false evidence and perjured testimony to the jury. The jury returned a verdict in favor of Venegas and awarded him $2 million in compensatory damages, $40,000 against each officer in punitive damages, and $117,000 in attorney's fees.

### ISSUE

Were the damage awards against the officers valid and proper? *Yes.*

### COURT DECISION

The evidence supported the conclusion that the officers procured false testimony from witnesses and denied Venegas a fair trial in his murder prosecution. The damage awards were therefore proper. The attorney's fees award of $117,000 did not constitute an abuse by the district court of its discretion; hence the award was proper.

### CASE SIGNIFICANCE

The procurement of false testimony by police officers for the purpose of prosecuting a suspect can lead to huge damage awards. In this case, the appellate court concluded that the record from the trial court contained evidence sufficient to support a jury verdict that the police officers had procured false testimony that lead to Venegas's being denied a fair trial. The appellate court refused to reverse that finding of fact. It also stated that attorney's fees awards are generally reviewed for abuse of discretion. Finding no such abuse in this case, the amount awarded was affirmed. Appellate courts generally do not review findings of fact but only review those of law. In civil liability cases, therefore, as is true in all court cases, the findings of facts in the trial court are extremely important, because they are seldom reversed on appeal.

# 9

# LIABILITY FOR
# SEARCHES AND SEIZURES

## INTRODUCTION

The Fourth Amendment to the United States Constitution provides,

> The right of the people to be secure in their persons, houses, papers, and effects, against unreasonable searches and seizures, shall not be violated, and no Warrants shall issue, but upon probable cause, supported by Oath or affirmation, and particularly describing the place to be searched, and the persons or things to be seized.

Cases against police officers for the violation of a plaintiff's right against unreasonable search and seizure are usually brought under Section 1983, because they involve a violation of the Fourth Amendment constitutional right. They are seldom brought under state tort law, and hence the cases discussed in this chapter are civil rights cases. Other than arrests, which also fall under the Fourth Amendment, most search and seizure cases involve minimal damage to person or property, and therefore lawsuits alleging illegal search and seizure have not been as numerous as those alleging illegal arrest. Nonetheless, several recent headlines from the *Liability Reporter* indicate the types of cases brought against the police:

FAILURE TO SECURE ARRESTEE'S APARTMENT AGAINST LOSS OF PROPERTY WAS MERE NEGLIGENCE INSUFFICIENT TO SUPPORT CIVIL RIGHTS LAWSUIT[1]

FEDERAL JURY AWARDS $140,000 FOR STRIP-SEARCH FOLLOWING TRAFFIC OFFENSE[2]

OPERATION COLD TURKEY RESULTS IN $500,000 SETTLEMENT[3]

WOMAN AWARDED $50,000 ON CLAIM THAT OFFICERS ORDERED HER TO LEAVE HER BED AND STEP OUTSIDE NAKED[4]

$235,000 AWARDED FOR OFFICERS' SEARCH OF HOME AND OFFICE USING REPOSSESSION ORDER[5]

APPEALS COURT UPHOLDS LIABILITY FOR STRIP SEARCH OF DISARMED MALE PRETRIAL DETAINEE (WHO WAS DEPUTY SHERIFF) CONDUCTED BEFORE FEMALE OFFICER[6]

To minimize Section 1983 lawsuits based on a violation of the constitutional right against illegal search and seizure, police officers must know what they can and cannot do under the Fourth Amendment. This chapter discusses the basic elements of the search and seizure law and identifies recent court decisions with which police officers must be familiar. A violation of the right against unreasonable search and seizure may lead to civil liability.

## I. SEARCH AND SEIZURE DEFINED

The terms *search* and *seizure* are often used together in such a way as to convey the impression that they refer to one and the same act. *Search and seizure* in fact have different meanings and refer to two separate acts.[7]

*A search is defined as any governmental intrusion into a person's reasonable and justifiable expectation of privacy.* Searches are not limited to homes, offices, buildings, or other enclosed places. Rather, they can occur in any place where a person has a "reasonable and justifiable expectation of privacy," even if the place is in a public area (meaning a place open to anyone). Katz v. United States, 389 U.S. 347 (1967). Thus, a search governed by the provisions of the Fourth Amendment can take place in an automobile, a telephone booth, or a public school locker room.

*A seizure is defined as the exercise of dominion or control by the government over a person or thing because of a violation of law.* A seizure occurs when there is some meaningful interference with an individual's possessory interests in the property seized. Maryland v. Macon, 37 CrL 3111 (1985). Although seizures by the police usually involve the taking of property, the arrest of a suspect is also a form of seizure governed by the provisions of the Fourth Amendment. This chapter, however, focuses on searches and seizures involving property and those that fall short of arrest, such as strip searches and electronic surveillance.

The law on searches and seizures is best understood if divided into two types: searches and seizures with warrant and searches and seizures without warrant. Each type is governed by different rules.

## II. SEARCH AND SEIZURE WITH WARRANT

*A search warrant is defined as a written order, issued by a magistrate, directing a peace officer to search for property connected with a crime and bring it before the court.*[8] In nearly all states, the police officer seeking a search warrant must state the facts establishing probable cause in a written and signed affidavit. The general rule is that a search or seizure is valid under the Fourth Amendment only if made with a warrant. Searches without warrant may be valid but they are the exception rather than the rule.

### A. Requirements

There are four basic elements of a valid search warrant: (1) the statement of probable cause, (2) the supporting oath or affirmation, (3) the particular description of the place to be searched and things to be seized, (4) and the signature of a magistrate.

**1. *Probable Cause.*** Probable cause in search and seizure cases is the same as in arrests. *Probable cause is generally defined as more than bare suspicion; it exists when the facts and circumstances within the officers' knowledge and of which they have reasonably trustworthy information are sufficient in themselves to warrant a person of reasonable caution in the belief that an offense has been or is being committed.* In searches and seizures (as contrasted with arrests), the issue of probable cause focuses on whether the property to be seized is connected with criminal activity and whether it can be found in the place to be searched.

**2. *Supporting Oath or Affirmation.*** A warrant is issued on the basis of a sworn affidavit presented to the magistrate and establishing grounds for the warrant. The magistrate issues the warrant only if satisfied by the affidavit that probable cause for a warrant exists. The contents of the affidavit must be sufficient to allow an independent evaluation of probable cause by the magistrate. To enable the magistrate to make an independent evaluation, the affidavit must contain more than mere conclusions by the officer. It must allege facts showing that seizable evidence will be found in the place to be searched. A warrant may be issued on the basis of affidavits containing only hearsay as long as there is probable cause.

**3. *Particular Description of Place to Be Searched and Persons or Things to Be Seized.*** The warrant must describe with reasonable certainty the place to be searched. For example, if the premises are an apartment in a multiple-dwelling apartment house, the warrant must specify which apartment is to be searched. The address of the apartment building is not sufficient. The rigid requirement of preciseness, however, has been weakened somewhat by a recent United States Supreme Court decision. In that case, the police had probable cause to believe that the search of an apartment would furnish evidence of drug crimes. The police knew that the suspect lived on the third floor of 2036 Park Avenue and reasonably believed that his was the only apartment on that floor. They asked for and received a warrant authorizing them to search "the premises known as 2036 Park Avenue, third floor apartment." It turned out that there were two apartments on the third floor, the other being occupied by X, another person who was not a suspect. The police executed the warrant by mistakenly searching X's apartment, where they discovered and confiscated drugs. The Court held that the warrant was valid, saying that "the validity of the warrant must be assessed on the basis of the information that the officers disclosed, or had a duty to discover and disclose, to the issuing magistrate." The police search was therefore held valid, although the warrant was overly broad. Maryland v. Garrison, 480 U.S. 79 (1987).

In another case, the Eighth Circuit held that the mistake of listing the address of a residence to be searched as "325 Atkinson Street" rather than "325 Short Street" did not render the warrant invalid, since the error was not misleading or confusing—the streets intersected in front of the residence and the warrant provided an accurate physical description of the premises to be searched. Lyons v. Robinson, 783 F.2d 737 (8th Cir. 1985).

Items for seizure must also be described with sufficient particularity that the officers will have to exercise little discretion over what may be seized. For example, the warrant cannot simply provide for the seizure of "stolen goods," since this language is too general and can lead to a "fishing expedition." An acceptable identification would be "a twenty-one-inch Panasonic television set." Contraband, however, does not have to be described with as much particularity, because it is in itself seizable. Therefore, the words "cocaine" or "prohibited substances" would be sufficient.

**4. *Signature of a Magistrate.*** As in the case of arrest warrants, search warrants must be issued only by a "neutral and detached" magistrate. The Supreme Court has said, "Inferences must be drawn by a neutral and detached magistrate instead of being judged by the officer engaged in the often competitive enterprise of ferreting out crime." Johnson v. United States, 333 U.S. 10 (1948).

The federal government and some states permit oral warrants. Under this procedure, the police may apply for the warrant in person or by telephone, stating facts under oath. A recording may be made, and the judge then orally authorizes the warrant, which may likewise be recorded. The practice is valid, since the Fourth Amendment does not specify that the supporting affidavit or complaint be in writing.

### B. Procedure for Service of Warrant

The search warrant is directed to a law enforcement officer and must state the grounds for issuance and the names of those who gave affidavits in support of it. The warrant usually directs that it be served in the daytime, but if the affidavits are positive that the property is on the person or in the place to be searched, the warrant may direct that it be served at any time. Some states, by law, authorize night searches. The warrant must designate the judge or magistrate to whom the warrant is to be returned. It must be executed and delivered within a specified number of days from the date of issuance. Some states specify ten days, others allow less time.

If the search warrant is not served during the time specified, it expires and can no longer be served. Search warrants differ in this respect from arrest warrants, which are usually valid until served. The officer executing the warrant must give a copy of the warrant and a receipt for any seized property to the person from whom it is taken or must leave a copy and receipt on the premises. A written inventory must be made, and the officer's report, accompanied by the inventory, must be submitted promptly.

### C. Announcement Requirement

The rule about announcements is the same as that applicable in arrests. Federal and many state statutes require that an officer making an arrest or executing a search warrant announce his or her purpose and authority before breaking into a dwelling. The idea is to allow voluntary compliance and avoid violence. Breaking into premises without first complying with the announcement requirement may or may not invalidate the entry and resulting search, depending on the law or court decisions in that state. Some states invalidate the entry and resulting search, others do not. There is no constitutional requirement that an announcement be made before entry; hence the validity of the search is governed by state law or court decisions.

In some cases, because of exigent circumstances, an announcement is not required. The usual instances are as follows:

1.  Announcing would create a strong threat of violence or danger to the officer.

2. There is danger that contraband or other property might be destroyed. Some states permit a magistrate to authorize so-called no knock searches, particularly in drug cases. In a no knock search, entry is made without announcement. The constitutionality of such statutes has not been fully tested, although they have been upheld by lower courts.

3. The officers reasonably believe that the persons within the premises are in imminent peril of bodily harm.

4. Then persons within are reasonably believed to be engaged in the process of destroying evidence or escaping because they are aware of the presence of the police.

5. The person to be arrested is in the process of committing the crime.

Exceptions to the announcement requirement are usually governed by state law, state court decisions, and agency regulations. They therefore vary from state to state.

### D. Scope of Search and Seizure

The search must not go beyond the premises described in the warrant and must be limited to locating the item or items described in the warrant.[9] It must not be used by the officer to conduct a "fishing expedition" for evidence that might later be used against the accused. For example, a warrant is issued for the search and seizure of "a .45-caliber pistol" in the home of a murder suspect. Once that pistol is seized, the police cannot explore other parts of the house to see if there might be other evidence to implicate the murder suspect.

Note, however, that although the police are limited in what they can do, it is valid and legal for the police to confiscate and seize evidence that is in "plain view" during a legitimate search. If, in the process of looking for the .45-caliber pistol in the suspect's home, the police see a bag of marijuana in the living room, they may seize it and introduce it against the suspect in court if the suspect is being prosecuted for marijuana possession.

The scope and manner of the search must be reasonable; that is, the officer's actions must be *reasonable in terms of the object of the search.* A convenient legal maxim is, "It is unreasonable for a police officer to look for an elephant in a matchbox." For example, a search warrant is issued for the recovery of a stolen twenty-five-inch Zenith TV set. In looking for the TV set, the officer cannot open lockers and drawers—unless, of course, the locker or drawer is big enough to contain the TV set. On the other hand, if the search warrant is for the confiscation of heroin, then the officer is justified in opening lockers and drawers in the course of the search. It follows that the smaller the item sought, the more extensive the scope of allowable search.

## III. SEARCH AND SEIZURE WITHOUT WARRANT

Although the constitutional rule is that searches and seizures must be made on the authority of a warrant, most searches and seizures by the police, like most arrests, are in fact made without a warrant.[10] Warrantless searches incident to arrest by themselves greatly outnumber searches made with a warrant. In a search or seizure without a warrant, the burden is on the police to establish testimony in court, if the legality of the search or seizure is challenged, that probable cause existed at the time the warrantless search or seizure was made. It is therefore essential for the law enforcement officer to be thoroughly familiar with the law on warrantless searches and seizures. *Generally, there are six exceptions to the rule that searches and seizures must be made with a warrant:*

1.  exception for search incident to a lawful arrest
2.  exception for search with consent
3.  exception for exigent circumstances
4.  exception for stop and frisk
5.  exception for automobiles
6.  exception for items in plain view

### A. Searches Incident to Lawful Arrest

As an exception to the warrant requirement, search incident to lawful arrest is widely used. In fact, it is invoked just about every time an officer makes an arrest, with or without a warrant. There are two requirements for this search to be valid:

1.  *The arrest itself must be lawful,* meaning that (a) there must be an arrest warrant based on probable cause or (b) the arresting officer must have had probable cause to make the arrest without a warrant.
2.  *The search must be limited in scope,* meaning that the search is reasonably required to protect the arresting officer from a possibly armed suspect or to prevent the destruction of evidence.

Once a lawful arrest has been made, the police may search any *area within the suspect's "immediate control,"* meaning the area within which the suspect would be able to grab a weapon or destroy evidence. Chimel v. California, 395 U.S. 752 (1969).

## B. Searches with Consent

Warrantless searches with consent are valid, but the consent must be *voluntary* and *intelligent*. Police must show that the accused's consent was not the result of force or coercion and that the accused knew what he or she was doing. Voluntariness and intelligence are determined by looking at the totality of circumstances. For example, consent given only after the officer demands entry cannot be deemed to be free and voluntary. A command to "open the door" will most likely be interpreted by the courts as giving the occupant no choice and therefore making the consent involuntary. The better practice is for the officer to "request" rather than "demand." Saying "Would you mind if I come in and look around?" is more likely to result in voluntary consent.

In one case, several deputy sheriffs looked for a woman for whom they had a number of felony arrest warrants. When they found her car parked across the street from a house, they conducted a two- to three-minute warrantless search of the house but did not find her. Subsequently, the woman filed a Section 1983 lawsuit against the police and the county, claiming that any consent she had given was ineffective and obtained at gunpoint from a visiting friend, who had no authority to consent to the search. The court disagreed, saying that there was effective consent. Testimony revealed that while the deputies carried guns, they did not point the guns at the homeowner or her friend. Moreover, when the deputies asked the two people in the house, "Do you mind us looking?" one of them said no, and both stepped aside and allowed the deputies to enter. The court added that even if the homeowner was not the one who said no, the fact that she did not challenge the deputies' entry demonstrated consent. Johnson v. Smith County, 834 F. 2d 479 (5th Cir. 1987).[11]

Who may give consent to a search? In general, the rules are as follows:

1. *Landlord.* No, except as to vacant rooms.

2. *Hotel clerk.* No.

3. *Wife or husband.* Yes, except with respect to areas where the other spouse has a reasonable expectation of privacy because only he or she uses it.

4. *College and university administrators.* No, with respect to the rooms or property of students.

5. *High school administrators.* Yes, with respect to student lockers.

6. *Business employer.* No, unless prohibition validly waived by the employee.

7. *Business employee.* No, with respect to property owned by the employer.

8. **Roommate.** Yes, but consent cannot extend to areas where another roommate has a reasonable expectation of privacy because only he or she uses it.

## C. Stop and Frisk

Several states have passed stop-and-frisk laws that allow an officer (1) to stop a person in a public place if the officer has reasonable suspicion that the person has committed or is about to commit a felony and (2) to demand the person's name and address and an explanation of his or her actions.[12] Other states, and some federal courts, have upheld such practices in judicial decisions even without statutory authorization. Although often used together, *stop* and *frisk* refer to two separate acts with different requirements.

A stop is justified and should take place only if the police officer has reasonable suspicion, in light of his or her experience, that criminal activity is about to take place. Therefore, the purpose of a stop is to prevent criminal activity. A stop for anything else is illegal unless it meets the standard of probable cause.

A frisk does not automatically follow a stop. It should follow only if there is nothing in the initial stages of the encounter (after the stop) that would dispel reasonable fear about the safety of the police officer or of others. The purpose of a frisk is protection; therefore frisking should take place only if protection is necessary. The totality of circumstances, meaning the whole picture, must be taken into account when determining the legality of a frisk. It is important for the police officer to note that the scope of a frisk is limited to a mere pat-down for weapons so as to remove physical danger, not to look for drugs, whereas the scope of a search after arrest is much wider in that it allows a full body search and therefore allows a search for evidence.

Although a stop and frisk is not an arrest, what the officer discovers while stopping or frisking may immediately give cause to make an arrest. For example, an officer stops a suspect and subsequently frisks him. In the course of the pat-down, the officer touches something that feels like a weapon. If it is in fact a prohibited weapon, the officer may confiscate it and immediately place the suspect under arrest. Once placed under arrest, the suspect may be searched in full and any contraband found on the suspect may be confiscated.

## D. Vehicle Stops

The general rule is that a seizure occurs every time a motor vehicle is stopped; the provisions of the Fourth Amendment therefore apply.[13] In one case the Court said: "The Fourth and Fourteenth Amendments are implicated in this case because stopping an automobile and detaining its occupants constitute a 'seizure' within the meaning of those Amendments, even though the purpose of the stop is limited and the resulting detention quite brief." Delaware v. Prouse, 440 U.S. 648 (1979). There must be at least a reasonable suspicion (a lower degree of certainty than probable cause) to justify an investigatory stop of a motor vehicle. A court has said, "The police do not have an unrestricted right to stop people, either pedestrians or drivers. The 'good faith' of the police is not enough, nor is an inarticulate hunch. They must have an articulable suspicion of wrongdoing, done or in prospect." United States v. Montgomery, 561 F.2d 875 (1977).

In a 1989 case, the Supreme Court said that the use of a stationary roadblock to effect a stop is a form of seizure; hence possible liability exists if the seizure ends in a fatal car crash rather than the simple stop the government may have intended. Brower v. Inyo County, 44 Crl. 3175. In *Brower*, the police blocked a speeding motorist's path with a tractor-trailer rig, which obstructed both lanes of the road. It was placed behind a curve and was not illuminated. Moreover, the motorist was "blinded" by lights from a police cruiser. As a result, instead of coming to a safe stop, the motorist crashed into the truck and died. The estate of the deceased motorist sued under Section 1983, alleging a violation of the Fourth Amendment constitutional right against unreasonable search and seizure. The Court decided that the use of a stationary roadblock constituted a seizure and could be the basis for a Section 1983 lawsuit.

As long as the stopping of the vehicle is lawful, what officers observe can evolve into probable cause to believe that the car contains the fruits and instrumentalities of crime or contraband, hence establishing a justification for a full warrantless search of the vehicle. Officers may also seize illegal items in plain view. The seizure then establishes probable cause, which justifies an arrest.

Once a driver has been arrested, the police may conduct a warrantless search of the passenger compartment of the vehicle for evidence related to the offense for which the arrest has been made. The scope of allowable search is broad, in that the police may examine the contents of any container found within the passenger compartment as long as it may reasonably contain something that might pose a danger to the officer or hold evidence in support of the offense for which the suspect has been arrested.

If the police legitimately stop a car and have probable cause to believe that it contains contraband, they may conduct a warrantless search of the car. The search can be as thorough as a search authorized by a warrant issued by a magistrate. Therefore, every part of the vehicle in which the contraband might be stored may be inspected, including the trunk and all receptacles and packages that could possibly contain the object of the search.

The rule allowing warrantless searches of cars probably does not extend to cars that are not "mobile," meaning those that are not being driven at the time of the search. These cars may or may not come under the automobile exception, and therefore a warrant may be needed for a search. United States Supreme Court decisions on this issue are unclear. Therefore, the better practice is to secure a warrant.

When the police lawfully impound a vehicle, they may conduct a routine inventory search without warrant or probable cause to believe that the car contains seizable evidence. This procedure is reasonable, since it protects the police against a claim that the owner's property was stolen and also protects them from potential danger.

### E.  The "Plain View" Doctrine

The "plain view" doctrine states that items that are visible to an officer who is legally in a place from which the sighting is made and who had no prior knowledge that the items were present may properly be seized without a warrant—as long as such items are immediately recognizable as subject to seizure.[14]

Although considered by most writers as an exception to the search warrant requirement, plain view is really not a "search" within the terms of the Fourth Amendment, because no search for any specific item is being undertaken. No warrant or probable cause is necessary, because the officer simply seizes what he or she sees, not something he or she has searched for. Moreover, seeing the item is accidental or unplanned.

The plain view doctrine has three basic elements:

1.  The item must be within the officer's sight, meaning that the awareness of the item must be gained solely through the sense of sight, not through the other senses—hearing, smelling, tasting, or touching.

2.  The officer must be legally present in the place from which he or she sees the item, meaning that the officer must have done nothing illegal to get to the spot from which he or she sees the item that is to be seized.

3.  The item must be immediately recognizable as subject to seizure, meaning that the recognition must be instantaneous and not the result of further inquiry or prying.

### F. Presence of Exigent Circumstances

The exception for exigent circumstances is a general catch-all category that encompasses a number of diverse situations.[15] What they have in common is some kind of an "emergency" that makes obtaining a search warrant impractical, useless, dangerous, or unnecessary. Among these situations are those involving danger of physical harm to the officer or destruction of evidence, danger to a third person, driving while intoxicated, and searches in hot pursuit.

**1. *Danger of Physical Harm to the Officer or Destruction of Evidence.*** The Supreme Court has implied that a warrantless search may be justified if there is reasonable ground to believe that delaying the search until the warrant is obtained would endanger the physical safety of the officer or would allow the destruction or removal of the evidence. Vale v. Louisiana, 399 U.S. 30 (1970). For example, an officer serves a warrant in a house for the seizure of a stolen TV set. If in the process the officer discovers an illegal weapon or drugs, the officer may also seize those, particularly if there is no time to obtain a warrant without the evidence being removed or destroyed by whoever might be in the house. Note, however, that in *Vale* the Court did not allow a warrantless search when there was merely a *possibility* that the evidence would be destroyed, thus giving *Vale* a narrow interpretation. The threat of danger or destruction must therefore be *real* or *imminent*.

**2. *Danger to a Third Person.*** An officer may enter a dwelling without a warrant in response to screams for help. In one case the Court said, "The Fourth Amendment does not require police officers to delay in the course of an investigation if to do so would gravely endanger their lives or the lives of others." Warden v. Hayden, 387 U.S. 294, (1967).

**3. *Driving while Intoxicated (DWI).*** The police may, without a search warrant and by force if necessary, take a blood sample from a person arrested for drunk driving, as long as the setting and procedures are reasonable (as when the blood is drawn by a medical doctor in a hospital). Exigent circumstances exist, because alcohol in the suspect's bloodstream might disappear in the time required to obtain a warrant. Schmerber v. California, 384 U.S. 757 (1966).

**4. *Searches in "Hot Pursuit" (or "Fresh Pursuit") of Dangerous Suspects.*** The police are not required to obtain a warrant if they are in the process of apprehending a suspect and the suspect enters a house. As long as the police have reason to believe that the suspect is in the house, a warrantless search is justified.

## IV. MISCELLANEOUS SEARCHES AND SEIZURES

There are other types of special searches and seizures that deserve discussion, among them are body searches, border searches, searches of prisoners, and strip and body cavity searches.[16]

### A. Body Searches

*Body searches incident to lawful arrests may be conducted.* A body search is valid in any situation in which a full custody arrest of a person occurs. There is no requirement that the officers fear for their safety or believe that they will find evidence of a crime before the body search can be made. United States v. Robinson, 414 U.S. 218 (1973). On the other hand, a strip search of an arrestee is more intrusive and cannot be conducted after every arrest. It can be conducted only if there is further justification for it.

### B. School Searches

*School searches do not require probable cause.* In a 1985 decision, the Supreme Court resolved an issue that had long bothered students, public school teachers, and administrators. Voting 6-2, the Court said that public school teachers and administrators do not need a warrant or probable cause to believe that a student is violating the law or school rule before searching that student. What is needed is *reasonable grounds* (a lower degree of certainty than probable cause) for suspecting that the search will turn up evidence that the student has violated or is violating either the law or the rules of the school. New Jersey v. T.L.O., 469 U.S. 325 (1985).

### C. Border Searches

*There is no need for probable cause in border searches.* The magnitude of smuggling and theft problems at international borders, airports, and seaports has led to a relaxation of the probable cause requirement for searches at such locations. Hence, a border patrol or customs officer is entitled to search on the basis of a *reasonable suspicion* (instead of probable cause) that the person is engaged in illegal activity. This rule applies to both American citizens and aliens.

### D. Searches of Prisoners

*The Fourth Amendment offers an inmate absolutely no protection against unreasonable searches and seizures of his or her cell.* This is because the inmate has no reasonable expectation of privacy there. The right to privacy is fundamentally incompatible with the close and continual surveillance of inmates and their cells required to ensure institutional security and internal order. In the words of Justice O'Connor, "All searches and seizures of the contents of an inmate's cell are reasonable." Hudson v. Palmer, 468 U.S. 517 (1984). Necessary surveillance does not, however, legitimize harassment tactics by prison guards. Such tactics may lead to liability in state and federal courts.

### E. Strip and Body Cavity Searches

Most of the search and seizure liability cases brought against police officers in the last few years have involved strip and body cavity searches; hence an extensive discussion is given to this topic. Headlines like the following, from the *Liability Reporter*, exemplify the types of cases filed:

FEDERAL JURY AWARDS $140,000 FOR STRIP-SEARCH FOLLOWING TRAFFIC OFFENSES[17]

POLICE DEPARTMENT POLICY REQUIRING VISUAL BODY CAVITY SEARCH FOR ALL PRETRIAL DETAINEES ARRESTED FOR FELONIES IS UNCONSTITUTIONAL[18]

DEFENDANTS NOT ENTITLED TO QUALIFIED IMMUNITY FOR STRIP SEARCHING MAN ARRESTED FOR NONPAYMENT OF PARKING TICKETS[19]

Civil liability cases on strip and body cavity searches may be divided into those that take place right after arrest—before an arrestee is taken to jail—and those that take place in jails and prisons. Also at issue are strip and cavity searches of jail or prison visitors.

**1. *Strip and Body Cavity Search after Arrest.*** Even if an arrest is proper and valid, a strip and body cavity search following the arrest is not always justified. There must be a reason for the search other than the mere fact of arrest. Each strip and body cavity search must be justified by the circumstances surrounding the arrest, meaning that an outright authorization to strip and body cavity search every arrestee will most likely be declared unconstitutional by the courts.

The Second Circuit has held that a strip search of a person arrested on misdemeanor charges is unconstitutional unless there is some reasonable basis to suspect that the person arrested is concealing weapons or other contraband. In the case in question, the suspect was arrested for nonpayment of parking tickets and was then allegedly subjected to a strip search and body cavity inspection. The court ruled that since there was no reasonable basis to suspect that the arrestee was concealing weapons or other contraband, the strip and body cavity search was improper. Walsh v. Franco, 849 F.2d 66 (2nd Cir. 1988).

The Fifth Circuit ruled that a county policy that permitted strip searches of any person arrested (including minor offenders awaiting bond) without a reasonable suspicion that the arrestee possessed contraband violated the suspect's Fourth Amendment right. Stewart v. Lubbock County 767 F.2d 153 (5th Cir. 1985). In a case that went to the Seventh Circuit, four women arrested for misdemeanor offenses brought a Section 1983 action against the city of Chicago challenging the constitutionality of that city's strip search policy. The court held that the city's full strip search of female misdemeanor arrestees who were not inherently dangerous and were detained only briefly while waiting to be bonded was unreasonable. Mary Beth G. v. City of Chicago, 723 F.2d 1263 (7th Cir. 1983).

In an unusual case, the Ninth Circuit held that *strip searches of police officers for investigative purposes* must be based on reasonable suspicion that evidence of wrongdoing will be uncovered. In that case, two Los Angeles police officers were taken behind a row of lockers in the corner of a police station locker room and strip-searched after a man arrested on DWI alleged that the officers took his money. The police officers subsequently filed a Section 1983 case against their superiors and the city. The court held that the officer's Fourth Amendment right against unreasonable searches was violated, because they were strip-searched despite the absence of a reasonable suspicion to believe they had the stolen money on them. Defendants were not held liable, however, because at the time the strip searches took place (in 1981), there was no clearly settled law establishing the rule that an investigative search could not be conducted without some suspicion that evidence would be uncovered. The court added, however, that such strip searches in the future would require reasonable suspicion; otherwise liability would ensue. Kirkpatrick v. City of Los Angeles, 803 F.2d 485 (9th Cir. 1986).

The above cases suggest that a departmental policy authorizing the strip and body cavity searches of all arrestees is unconstitutional and exposes the officer and the department to civil liabilities. Such searches may be justified, however, under the following circumstances:

1.  There is a reasonable basis to suspect that the person arrested was concealing weapons or other contraband, regardless of the offense.

2.  There is a reasonable basis to suspect that the arrestee is inherently dangerous, regardless of the offense. The term *inherently dangerous* is subjective and open to varying interpretations. In one case, the Fifth Circuit held that if the police arrested a suspect on a minor charge, such as passing a bad check, and found, before placing the suspect in jail, that he or she had been arrested before and was then awaiting trial on a major narcotics trafficking charge, a strip search would be justified. Watt v. City of Richardson Police Department, 849 F.2d 195 (5th Cir. 1988).

The above cases deal specifically with strip and body cavity searches. The rule is that once a valid arrest has been made for any offense, felony or misdemeanor, a mere body search (as opposed to a strip and body cavity search) may be conducted by the police and any evidence obtained from the search will be admissible as evidence in court. The justification for the more restrictive policy in strip and body cavity searches is that these types of search are much more intrusive of a person's privacy and carry more potential for humiliation and embarrassment.

**2. *Strip and Body Cavity Search in Jails and Prisons.*** Strip and body cavity searches of detainees and prisoners often occur in prisons and jails. In these cases, the United States Supreme Court has set a balancing test between institutional security and inmate privacy. The rule is that such searches are permissible so long as they are conducted in a reasonable manner and are justified under the circumstances. The Court said,

> We do not underestimate the degree to which these searches may invade the personal privacy of inmates. The searches must be conducted in a reasonable manner. We deal here with the question of whether visual body-cavity inspections contemplated by prison rules can ever be conducted on less than probable cause. Balancing the significant and legitimate security interest of the institution against the privacy interest of inmates, we conclude that they can. Bell v. Wolfish, 441 U.S. 520, at 560 (1979).

The Court added that the prison administrators had shown that the inmates had tried to smuggle money, weapons, drugs, and other forms of contraband in their body cavities and therefore the searches were justified.

The above cases suggest that strip and body cavity searches in jails and prisons are valid only if (1) there is individualized suspicion, or (2) a special institutional need can be established by the jail or prison authorities (e.g., based on the occurrence of the past smuggling by inmates of contraband into the institution or easy access by inmates to contraband). In either case, the search must be conducted in a reasonable and proper manner so as not to subject the person searched to embarrassment or humiliation.

**3. *Strip and Body Cavity Searches of Jail or Prison Visitors.*** The strip and body cavity searches of jail or prison visitors has also been the subject of liability lawsuits. In one case, the First Circuit held that the requirement that all prison visitors submit to a strip and body cavity search without the existence of an individualized suspicion or a special institutional need violated the visitors' Fourth Amendment right against unreasonable search and seizure. Blackburn v. Snow, 771 F.2d 556 (1st Cir.

1985). The Fifth Circuit has gone even further and held that random strip searches of prison visitors are unreasonable under the Fourth Amendment, even if the visitor consents to being searched. The court held that for a strip search of a visitor to be valid, prison officials must have a particular and reasonable suspicion concerning the visitor. Such reasonable suspicion must be based on specific objective facts and rational inferences. Johns v. Thorne, 765 F.2d 1270 (5th Cir. 1985).

## V.  DEFENSES IN SEARCH AND SEIZURE CASES

Other than outright denial, three types of defenses are often invoked in search and seizure cases: (1) the probable cause defense, (2) the good faith defense, and (3) possession of a warrant.

### A.  The Probable Cause Defense

As in the case of false arrest and imprisonment, the existence of probable cause is a defense in illegal search and seizure cases. The relevant definition of probable cause is the same as that used in arrest and false imprisonment cases, namely, whether or not the officer had a "reasonable good faith belief in the legality of the action taken." That standard is lower than the standard set for probable cause in the issuance of arrest or search and seizure warrants and is hardly distinguishable from the standard required under qualified immunity.

Again, as in the case of arrests, the presence of probable cause is not a defense if the charge is for an improper execution of an otherwise valid warrant. The officer, in search and seizure civil liability cases, must be able to establish (1) that the warrant was valid, and (2) that it was executed properly. Failure to prove one or both may lead to civil liability.

### B.  The Good Faith Defense

The good faith or qualified immunity defense is available to police officers in search and seizure cases. In one case, the United States Supreme Court held that a federal law enforcement agent who participates in a warrantless search that violates the Fourth Amendment may not be held personally liable for money damages if a reasonable officer could have believed that the search was in accordance with the Fourth Amendment. In that case, an FBI agent participated with other law enforcement officers in a warrantless search of a third person's home. The search was conducted because the agent believed that the suspect might be found there, but he was not. The homeowner later brought suit alleging a violation of his Fourth Amendment right. On appeal, the Court rejected outright liability saying that an officer is entitled to a dismissal of the case if he can establish as a matter of law that a reasonable officer could have believed that the search comported with the Fourth Amendment even though in reality it did not. The Court added that "the objective question [here is] whether a reasonable officer could have believed petitioner's warrantless search to be lawful, in light of clearly established law and information the searching officers possessed." Anderson v. Creighton, Jr., 483 U.S. 635 (1987). Significantly, the decision rejected the homeowner's claim that it is not appropriate to give officials alleged to have violated the Fourth Amendment (and thus to have made an unreasonable search or seizure) the protection of qualified immunity.

In another case, the police mistakenly entered the wrong apartment (the apartment entered was in fact the apartment described in the search warrant but was not the premises the police sought to search) and were sued for damages. The court held that the police were entitled to qualified immunity and refused to impose liability. Dunday v. Barnes, 592 F.2d 1336 (5th Cir. 1979). The court added, however, that liability might ensue if, despite a valid warrant, the search was done in an unreasonable manner.

Clearly, then, the court used good faith immunity to shield officers from liability, meaning that liability does not ensue if the officers could have believed that what they did was valid under the Fourth Amendment. Also rejected by the court was the concept that no immunity should be provided to police officers who conduct unlawful warrantless searches of the homes of innocent third parties in search of fugitives.

### C. Possession of a Search Warrant as a Defense

As is also true in arrest cases, the mere possession of a warrant is not an absolute defense in search and seizure cases. In a Ninth Circuit decision, plaintiffs sued county law enforcement officers for the issuance of a search warrant without probable cause, for mistaken execution at their residence, and for carrying out the search in an unreasonable and excessive manner. The defendants contended that they were insulated from liability because their actions were based on a warrant issued by the magistrate. The court rejected this defense, saying that the standard to be used for liability was whether a reasonably well-trained officer in the defendants' position would have known that this affidavit failed to establish probable cause and that therefore a warrant ought not to have been applied for. Moreover, the court said that the officers' conduct in allegedly destroying the property of rural residence owners during the search pursuant to the warrant, which was executed at the wrong residence, also had to be judged based on a reasonableness standard. Bergquist v. County of Cochise, 806 F.2d 1364 (9th Cir. 1986).

In another case involving issuance of a search warrant, the First Circuit upheld a jury's award of $75,000 against a police officer for the wrongful search and seizure of the plaintiff's property. The plaintiff's business, which had netted a thousand dollars a week prior to the search, was destroyed as a business entity because of the search and resulting publicity stemming from an alleged victim's charge that he was held against his will with force of arms and made to work without pay. The officer contended that since the magistrate issued the warrant, this judicial issuance formed "an impregnable shield against any attack on the sufficiency of the underlying affidavit." The court said that while it is true that probable cause determinations based on information furnished by a victim are generally considered to be reliable, no court has ever adopted the per se approach advocated by the police officer. Whether probable cause exists in any given case invariably depends on the particular facts and circumstances of that case and is a question to be resolved by either the judge or jury. In this particular case, the appellate court upheld the award, because there was sufficient evidence from which the jury could have found that the officer acted without probable cause. The alleged victim who supplied the information was a drifter who had behaved incoherently while in police custody and sounded as if he was on drugs; hence the alleged victim's credibility was low. Therefore, even though the officer may have been acting on information provided by an alleged victim of a crime, this fact alone did not preclude the jury from finding, as it did here, that probable cause did not exist. BCR Transport Co., Inc., v. Fontaine, 727 F.2d 7 (1st Cir. 1984).

Taken together, the above cases indicate the following:

1. A warrant does not always exempt an officer from liability, particularly if such warrant was issued upon complaint of the police officer himself, who should have known that probable cause did not exist.
2. An officer should not apply for a warrant if he or she is convinced that probable cause does not in fact exist.
3. Even if the warrant is valid, it must be executed in a manner that meets the reasonableness standard.

## SUMMARY

A search is defined as any governmental intrusion into a person's reasonable and justifiable expectation of privacy; a seizure is defined as the exercise of dominion or control by the government over a person or thing because of a violation of law. Cases against police officers for the violation of a plaintiff's right against unreasonable search and seizure are usually brought under Section 1983, not under state tort, because they involve a violation of the Fourth Amendment constitutional right.

Searches and seizures may be divided into two types: searches and seizures with warrant and searches and seizures without warrant. Each type is governed by different rules. Search and seizure warrants have four basic elements: (1) the probable cause, (2) the supporting oath or affirmation, (3) the particular description of the place to be searched and persons or things to be seized, and (4) the signature of a magistrate. The constitutional rule is that searches and seizures must be made on the authority of a warrant. In reality, however, most searches and seizures are made without a warrant and therefore fall under the exceptions to the warrant requirement. Six exceptions to the warrant requirement are discussed in this chapter: (1) searches incident to a lawful arrest, (2) searches with consent, (3) exigent circumstances, (4) stop and frisk, (5) automobile searches, and (6) plain view situations.

Among the miscellaneous forms of searches and seizures, strip and body cavity searches invite particular attention, because the courts have decided numerous liability cases on this topic involving police officers. The rule is that authorizing strip and body cavity searches of all arrestees is unconstitutional. Such searches may be justified, however, if there is reasonable basis to suspect that the arrestee is concealing weapons or contraband or that the arrestee is inherently dangerous. Strip and body cavity searches of prison visitors are constitutionally valid only if there is individualized suspicion or a special institutional need that can be established by jail or prison officials.

Other than an outright denial, three types of defense are often invoked in search and seizure cases: (1) probable cause, (2) good faith, and (3) possession of a warrant. Probable cause as a defense in search and seizure cases is defined as "reasonable good faith belief in the legality of the action taken." Good faith means that there is no liability if a reasonable officer, under similar circumstances, could have believed that the search comported with the Fourth Amendment. Possession of a search warrant is not an absolute defense. It is a defense only if the warrant is in fact valid and was executed in a manner that meets the reasonableness standard.

## NOTES

1.  *Liability Reporter*, March 1988, at 10.
2.  *Liability Reporter*, December 1987, at 11.
3.  *Liability Reporter*, January 1987, at 14.

4. Liability Reporter, October 1988, at 12.
5. Liability Reporter, October 1988, at 13.
6. Liability Reporter, February 1988, at 13.
7. This discussion of searches and seizures is largely taken, with modification, from R. V. del Carmen, Criminal Procedure for Law Enforcement Personnel (Brooks/Cole Publishing Company, 1987), chap. 7.
8. Ibid., at 139–144.
9. Ibid., at 144.
10. Ibid., at 145–147.
11. Liability Reporter, 1988, No. 184, at 13.
12. This discussion of stop and frisk is largely taken from del Carmen, Criminal Procedure for Law Enforcement Personnel, chap. 6.
13. This discussion of vehicle stops is largely taken from del Carmen, Criminal Procedure for Law Enforcement Personnel, chap. 8.
14. This discussion of the "plain view" doctrine is largely taken from del Carmen, Criminal Procedure for Law Enforcement Personnel, chap. 9.
15. del Carmen, Criminal Procedure for Law Enforcement Personnel, at 150–152.
16. This discussion of miscellaneous searches and seizures is largely taken from Criminal Procedure for Law Enforcement Personnel, at 152–156.
17. Liability Reporter, April 1987, at 13.
18. Liability Reporter, January 1988, at 13.
19. Liability Reporter, August 1988, at 14.

## CASE BRIEFS

### ANDERSON v. CREIGHTON
### 41 CrL 3396 (1987)

#### FACTS

On November 11, 1983, Russell Anderson, an agent of the FBI, and other state and federal law enforcement officers conducted a warrantless search of the home of R. Creighton, Jr. The search was conducted in belief that a suspected bank robber, V. Dixon, might be found there. He was not. Creighton filed suit for damages, claiming that Anderson had violated his Fourth Amendment rights to be secure in his home from unreasonable searches. Anderson filed a motion for dismissal or summary judgment based on his qualified immunity from civil damages pursuant to the decision in Bivens v. Six Unknown Named Agents of the Federal Bureau of Investigation, 403 U.S. 388 (1971). The federal district court held for Anderson. Creighton appealed to the Eight Circuit Court of Appeals, which overturned the decision. The Supreme Court granted certiorari.

ISSUE

May a federal law enforcement officer who participates in a search that violates the Fourth Amendment be held personally liable for damages if a reasonable officer could have believed that the search was in compliance with the Fourth Amendment? *No.*

SUPREME COURT DECISION

A law enforcement officer is exempt from liability in search and seizure cases if he can establish as a matter of law that a reasonable officer could have believed that the search comported with the Fourth Amendment even though it actually did not.

CASE SIGNIFICANCE

This case reiterates the ruling in Harlow v. Fitzgerald, 457 U.S. 800 (1982), which states that liability ensues only if the officer violated a clearly established right of which a reasonable person would have known. The Court then added that "in order to conclude that the right which the official allegedly violated is 'clearly established,' the contours of the right must be sufficiently clear that a reasonable official would understand that what he is doing violates that right." It also said that the "relevant question. . . is the objective question whether a reasonable officer could have believed petitioner's warrantless search to be lawful, in light of clearly established law and the information the searching officer possessed. Petitioner's [the officer's] subjective beliefs about the search are irrelevant." Clearly the Court in this case rejected the "subjective" standard of the legal reasonableness of the action and used instead the "objective" standard, which focuses on the legal rights that were clearly established at the time the action was taken.

This case sought liability for what federal law enforcement officials did, and therefore it was filed as a *Bivens*-type action (constitutional tort against federal officials) rather than under Section 1983 or state tort. As a *Bivens*-type action, however, Section 1983 principles apply.

### BERGQUIST v. COUNTY OF COCHISE
### 806 F.2d 1364 (9th Cir. 1986)

FACTS

Federal agents from the DEA informed the Cochise County Sheriff's Office about a sighting by an informant of marijuana plants in a greenhouse. The confidential informant also said he had encountered vicious Doberman pinschers on the property. Based on this information and acting on a warrant, thirteen officers from the DEA and Cochise County arrived at the

Bergquist residence to execute a search actually authorized for another farm, the Burwell Hatch Farm. The officers failed to find any Doberman pinschers but threatened to shoot the pet dogs of the Bergquist children, who were home. The officers then searched the greenhouse but found no marijuana plants. In the process of searching other buildings on the property, the officers damaged or destroyed photographic equipment and ceramic artworks in the Bergquists' studio. The Bergquists complained in the district court that the warrant was issued without probable cause, and was mistakenly executed at their residence, and was carried out in an unreasonable and excessive manner. The complaint also alleged that the DEA and the county failed to properly train and instruct their officers on the need for corroboration of informant data and that the county failed to train its magistrates adequately. The district court granted the defendants' motion to dismiss. The Bergquists appealed.

## ISSUE

Could the officers be held liable for the mistaken search and seizure, based on a warrant, conducted on the Bergquist residence? *Yes.*

## COURT DECISION

The court of appeals held that (1) the officers could be held liable for wrongfully seeking and obtaining a warrant, (2) the officers' conduct in allegedly destroying property in a wrong residence had to be evaluated against a reasonableness standard, and (3) the complaint sufficiently alleged a link between the policy of inadequate training and supervision by the supervisors and the harm caused to plaintiffs' property.

## CASE SIGNIFICANCE

In this case, the court said that the mere possession of a warrant is not an absolute defense in wrongful search and seizure cases. There was a search warrant issued by a magistrate, but that warrant did not protect the officers from liability if it was improperly obtained by the officers. The standard to be used for liability is whether a reasonably well trained officer in the defendants' position would have known that the affidavit failed to establish probable cause and that therefore a warrant should not have been applied for. Also, the officers' conduct in allegedly destroying the property of the plaintiffs and the warrant's having been served on the wrong premises had to be judged on the basis of a reasonableness standard. If the officers' conduct is deemed reasonable under the circumstances, then no liability ensues, despite the illegality or impropriety of the search and seizure. The officer is therefore well advised to use reasonableness in the execution of search warrants.

## BROWER v. INYO COUNTY
### 57 U.S.L.W. 4321 (1989)

### FACTS

Police officers placed an eighteen-wheel tractor-trailer across both lanes of a highway in an effort to stop Brower, who had stolen a car and eluded the police in a twenty-mile chase. The tractor-trailer was placed behind a curve, with a police car's headlights pointed in such a manner as to blind Brower. Brower was killed when his car crashed into the roadblock. His heirs and estate brought a Section 1983 action for damages against the police, alleging that his constitutional right against unreasonable search and seizure was violated by the use of such a roadblock.

### ISSUE

Is a roadblock set up by the police to stop a fleeing suspect a form of seizure under the Fourth Amendment? *Yes.*

### SUPREME COURT DECISION

A seizure occurs when there is a "governmental termination of freedom of movement through means intentionally implied." Because Brower was stopped through means intentionally designed to stop him, such a stop constituted a seizure.

### CASE SIGNIFICANCE

This case, decided in 1989, gives the most authoritative guidance to police officers as to when "seizure" in police work takes place, particularly in the context of roadblocks. The Court said that there is seizure when there is a "governmental termination of freedom of movement through means intentionally applied." Under this definition, a roadblock is a form of seizure. Since the roadblock in this case was set up in such a manner that it was likely to kill Brower, the Court decided that there was cause of action to recover for Brower's death. The Court did not say, however, that the police were automatically liable. Instead, it remanded the case to the court of appeals to determine whether the district court erred in concluding that the roadblock was reasonable. If the roadblock was unreasonable, then liability could be imposed, because the police would be deemed to have deprived Brower of a constitutional right resulting in his death.

# 10

# Liability for Negligence

## INTRODUCTION

As discussed in Chapter 2, civil liability generally arises under state tort law or Section 1983. State tort may be divided into *intentional tort* and *negligence tort*. Intentional tort involves the commission of an act the results of which the officer intended or should have expected. In contrast, negligence tort generally involves omission—the failure to do something that ought to have been done.

## I. NEGLIGENCE DEFINED

In simplest terms, negligence may be defined as the failure "to do something that a reasonable man would do or the doing of something which a reasonable man would not do under the existing circumstances."[1] This general definition may be modified or superseded by specific state laws or judicial decisions that provide for a different definition, usually in terms more restrictive than the above.

Negligence tort applies in many aspects of police work but particularly in the following instances: general failure to protect the public from harm or injury, failure to protect against drunk drivers, failure to respond to 911 calls, negligence in traffic and DWI cases, negligence in police use of motor vehicles, failure to give proper medical aid, negligent traffic control, negligent use of weapons, failure to warn of hazardous road conditions, and failure to protect against domestic violence. Many of these topics are discussed in the next chapter. This chapter discusses negligence in general, including the levels of negligence, the elements of negligence tort, possible liability for negligence under Section 1983, and defenses in negligence cases.

## II. LEVELS OF NEGLIGENCE IN CIVIL LIABILITY CASES

Negligence is classified in various ways by different jurisdictions, but for purposes of police civil liability it is best classified according to levels of negligence. Using this framework, negligence may be classified as slight negligence, gross negligence, and negligence per se. *Black's Law Dictionary* defines these types of negligence as follows:

1.  *Slight negligence:* "an absence of that degree of care and vigilance which persons of extraordinary prudence and foresight are accustomed to use."

2.  *Gross negligence:* "the intentional failure to perform a manifest duty in reckless disregard of the consequences as affecting the life or property of another; such a gross want of care and regard for the rights of others as to justify the presumption of willfulness and wantonness."

3.  *Negligence per se:* "conduct, whether of action or omission, which may be declared and treated as negligence without any argument or proof . . . either because it is in violation of a statute or valid municipal ordinance, or because it is so palpably opposed to the dictates of common prudence that it can be said without hesitation or doubt that no careful person would have been guilty of it."[2]

Definitions may vary from state to state, and the terms may also vary. Such variations may be due to specific categorizations and definitions provided by state laws or court decisions. For example, some states use such terms as *mere negligence, simple negligence,* and *criminal negligence.* The type of negligence needed to hold an officer civilly liable also differs from state to state and may vary with the type of legal action, dependent on state or case law. In some states, slight negligence may suffice to establish liability, while in others gross negligence is required.

In some negligence cases, the standards of care prescribed in police departmental rules and regulations are used by the court to define the level of care expected from police officers. For example, in a wrongful death action filed against a police officer by the parents of a man who was shot and killed by that officer in response to a radio call that erroneously reported a burglary in progress, the officer's failure to comply with police department guidelines as provided for in the department's manual by using deadly force when such ought not to have been used was considered by the court to have raised a presumption of negligence. Peterson v. City of Long Beach, 155 Cal. Rptr. 360 (1979). It is therefore important for police officers to know and follow departmental rules and regulations if they are to avoid possible charges of negligence in the performance of responsibilities. In some jurisdictions, violations of departmental rules may not lead to civil liability, but they can be the basis for disciplinary action by the agency.

## III. ELEMENTS OF NEGLIGENCE UNDER STATE TORT LAW

For a negligence tort under state law to succeed, four elements must be present: (1) a duty on the part of the defendant, (2) a failure to conform to that duty, (3) a proximate cause, and (4) actual damage. All four must be present for liability to ensue, which is to say that the absence of one precludes liability. These four elements are illustrated below, using the case of negligent use of a motor vehicle by an officer who, against departmental policy, speeds excessively and drives carelessly on a crowded freeway, causing harm to an innocent motorist.

1. *Duty on the part of the defendant.* This means that there must be a legal duty that requires a defendant to act according to certain standards in order to avoid unreasonable risks to others. In the example above, the officer has a legal duty to make sure that his or her use of the motor vehicle does not pose an unreasonable risk to others, a duty that has been strengthened by departmental policy.

2. *Failure to conform to that duty.* This means that the defendant failed to act in accordance with legal expectations, such failure resulting in an unreasonable risk to others. In the example above, the officer, by driving carelessly on a crowded freeway, violates that legal duty.

3. *Proximate cause.* The plaintiff must prove that there is a close or causal link between the defendant's negligence and the consequent harm to the plaintiff. In the example above, the plaintiff must prove that the injury was caused by the officer's negligent conduct, that the injury, for instance, was caused by a collision or pileup resulting from the officer's speeding.

4. *Actual damage.* The plaintiff must prove that damages were incurred as a result of the officer's negligent conduct. If no such damages are proved in court, there is no recovery. In the example above, the plaintiff must prove that hospital fees, doctor's fees, loss of earnings, suffering, and so on, were due to the officer's negligence.

## IV. MAY OFFICERS BE LIABLE FOR NEGLIGENCE UNDER SECTION 1983? MAYBE.

Negligence cases against the police are usually filed under state tort law. Most cases in this and the next chapter are state tort negligence cases. A second source of possible negligence liability is Section 1983, but on this issue there is disagreement among the courts. Admittedly, there is liability under Section 1983 for intentional acts, but whether Section 1983 liability can be based on negligence (usually a nonaction) is a question that has generated considerable controversy in the courts. In Smith v. Wade, 33 CrL 3021 (1983), the United States Supreme Court said;

> We hold that a jury may be permitted to assess punitive damages in an action under Section 1983 when the defendant's conduct is shown to be motivated by evil motive or intent, or when it involves reckless or callous indifference to the federally protected rights of others.

This statement appears to indicate that negligence, at least the kind of negligence that involves reckless or callous indifference, may be a basis for liability under Section 1983. A number of scholars maintain that "negligence may be actionable under Section 1983,"[3] although "an isolated act of negligence is not actionable because it does not violate the Eighth Amendment prohibition against cruel and unusual punishment."[4]

The United States Supreme Court made it clear, however, that there is no liability under Section 1983 for actions that allege that the due process right of a plaintiff was violated by acts of public officials that constituted "mere negligence." Daniels v. Williams, 474 U.S. 327 (1986), and Davison v. Cannon, 474 U.S. 344 (1986). But what about "gross negligence"? In a 1989 case, DeShaney v. Winnebago County Department of Social Services, 57 U.S.L.W. 4218 (1989), liability under Section 1983 was ruled out by the Court in failure-to-protect cases except when the person is under the custody of the state.

Some lower courts have allowed Section 1983 liability based on negligence. Typical are cases in which a police chief negligently failed to train and supervise police officers under his control, a prison official negligently failed to provide necessary medical care for inmates, and mental health officials negligently failed to prevent some inmates from beating another inmate.[5] Most courts that allow recovery require gross, reckless, or culpable negligence, as opposed to mere or simple negligence, on the part of the officer-defendant. Whether these enhanced forms of negligence have been proven—or even what the terms mean—is up to the courts to determine. Moreover, the rule appears to be that an isolated act of negligence does not lead to liability under Section 1983. Griffin v. Hicks, 804 I.2d 1052 (8th Cir. 1986). It is not clear, therefore, whether officers may be liable for negligence under Section 1983. This has yet to be decided by the United States Supreme Court.

## V. MAY NEGLIGENCE THAT IS NOT ACTIONABLE UNDER SECTION 1983 SUCCEED UNDER STATE TORT? YES.

If a lawsuit under Section 1983 based on negligence fails, may it nonetheless succeed under state tort? The Fifth Circuit Court of Appeals has said yes—in the case of Young v. City of Killeen, 775 F.2d 1349 (5th Cir. 1985). In that case, a police officer was held liable in the amount of $202,295.80 for shooting and killing a person who was suspected of drug dealing. The officer claimed he shot in self-defense when he saw the suspect reach for something under the seat of the car. The court held, however, that the officer was negligent because he did not follow good police procedure:

- He failed to use his radio.
- He failed to use a back-up unit.
- He placed his car dangerously in a "cut off" maneuver.
- He ordered the two suspects to exit their car rather than issuing an immobilization command to remain in the car with their hands in plain view.
- He abandoned a covered position and advanced into the open, where the odds of overreacting were greater.

The court rejected the plaintiff's claim for liability under Section 1983 but upheld it based on state tort law, the principle being that what may not be a violation of a constitutional right may nonetheless lead to liability based on a violation of proper police procedure. In this case, the judge concluded that the officer's fault in not following proper police procedure not only placed the officer in a position of greater danger but also imperiled the deceased suspect by creating a situation in which a fatal error was likely. Damages were therefore awarded in a wrongful death case under state tort.

## VI. DEFENSES IN NEGLIGENCE TORT CASES

The absence of one of the four elements in negligence cases is a common defense in state tort cases. Another defense often used is the discretionary acts defense (a form of immunity defense). Finally, there are several defenses that may be categorized under the term "other defenses."

### A. The Discretionary Acts Defense

This defense was first enunciated in the case of South v. Maryland, 59 U.S. (18 How.) 396 (1856), where the court referred to the "ministerial functions of the sheriff."[6] The discretionary acts defense holds that if a governmental function is discretionary—that is, involves planning or policy-level decisions—there can be no liability for negligent decisions. Conversely, if a governmental function is ministerial—that is, involves operational-level behavior or decisions—liability may exist if negligence is established. This is therefore a form of immunity defense, with the officer claiming immunity because that act performed is discretionary instead of ministerial. A discretionary function may be defined as a function that is not required or, if required, for which the time, manner, or extent of performance is left to the officer. In contrast, a ministerial function is a function that is done under the authority of a superior; it is a function that demands no special discretion, judgment, or skill.[7] In practice, these definitions tend to be subjective and are difficult to apply with precision. The determination of whether the act is discretionary or ministerial is made by the judge or jury. Decided cases indicate that in police negligence cases immunity exists for discretionary functions but not for ministerial functions. This principle has been used by state courts when considering police and municipal liability for negligent failure to arrest intoxicated drivers.

Applying the discretionary acts exception, the Florida Supreme Court, in Everton v. Willard, 468 So.2d 936 (Fla. 1985), held that a peace officer's decision to arrest or not to arrest a drunk motorist is a discretionary function. As such, police and municipalities cannot be held liable for damages resulting from police failure to arrest intoxicated drivers where there exists only a general duty. The court stated that "discretionary power is considered basic to the police power function of governmental entities and is recognized as critical to a law enforcement officer's ability to carry out his duties." The court added that "merely because an activity is operational, it should not necessarily be removed from the category of governmental activity which involves broad policy or planning decisions."[8]

### B. Other Defenses

There are other defenses in negligence tort cases, the most common of which are sudden emergency (or sudden peril), contributory negligence, comparative negligence, and assumption of risk.[9] The types of negligence defenses vary from state to state.

**1. *Sudden Emergency.*** This defense is based on the principle that an officer cannot be held accountable under a general reasonable standard if he or she had to act instinctively and with only a minimum exercise of judgment.

EXAMPLE: In one case, an officer who was shot during a robbery of a bar returned fire from the floor where he had fallen. One of the bullets from the officer's gun hit and killed the plaintiff, who was 110 feet away. The court said that the jury could find that this was an emergency situation in which there was no opportunity to think and therefore a speedy decision was necessary. Scott v. City of Opa Locka, 311 So. 2d 825 (Fla. Dist. Ct. App. 1975). In another case, however, a court held that this defense is not available when the actions of the officer themselves create the emergency. London v. Ryan, 349 So. 2d 1334 (La. App. 1977).

**2. *Contributory Negligence.*** If the plaintiff's negligence contributed proximately to his or her injuries, no recovery of any kind is allowed. It is therefore an absolute defense in state tort actions.

EXAMPLE: Damage and injury are inflicted on the plaintiff as a result of negligent use by the police of a motor vehicle when chasing a suspect. If the police can prove that the plaintiff is not blameless and in fact contributed to the injury (e.g., in not properly giving way despite hearing the police siren during the chase), then no liability is imposed on the police. Less than half of the states, however, recognize contributory negligence as a defense. Most states follow the comparative negligence rule.

**3. *Comparative Negligence.*** Applying the rule of comparative negligence requires rejecting the "all or nothing" approach and instead apportioning liability between the plaintiff and the defendant on the basis of relative degrees of fault. For example, an officer is sued for injury to a motorist arising from the officer's negligence in directing traffic. Assume that the amount of damage is a thousand dollars. If the officer is 40 percent negligent and the motorist is 60 percent negligent, recovery by the plaintiff will be limited to four hundred dollars.

**4. *Assumption of Risk.*** There is no liability if the plaintiff is considered to have assumed the risk of certain harm by voluntarily taking chances that led to the harm.

EXAMPLE: A police officer warns a motorist that it is extremely dangerous to cross a certain road because of high water conditions. The motorist goes ahead anyway despite the warning. Should injury or damage occur, the motorist will likely be considered to have assumed the risk; hence recovery will not be allowed.

## SUMMARY

Negligence is defined as "the omission to do something which a reasonable man, guided by those ordinary considerations which ordinarily regulate human affairs, would do, or the doing of something which a reasonable and prudent man would not do." Negligence may be classified as slight negligence, gross negligence, and negligence per se. Definitions may vary from state to state, and the type of negligence needed to hold an officer civilly liable also varies from state to state, depending on state or case law.

Negligence tort has four elements that must be present for liability to ensue: (1) a duty on the part of the defendant, (2) a failure to conform to that duty, (3) a proximate cause, and (4) actual damage. Negligent tort cases are usually filed under state tort law, but court decisions are unclear as to whether or not liability can arise under Section 1983. An action may succeed under state tort law even if it fails under Section 1983.

Various defenses are available in negligence tort cases. The discretionary acts defense holds that if a governmental function is discretionary, there can be no liability for negligent decisions; conversely, if a governmental function is ministerial, then liability may exist if negligence is established. Other defenses include sudden emergency, contributory negligence, comparative negligence, and assumption of risk.

## NOTES

1. H. Black, *Black's Law Dictionary*, 5th ed. (West Publishing Co., 1979) at 931–933.
2. *Ibid.*, at 1184–1187.
3. See I. Silver, *Police Civil Liability* (Matthew Bender, 1989), at 8–37. See also Penland and Boardman, "Section 1983: Contemporary Trends in Police Misconduct Arena," *Idaho Law Review* 20 (1984), at 660.
4. Silver, *Police Civil Liability*, at 8–33.
5. R. V. del Carmen, *Potential Liabilities of Probation and Parole Officers* (National Institute of Corrections, August 1985, revised edition), at 51.
6. V. E. Kappeler and R. V. del Carmen, "Police Civil Liability for Failure to Arrest Drunk Drivers, *The Police Chief*, October 1988, at 102.
7. The Attorney's Pocket Dictionary, at 315.
8. Kappeler and del Carmen, "Police Civil Liability," at 124.
9. R. V. del Carmen, *Criminal Procedure for Law Enforcement Personnel* (Brooks/Cole Publishing Company, 1987), at 414–415.

# 11

# SPECIFIC INSTANCES OF NEGLIGENCE IN POLICE WORK

## I. ARE THE POLICE LIABLE FOR FAILURE TO PROTECT? GENERALLY NO, BUT EXCEPTIONS EXIST

One of the most bothersome legal issues confronting the police in the last few years is the issue of liability for failure to protect. The nature of their work constantly exposes police officers to lawsuits from the public for failure to prevent harm and injury, whether the harm or injury is reasonably foreseeable or not. In view of a significant recent United States Supreme Court decision, any discussion of possible police liability for failure to protect must separate liability *under state tort law* from liability *under Section 1983*. This is because, whereas liability under state tort law for failure to protect is alive and well, liability under Section 1983 for failure to protect no longer exists—at least under the due process clause of the Fourteenth Amendment.

### A. Under State Tort Law

The rule under state tort law may be summarized as follows: In general, because of the public duty doctrine, there is no liability for failure to protect; however, liability may be imposed if a "special relationship" exists between the officer or agency and the injured party.[1]

**1. *In General, No Liability for Failure to Protect Because of the Public Duty Doctrine.*** The public duty doctrine holds that government functions, such as police protection, are duties owed to the general public and not to specific individuals; therefore, police officers who breach a general duty while acting within the scope of their official capacity are not liable for injury or harm to particular individuals that may have been caused by a third party.[2]

The public duty doctrine was first enunciated by the United States Supreme Court in the case of South v. Maryland, 59 U.S. (18 How.) 396 (1896). In that case, an individual requested that a Maryland county sheriff provide him with protection from a violent mob. The sheriff refused, the citizen was seriously injured, and a lawsuit was filed against the sheriff. The Court ruled that "the duty of conservator of the peace exercised by the sheriff is a public duty a breach of which is to be punished by indictment." The Court added, however, that in cases where a law enforcement officer acts "ministerial and is bound to render certain services to individuals, he is liable for acts of misfeasance or non-feasance to the party who is injured. . . ." This case introduced the public duty doctrine into American case law.

The public duty doctrine currently prevails in a great majority of states; hence in most states there is no liability for harm or injury to a member of the general public resulting from police failure to protect. Illustrative is a recent California case where a massacre took place at a McDonald's restaurant in which a deranged man shot and killed twenty-one people. The city, its mayor, and the police chief were sued for an alleged inadequacy in the training and supervision of police officers, which supposedly resulted in inadequate and untimely efforts to protect the patrons at McDonald's who were killed. The court held that there was no liability for the killings in the absence of a special relationship between the police and the twenty-one victims who were killed. Lopez v. City of San Diego, 235 Cal. Rptr. 583 (Ct. App. 1987).

In another case, the Seventh Circuit Court of Appeals decided that undercover police officers who saw a mugging and pursued the attackers only after the victim had been robbed and beaten were not liable for failure to prevent the injury. In that case, Chicago police detectives conducted surveillance at a parking lot after several reports of attacks there. A woman, who was attacked by robbers during the surveillance and who suffered a broken leg and had her purse stolen, filed suit, alleging that the police waited until the attack had ended before chasing the suspects. The appellate court refused to hold the officers and their supervisor liable, saying that the mere fact that the police were in a position to observe the attack did not create liability based on failure to protect. Simack v. Risely, 804 F. 2d 143 (7th Cir. 1986).

The practical justification for the public duty doctrine is that it insulates police officers from lawsuits from any and all members of the public whose injury might somehow be attributed to lack of police protection. Without the protection provided by the public duty doctrine, the task of policing would be legally risky and time consuming. A second justification is that the doctrine affords police officers wide discretion in the performance of day-to-day responsibilities. An officer's decision not to provide protection might prove to be a mistake if an individual is subsequently exposed or subjected to harm, but what in retrospect may be poor judgment cannot be the basis for civil liability, particularly because sometimes crucial decisions need to be made by the police in a matter of seconds.

**2. The Special Relationship Exception to the Public Duty Doctrine.** The public duty doctrine admits of one major and multifaceted exception: the exception based on a "special relationship." As a result of this exception, if a duty is owed to a particular person rather than to the general public, a police officer or agency that breaches that duty can be held liable for damages. Court decisions indicate that there are various ways in which a special relationship may be established in police work, including these:

- The police deprive an individual of liberty by taking that individual into custody.
- The police assume an obligation that goes beyond police duty to protect the general public.
- Protection is mandated by law.
- Protection is ordered by a court.

The above list is merely illustrative, not inclusive. The courts of each state determine which ways of establishing a special relationship are valid in that state.

**a) Depriving an Individual of Liberty by Taking Him or Her into Custody.** In DeShaney v. Winnebago County Department of Social Services, 57 U.S.L.W. 4218 (1989), discussed at the end of this chapter, the United States Supreme Court said that an individual has a constitutional right to be protected by the police when the state has imposed limitations on a person's freedom to act on his own behalf "through imprisonment, institutionalization, or other similar restraint of personal liberty." The Court specifically mentioned prisoners and committed mental patients as falling under this category. Hence, if an officer arrests a suspect or if a suspect is detained in jail, the duty to protect that suspect from harm exists, because a special relationship has been created by the act of depriving the suspect of liberty.

In a Florida case, a person was arrested for possession of a lottery ticket. He was handcuffed by the police but then was stabbed by a third party. The court ruled that once the suspect was handcuffed and taken

into custody, a special relationship was created that made the city responsible for his safety as though he was incarcerated in the city jail. In this
case, however, the court did not find the officers liable, because there
was no negligence in the officers' handling of the suspect—they were just
as surprised as the arrested person was when a woman ran by and
stabbed him. Sanders v. City of Belle Glade, 510 So. 2d 962 (Fla. App.
1987).[3] Similarly, police officers were not held liable for a severe attack on
a suspect who was accused of the rape of an eight-year-old girl and who
was shot five times and killed by the girl's mother while handcuffed in an
interrogation room. The court found that the police officers were unaware that the victim's mother presented an imminent danger to the suspect's safety. The mother had previously been arrested for aggravated
battery and was the registered owner of a handgun, but those facts alone
did not create liability, because it would have been unreasonable to expect the officers to have knowledge of all records in the possession of the
department.[4] Rush v. City of Chicago, 517 N.E. 2d 17 (Ill. App. Ct. 1987).
The key element in these cases is negligence by the police. If no negligence can be proved by the plaintiff, then no liability ensues, even if a
person is injured by a third party while in police custody.

   **b) *Assuming an Obligation That Goes beyond Police Duty to Pro-
tect the General Public.*** The case of Schuster v. City of New York, 154
N.E. 2d 534 (N.Y. 1958), illustrates this category of special relationship. In
this case, a young man provided New York City police officers with information that led to the arrest of a fugitive. The incident received considerable media attention, exposing Schuster as the individual who had
assisted in the fugitive's apprehension. When Schuster received life-
threatening phone calls, he notified the police. Several weeks later,
Schuster was shot and killed. A subsequent lawsuit by Schuster's family
alleged that city police failed to provide Schuster with adequate protection and that New York City breached its special duty owed to individuals
who provide the police with information about a crime. A New York
court imposed liability, stating that "in our view the police owe a special
duty to use reasonable care for the protection of persons who have col-
laborated with it in the arrest or prosecution of criminals."
   In another New York case, the court held that a special relationship
exists when a citizen assists police officers in the apprehension of a suspect. Mohan v. State of New York, 516 N.Y.S. 2d 787 (A.D. 1987). In this
case, the court allowed the estate of a man killed by his brother to file a
negligence suit against the state. The dead man had been asked by state
troopers to help them find his brother, who had been reported to be
armed with a gun. The man did help in the search, during which the
brother shot him. The court said that the state was potentially liable because the request to help created a special relationship.

Some courts have held that the failure to protect an informant creates police liability. This is because the agreement by a person to help the police secure information that otherwise would not be available takes that person out of the general public and places him or her in a category where police protection is needed. One example would be where a witness in a witness protection program was subsequently killed as a result of negligent police protection. Another example would be where a current informant is exposed to unnecessary danger and is in fact injured because of police negligence.

The problem with this category of special relationship is that courts in various states give it different interpretations. For example, the courts in Illinois have said that liability based on a special relationship (which the courts also call a *special duty*) exists if the following conditions are met:

1. The municipality was aware of the particular danger or risk to which the plaintiff was exposed.

2. Specific acts or omissions by the municipality were alleged by the plaintiff.

3. The acts or omissions were affirmative or willful in nature.

4. The injury occurred while the plaintiff was in the direct and immediate control of employees or agents of the municipality.[5]

Using those standards, an Illinois court ruled that a plaintiff had been brought into a position of danger by the police when he was attacked, while police officers were present, by four individuals whom the police had asked him to identify. Liability was imposed. Gardner v. Village of Chicago Ridge, 219 N.E. 2d 147 (1966). By contrast, no liability was imposed for a police officer's failure to accompany the plaintiff to a subway station upon request. The plaintiff was earlier accosted by six young men who were chased away by the officer. The officer later declined to go with this passenger down to the train waiting area, saying that there would be no problem because the youths would be using a different platform. The plaintiff was attacked by the youths, but the court found no liability for failure by the police to provide protection, saying such did not fall under the special relationship doctrine.[6] Marvin v. Chicago Transit Authority, 446 N.E. 2d 1183 (1983).

c) *Protection Mandated by Law.* Some states enact laws expressly protecting special groups or individuals. In other states, judicial interpretations consider certain laws as protecting special groups or individuals despite that such protection is not expressly provided for by law. Laws prohibiting drunk driving sometimes fall under this category of special relationship, as determined by the courts. For example, in Irwin v. Town of Ware, 467 N.E. 2d 1292 (Ma. 1984), the court found that a cause of action existed due to the special relationship between the police and the plaintiff; hence the police were liable for failure to arrest a drunk driver who subsequently caused injury to the plaintiff. Such special relationship was deemed created by the legislature in a state statute that prohibited drunken driving. The court reasoned that "statutes which establish police responsibility in such circumstances evidence a legislative intent to protect both intoxicated persons and users of the highway."

In another case, police officers and the city were held potentially liable for failing to take a drunk person into protective custody. The court found that state law clearly required police officers to take such incapacitated persons into custody, which in this case the officers failed to do. Instead, they turned the man over to his two companions, who later abandoned him. As a result, the man died of suffocation. Morse v. City of Mount Pleasant, 408 N.W. 2d 541 (Mich. App. 1987).

Some cases in various states have been settled in favor of plaintiffs who established that law enforcement officials failed to comply with state laws mandating protection in family violence cases. These laws usually require the police to advise victims and potential victims, in writing, of their rights and the availability of shelters. They also establish departmental procedures requiring that information be provided to officers, such information to include the names of persons protected by protective orders and the persons to whom the protective orders are directed. Failure to comply with these statutory requirements can result in liability.

**d) *Protection Ordered by a Court.*** This is illustrated in the case of Sorichetti v. City of New York, 482 N.E. 2d 70 (1985), a much-publicized case wherein the New York Court of Appeals upheld a judgment for two million dollars against the New York police for failure to protect a child who was under an order of protection issued by the court. In that case, a mother had obtained an order for protection curtailing her husband's access to their child because of the husband's violent tendencies. One weekend, the mother agreed to permit the husband to keep the child if he met her at the police station. At the station, the husband yelled to the wife that he was going to kill her, and then pointed to the daughter and said, "You better do the sign of the cross before this weekend is up." The wife immediately asked the police to arrest her husband; the police replied that there was nothing they could do. The wife went again to the police the next day and demanded that they return her daughter and arrest her husband, but the police denied her request. That same weekend, the child was attacked by the father and suffered severe wounds. The appellate court upheld the huge damage award, saying that the court-issued protective order created a special relationship that required the police to take extra steps to protect the daughter from harm from a known source.[7]

**3.** *Special Relationship versus Special Duty.* In most negligent-use-of-motor-vehicle cases, the courts use the term *special duty* instead of *special relationship* in describing the basis for liability. Is there any difference between these two terms? The answer is not clear, because most courts tend to use the two terms loosely and interchangeably. If there is any distinction at all, it is that the term *special relationship*, as used by most courts, is broader: It encompasses those situations where the narrowing of the target (from the general public to a particular individual) is triggered by a number of factors, including but not limited to a mandate by law or regulation. Other special relationship factors that create police obligations include being placed under police custody and consenting to act as a police informant. By contrast, while a special duty also involves a shift of the duty to protect from the general public to a particular individual or a group of individuals, that narrowing of relationship usually stems from statute, case law, or departmental rules. A special duty therefore stems from a specific mandate rather than from situational relationships; hence it is narrower and more limited.

**4.** *Domestic Abuse Situations under State Tort Law.* The general rule is that the police do not have any liability in domestic abuse situations, but liability can arise if a special relationship has been created between the police and the abused spouse. This is because the duty to protect a spouse comes under the public duty doctrine—it is the same duty an officer owes to the general public. An example is the case of Turner v. City of North Charleston, 675 F. Supp. 314 (D.S.C. 1987). In that case, the spouses had a history of disputes and violence. The husband had been charged earlier with rape, battery, abduction, and assault. The wife later filed for divorce after an abduction during which she was shot. A restraining order was issued, but the husband entered the wife's home despite the restraining order, threatened her with a knife, and then made harassing telephone calls. The state had a domestic abuse statute, but that statute, according to the court, did not in itself establish a special relationship that mandated the police to give the wife the protection she needed. Besides, even if it did, the officers had no knowledge of the actual danger to which the wife was exposed; hence the officers were not negligent in failing to act.

There are instances, however, when a special relationship has been established and failure to protect would therefore lead to liability. Foremost among these are cases where the state has passed legislation authorizing courts to issue protective orders to spouses in domestic abuse situations. In these cases, the existence of a statute and the issuance of a judicial order to protect a particular spouse creates a special duty on the part of the police to extend protection. Failure to afford the necessary level of protection despite a judicial order may create liability.

## B. Under Section 1983

The leading case on liability under Section 1983 for failure to protect is DeShaney v. Winnebago County Department of Social Services, 57 U.S.L.W. 4218 (1989), which says there is no constitutional right to protection under the due process clause.

**1. *The DeShaney Case.*** In addition to possible liability under state tort law for failure to protect, a second possible source of liability is Section 1983, the federal civil rights statute. For a long time federal courts were not sure whether or not liability existed. On February 22, 1989, the United States Supreme Court resolved the issue in favor of public officials, holding that, with some exceptions, the state and its officers are not liable under Section 1983 for failure to protect individuals from injury caused by private persons. DeShaney v. Winnebago County Department of Social Services, 57 U.S.L.W. 4218 (1989).

The facts in *DeShaney* are indeed touching. Joshua DeShaney, a four-year-old, was beaten and permanently injured by his father to whose custody he was awarded after a divorce. Over a period of time, the county department of social services and several social workers received complaints that the child was being abused by his father. They took various steps to protect the boy, but they did not remove him from the father's custody despite knowledge and proof that violence was inflicted by the father. Subsequently, the child was beaten so badly that he suffered permanent brain damage and was rendered severely retarded. He is expected to spend the rest of his life in an institution. The father was tried and convicted of child abuse in criminal court. The mother, acting for and as guardian of the child, later sued the officials of the county department of social services of Winnebago County (Wisconsin) under Section 1983, claiming that social services officials violated the child's constitutional right to due process by failing to intervene to protect the child against his father's violence. The district court decided for the county and the court of appeals affirmed that decision.

On appeal, the United States Supreme Court said that the Fourteenth Amendment right to due process does not impose an affirmative duty on the state to protect individuals who are not in state custody from harm by private persons (the father in this case). Therefore, the county's social services officials could not be held liable civilly under Section 1983, because no constitutional right was violated by the lack of protection. There was no liability even though these officials had knowledge of the abuse and had continuing contact with the family. Significantly, the Court stated that there are instances when the state does have an affirmative duty to protect under the due process clause, in particular, when the state has imposed limitations on a person's freedom to act on his or her own behalf "through imprisonment, institutionalization, or other similar restraint of personal liberty." Examples would include prisoners and committed mental patients. Other than those instances, the state cannot be held liable for failure to protect under Section 1983.

**2. *The Implications of the DeShaney Case.*** What is the impact of *DeShaney* on police civil liability cases? The answer is that the case settles for now an issue that has bothered courts and police officers for years. During the last few years, the number of cases filed against the police for failure to protect based on a variety of situations has risen. Among these are cases where the police allegedly failed to protect against drunk drivers, reckless drivers, home violence, robberies, and other criminal acts. *DeShaney* precludes recovery except in cases when the person is under the custody of the state.

Although *DeShaney* involved county social services officials and not police officers, the principle should apply equally to law enforcement work. The Court's decision did not make any distinction based on the type of public services provided; what it emphasized instead was the absence of a constitutional right to protection under the due process clause of the Fourteenth Amendment. The pervading theme in the decision is the absence of a constitutional right to protection from the state for harm inflicted on an individual from third persons (meaning non-public-officers).

*DeShaney*, although doubtless a favorable decision for public officials, should not be interpreted to mean that no civil liability of any kind may be imposed on law enforcement officers. Civil liability was sought under Section 1983 based on due process. The Court said that there could be no liability under that law, because one element of a Section 1983 case was missing—the violation of a constitutional right. Since no constitutional right to due process exists based on failure to protect from harm inflicted by a third person, a Section 1983 case could not succeed. Toward the end of the decision, however, the Court said this: "It may well be that, by voluntarily undertaking to protect Joshua [the child] against a danger it concededly played no part in creating, the State acquired a duty under state tort law to provide him with adequate protection against that danger." Clearly, the Court indicates that liability might ensue, not under Section 1983, but under state tort law. The Court concluded by saying, "The people of Wisconsin may well prefer a system of liability which would place upon the State and its officials the responsibility for failure to act in situations such as the present one. They may create such a system by changing the tort law of the State in accordance with the regular law-making process."

**3. *Possible Liability If Other Constitutional Rights Are Violated.*** The Court, in *DeShaney*, did not say whether or not a right to protection might successfully be invoked under the other constitutional rights. For example, might failure to protect come under the equal protection clause or the right against cruel and unusual punishment? Although most failure-to-protect cases should come under the due process clause, there might be cases when failure to protect constitutes discrimination (hence a violation of equal protection) or cruel and unusual punishment.

For example, at least one federal court of appeals has ruled that lack of protection in domestic abuse cases is actionable under Section 1983 if it involves a violation of a constitutional right, such as the right to equal protection. Watson v. City of Kansas City, Kansas, 857 F. 2d 690 (10th Cir. 1988). In the case in question, the wife of a police officer and her son filed a Section 1983 suit against the city, its police chief, and some officers, alleging that they failed to provide police protection against domestic violence. The woman alleged that a few days before their divorce, her police officer-husband threatened her with a knife. She called the police, but allegedly a police captain, accompanied by other officers who responded to the call, told her that if she ever called the police again, she would be arrested and would never see her two children again. The husband beat her and her children many times but no arrest was made; neither was the husband ordered to leave. In another incident, the woman drove to the police station to ask for assistance, which the officers did not give. The husband followed her home, beat, stabbed, and then raped her. In one of her calls, the officer responding allegedly said that the whole situation was her fault because she married her husband. The husband later committed suicide.

The Tenth Circuit Court of Appeals held that although in general there is no constitutional right to protection by the police, the state cannot discriminate in providing such protection. Evidence in this case showed that the police department discriminated against victims of domestic violence and afforded them less protection than that given to the general public in violence cases: Whereas the arrest rate for nondomestic assault cases in that city was 31 percent, the rate for domestic violence was only 16 percent. Such discrimination violated the equal protection clause of the Constitution and was therefore actionable.

**4. Summary.** To summarize, the United States Supreme Court, in *DeShaney v. Winnebago County Department of Social Services*, decided as follows:

1. The Fourteenth Amendment right to due process does not impose an affirmative duty on the state to protect individuals who are not in state custody from harm by private persons. Since no constitutional right is violated, there is no liability for failure to protect.

2. Liability under Section 1983 based on due process ensues only in cases where an individual is imprisoned, institutionalized (as when committed to a mental hospital), or is under similar restraint of personal liberty.

3. Liability might ensue under state tort law, but that is to be determined by the statutes or court decisions of the state.

4. In *DeShaney*, the Court rejected police liability based on an alleged violation of a due process right. The case does not rule out possible liability based on a violation of other constitutional rights, notably the right to equal protection.

5. The principles in *DeShaney* apply only to police liability for failure to protect individuals from harm inflicted by third parties, not from liability for injury or harm inflicted by law enforcement officials themselves.

## II. ARE THE POLICE LIABLE FOR FAILURE TO ARREST DRUNK DRIVERS? GENERALLY NO, BUT EXCEPTIONS EXIST

Most states hold that police officers, because of the public duty doctrine, are not liable for injuries inflicted on the public by drunk drivers whom the police fail to arrest. In some states, however, liability is now being imposed by the courts based on exceptions to the public duty doctrine. The cases below illustrate the general rule and the exceptions.[8]

### A. The General Rule: Cases Where No Liability Was Imposed

In Ashburn v. Ann Arundel County, 510 A. 2d 1078 (Md. 1986), a Maryland court of appeals held that the officer, the county, and the police department could not be held liable for injuries caused by a drunk driver. In that case, a police officer found John J. Millham in a pickup truck in the parking lot of a 7-Eleven store. Millham was intoxicated and sitting behind the wheel of the truck, which had its engine running and its lights on. Millham was driving the vehicle, and under Maryland law he could have been charged with drunk driving. The officer told Millham to pull his truck to the side of the lot and to refrain from driving that evening, but he did not make an arrest. As soon as the officer left, Millham drove the truck and a short distance later collided with the plaintiff-pedestrian. Losing his left leg and suffering other injuries, the plaintiff brought suit. On appeal, the court of special appeals, in a sweeping decision, held as follows:

1. The police officer was acting in a discretionary capacity and hence was immune from liability.

2. The police officer was not in "special relationship" with pedestrians and therefore did not have a duty to prevent a driver from injuring pedestrians.

3. The law that requires police officers to detain and investigate a driver did not impose any duty on the police to prevent drivers from injuring pedestrians.

Like most states, Maryland adheres to the general rule that the public duty doctrine precludes liability unless a special relationship between the police and the victim is established. No such relationship existed in this case.

In Massengill v. Yuma County, 456 P. 2d 376 (1969), the Arizona Supreme Court held that the duty to arrest a drunk driver is a duty owed to the general public and not to a particular individual; consequently, a third party who is injured by a released drunk driver cannot recover damages from governmental entities. In this case, a lawsuit was filed against a sheriff, his deputy, and the county for failure to arrest two traffic violators who became involved in a head-on collision resulting in the deaths of five persons. According to the testimony, the deputy knew or should have known that the drivers were impaired, but he failed to intervene until after the incident had occurred. The Arizona Supreme Court applied the public duty doctrine, ruling that the circumstances of the case did not demonstrate any greater duty to the injured drivers than that owed to the public as a whole; hence recovery was denied.

In a similar case, Fusilier v. Russell, 345 So. 2d 543 (La. App. 1977), a state tort case was brought against two Louisiana deputy sheriffs for failure to arrest an intoxicated person who later became involved in a collision, leaving a victim severely burned. Before the accident, deputy sheriffs responded to a call to evict a disorderly person from a local nightclub. Upon arrival the officers observed an intoxicated man staggering around the nightclub's parking lot. Although the officers knew the subject was impaired, they failed to arrest him. Without the knowledge of the officers, the subject left the area driving a motor vehicle. Ten minutes later, the deputies saw an accident in which two vehicles were on fire. The drunk driver had struck another vehicle. The Louisiana Court of Appeals, applying the public duty doctrine, ruled that the police duty to arrest is a duty owed to the general public and that an individual duty was not owed to the injured party under the circumstances of the case.

In Crosby v. Town of Bethlehem, 457 N.Y.S. 2d 618 (A.D. 1982), a New York case, a pedestrian was killed by an intoxicated motorcyclist; a lawsuit was brought against a police officer and the municipality for alleged negligent failure to arrest a drunk driver. Before the accident, an off-duty police officer, who lived next door to the site of a lively party, conversed with and watched an intoxicated subject mount his motorcycle. The officer called the police department and reported the violation but failed to intervene at the scene. The driver subsequently became involved in a fatal accident that led to the filing of a lawsuit against the officer and the city. The New York Supreme Court failed to find a breach of duty, saying that although the "ultimate tragedy was entirely foreseeable . . . foreseeability is not to be confused with duty, and foreseeability may not be used to create a duty where none existed before." The court in effect ruled that police officers have no duty to arrest intoxicated would-be motorists.

### B. The Exception: Cases Where Liability Was Imposed

The four cases discussed above exemplify the reluctance of the courts to impose liability on police officers who fail to arrest intoxicated drivers. Most state courts, because of the public duty doctrine, refuse to impose liability. Recently, however, at least eight states have rejected the public duty doctrine, some in drunk driving cases. For example, thirteen years after the Arizona Supreme Court established the *Massengill* rule (no liability because of the public duty doctrine), the same court reversed that decision in Ryan v. State, 656 P. 2d 597 (Ariz. 1982). In *Ryan*, the Arizona Supreme Court stated that "we shall no longer engage in the speculative exercise of determining whether the tortfeasor has a general duty to the injured party, which spells no recovery, or if he had a specific individual duty which means recovery." The court then rejected the blanket immunity afforded by the public duty doctrine in favor of a case-by-case analysis, a position that might establish liability in future cases.

A similar position was taken by the Wyoming Supreme Court in 1986. In DeWald v. State, 719 P. 2d 643 (Wyo. 1986), state police officers were involved in the pursuit of an intoxicated motorist. The officers activated their emergency equipment and chased the suspect into a nearby town, where the eluding driver increased his speed, causing the officers to curtail their pursuit. Shortly thereafter, however, the subject became involved in an accident, killing another motorist. A lawsuit was filed against the state and the officers, alleging negligence. The Wyoming Supreme Court refused to apply the public duty doctrine and ruled that the doctrine was no longer applicable in the state of Wyoming. The court concluded, as did the New Mexico Supreme Court in Schear v. Board of Bernalillo County, 687 P. 2d 728 (N.M. 1984), that the trend in this area is toward allowing liability. In fact, as of 1988, four of the last eight jurisdictions deciding the liability issue have rejected the public duty doctrine on the grounds that such doctrine amounts to duty to no one.

In a Kansas case, the Kansas Supreme Court concluded that a general order requiring arrests of drunken drivers created a special duty on the part of the police to make such arrests; failure to make arrests would lead to liability. The Kansas Supreme Court said,

> Where the police are subject to guidelines or owe a specific duty to an individual, the general rule does not apply and the police owe a special duty accordingly. Here the Kansas City Police Department had a standard operating procedure manual which detailed mandatory procedures for handling a variety of police situations. This manual was not made a part of the record. However, the police were also subject to a General Order which set out the procedures to be followed by the police in handling individuals incapacitated by alcohol or drugs. . . . Thus, the police officers had a duty to take the intoxicated (driver) into protective custody.[9]

In this Kansas case, the police, instead of taking an intoxicated man into custody, told the man and his friends to clear out of the parking lot. The court said the police should have realized that taking the intoxicated man into custody was necessary for the protection of third persons. The police were four or five feet from the intoxicated man and therefore ought to have known that he was drunk. An examination after the car crash, which killed the plaintiff's husband, showed that the man had an alcohol level of .26 percent. The court held the city and the police liable for 18 percent of the $1,095,103.66 damage award, the intoxicated man liable for 75 percent, and the deceased liable for 7 percent. Fudge v. City of Kansas City, Kansas, 720 P. 2d 1093 (Kan. 1986).

In summary, the public duty doctrine, although alive and well in cases of police failure to arrest drunk drivers, is starting to erode. Some states now impose liability based on the concept of duty as a mandatory function or on the special relationship exception to the public duty rule. Although only a few states thus far have imposed liability, it is probable, given the impetus of the victims' rights movement, that other states might follow suit and carve out exceptions that would make police officers liable for failure to arrest drunk drivers. Police officers need to know the rule used by the courts in their state.

## III. ARE THE POLICE LIABLE FOR USE OF MOTOR VEHICLES? GENERALLY NO, BUT EXCEPTIONS EXIST

As in other cases of police work, the general rule is that, because of the public duty doctrine, there is no liability for use of motor vehicles, but there are notable exceptions. This topic is best discussed under two headings: liability under state tort law and liability under Section 1983, the federal law. In both cases, liability exists under the exceptions, but the basis for liability differs.

### A.  Under State Tort Law, No Liability Unless a Special Duty Exists

The crucial factor that determines whether or not liability ensues when the police injure a third party as the result of the use of motor vehicles is the existence or nonexistence of a special duty. Simply stated, there is no police or agency liability unless the plaintiff can prove that a special duty exists. The question in each case is whether a special duty is owed to the injured individual such that the individual is in effect set apart from the general public and is therefore entitled to recover damages. Note that the term *special duty*, as used in negligent-use-of-motor-vehicle cases, is really synonymous with the term *special relationship* used in most cases of police negligence. An important question, therefore, is, When does such a special duty exist? One writer states that there are three ways in which a special duty is created: by law, by court decisions, and by departmental policy.[10]

1. *Special Duty Created by Law.* Most states have laws covering police use of vehicles in the course of police work. These laws usually exempt police vehicles from traffic regulations (such as speed limits, traffic signals, and the right of way) in emergencies, as long as proper procedures are followed. According to one writer, these statutes generally make these exceptions based on (1) the existence of an actual emergency, (2) the use of adequate warning devices, and (3) the continued exercise of due care for the safety of others.[11] These statutes, however, do not exempt an officer from liability even in emergency cases if the conduct of the officer amounts to reckless driving.

2. *Special Duty Created by Court Decisions.* In the absence of specific statutes governing the decisions and conduct of the police in the use of motor vehicles during emergencies, courts have set a standard by which a special duty will be considered to have existed. The standard is that care which "a reasonable prudent officer would exercise in the discharge of official duties of a like nature."[12] The standard, therefore, is one of *reasonableness*. Court decisions have categorized the many important factors involved in determining whether there has been negligent operation of a police emergency vehicle into four:[13]

a) *The justification for the chase.* The courts will look into such matters as (1) whether there existed a real or apparent emergency, (2) whether the offender's conduct was serious enough to justify the chase, (3) whether alternatives to pursuit were available to the officer, and (4) whether apprehension of the suspect was feasible.

b) *The actual physical operation of the vehicle.* The courts will look at such considerations as (1) the speed at which the vehicle was operated, (2) the use of emergency equipment, (3) violations of traffic regulations, and (4) disregard of traffic control devices.

c) *The circumstances surrounding the operation.* The courts will look into such items as (1) the physical conditions of the roadway, (2) the weather conditions, (3) the density of traffic, (4) the presence of pedestrians; (5) the presence of audio or visual warning devices, and (6) the area of pursuit.

d) *Departmental considerations.* The courts will look into such concerns as (1) whether there was a violation of departmental policy regarding police pursuits, (2) whether the officer had been trained in pursuit driving, and (3) the physical and visual condition of the police vehicle.

**3. *Special Duty Created by Departmental Policy.*** Departmental polices are a source of obligation; therefore attention must be paid to them by police officers. This is because, by creating standards for officers to follow, an agency also creates expectations on the part of the public that those standards will be followed. One writer notes, "A law enforcement organization's policies, procedures, and training material concerning high-speed pursuits are generally admissible as evidence in lawsuits against the department or its officer for the negligent operation of a pursuit vehicle."[14] The weight given to these policies, once admitted into evidence in a civil liability trial, would depend on the case law or practice in that jurisdiction. Some jurisdictions consider these policies as actually *creating a special duty,* while others view them merely as *guidelines* to help a jury determine whether or not the pursuit was reasonable.[15]

### B. Under Section 1983, No Liability Unless What Happened Amounts to a Violation of a Constitutional Right

As discussed in previous chapters, one requirement of a Section 1983 suit is the violation of a constitutional right. An injury or harm caused during a vehicular pursuit may be compensable under Section 1983, but the plaintiff must establish that the behavior of the police amounted to a violation of a constitutional right. In the absence of such proof, an injury may be compensable only under state tort law.

Most courts have decided that no liability exists under Section 1983.

For example, in Cannon v. Taylor, 782 F. 2d 947 (11th Cir. 1986), the Eleventh Circuit Court of Appeals held that the city was not liable, because what happened to the plaintiff did not amount to a violation of a constitutional right. In this case, the police officer negligently operated his motor vehicle without using lights or a siren during an emergency pursuit, which resulted in an injury. No liability was imposed, despite (1) the finding that the injury was caused by the negligent or even grossly negligent operation of a motor vehicle by a police officer acting in line of duty, and (2) some evidence proving that the agency took no corrective action or disciplined officers for past incidents involving the failure to activate lights or sirens (both in violation of state law).

In Allen v. Cook, 668 F. Supp. 1460 (W.D. Okl. 1987), a suspect was killed when his car ran a roadblock set up by the police in an effort to stop the car from drag racing. A subsequent lawsuit alleged that the sheriff failed to train and supervise his deputies adequately in matters involving high-speed pursuits and that this failure amounted to deliberate indifference and gross negligence. The court held, however, that the allegation that a deputy sheriff had relayed erroneous information to the dispatcher (encouraging other officers to continue the pursuit) and called for the setting up of a roadblock constituted mere negligence that did not amount to a violation of a constitutional right; hence there was no liability under Section 1983.

Despite the general rule of no liability under Section 1983, some cases have held that certain acts by police officers in the course of vehicular pursuits may constitute a violation of constitutional rights, making any resulting injuries compensable under Section 1983. Three cases serve as examples. In Jamieson v. Shaw, 772 F. 2d 1205 (5th Cir. 1985), the Fifth Circuit Court of Appeals held that "the constitutionally permissible use of force standard set forth by the Supreme Court in *Tennessee v. Garner* was violated when a passenger in a fleeing vehicle was hurt when the vehicle hit a so-called deadman roadblock after officers allegedly shined a bright light into the driver's eyes as the vehicle approached the roadblock."[16] In a second case, City of Miami v. Harris, 480 So. 2d 69 (Fla. App. 1985), the court held that a city can be held liable "for a pursuit policy that is adopted with a reckless disregard of whether such policy would cause loss of life without due process."[17] In both cases, the courts said that the behavior of the police was so bad that it amounted to a violation of the constitutional right either against due process or unreasonable search and seizure. What kind of behavior is so bad as to amount to a violation of a constitutional right is essentially a question of fact for the judge or jury to decide.

In a third and more significant case, the United States Supreme Court said that stopping motorists by means of a roadblock established for that purpose constitutes a seizure under the Fourth Amendment. Brower v. Inyo County, 57 U.S.L.W. 4321 (1989). In that case, a suspect was killed when the stolen car he had been driving at high speed crashed into a police roadblock. The administrator of the deceased suspect's estate brought a Section 1983 suit in federal district court, claiming, among other things, that the county of Inyo and its officers violated the suspect's Fourth Amendment rights by effecting an unreasonable seizure using excessive force. The complaint alleged that the defendants placed an eighteen-wheel tractor-trailer completely across the highway in the path of Brower's car, they placed it behind a curve, and they aimed the headlights of a police cruiser in such fashion as to blind the suspect on his approach. The result of this act was that Brower crashed into the roadblock and died. The court remanded the case to the trial court (which had dismissed the case for failure to state a claim) to determine whether the seizure was in fact unreasonable under the Fourth Amendment. More importantly, however, the court categorically held that stopping a motorist by means of a roadblock constitutes seizure under the Fourth Amendment and that therefore liability might ensue under Section 1983 if the police action is unreasonable and amounts to a violation of a constitutional right.

### C. Liability for Injury Caused by Fleeing Motorist-Suspect

Some cases have been filed by third parties against police officers and departments seeking damages for injuries caused by a fleeing motorist-suspect who is being pursued by the police. For example, the police pursue a suspect who, in the course of the pursuit, hits and injures a pedestrian. Will the officers or the department be held liable for the pedestrian's injury? The answer usually hinges on whether or not the "police conduct in breaching a duty owed was the proximate cause" of the injury to the third party.[18] Most states hold that the police are not liable for injuries or harm cause by a fleeing violator, because the proximate cause of the injury was not the conduct of the police in effecting the chase but the negligent behavior of the fleeing violator. Although the police caused the violator to flee, the subsequent negligent conduct by the violator in the course of that flight could not be directly attributed to the chase by the police.[19]

### IV. ARE THE POLICE LIABLE FOR FAILURE TO RESPOND TO CALLS? GENERALLY NO, BUT EXCEPTIONS EXIST

Numerous cases have been filed against the police based on alleged negligent failure to respond to calls for police help, including 911 calls. Many police departments encourage the public to call 911 in cases of emergency and have assured the public that such calls will be given priority and responded to promptly. The public has come to expect quick response to these calls and, in most cases, have gotten it. What happens, however, if that response is slow or improper or if there is no response at all?

The general rule, based on court decisions, is that the police cannot be held liable for either slow or improper response to calls for police help, including 911 calls, except where a special relationship exists between the police and the caller. When such a special relationship exists is determined by the courts on a case-by-case basis. It may be based on law, court decisions, or department policy.

### A. The General Rule: Cases Where No Liability Was Imposed

In Galuszynski v. City of Chicago, 475 N.E. 2d 960 (1985), the police were not held liable, because what they did or did not do was not the proximate cause of the harm suffered by the plaintiff. In that case, plaintiff Sylvia Galuszynski called the Chicago Police Department through the 911 emergency telephone system to report the presence of an intruder who was attempting to break into her home. After obtaining the necessary information, an employee of the department informed Galuszynski that police officers were on the way and told her to "watch for the police." The officer, however, did not respond until twenty-four minutes after plaintiff placed the call. During that time, armed intruders entered plaintiff's home and attacked her and her mother, injuring both of them. The intruders also stole money, jewelry, and other personal property.

The plaintiff brought suit, seeking recovery for injuries suffered as a result of the city's failure to promptly respond to the 911 emergency call. On appeal, the Appellate Court of Illinois held that the plaintiff failed to allege the existence of a "special duty" exception to governmental immunity in that the complaint failed to allege facts showing that the plaintiffs were under the direct and immediate control of the police at the time the injuries occurred.

In a second case, Trezzi v. City of Detroit, 328 N.W. 2d 70 (Mich. App. 1983), the court refused to impose liability for failure to respond to an emergency call. In that case, several 911 calls were made to police operators requesting emergency assistance at the home of the plaintiff. In the emergency dispatch system, the operators attached priority ratings to calls based on their nature, and police units were dispatched in accordance with the priority ratings. The plaintiff alleged that the 911 operators attached an unjustifiably low priority rating to her calls, as a result of which no police vehicles came until approximately one and a half hours after the first call. The plaintiff maintained that as a result of police negligence, Rosa and Gino Brigolin sustained numerous injuries that led to their deaths. The court of appeals held that (1) the city's operation of the emergency dispatch system was a governmental function and therefore entitled to immunity from tort liability, and (2) the complaint alleging that operators and dispatchers failed to correctly interpret emergency calls and failed to promptly dispatch police vehicles did not constitute a claim for intentional tort; hence no liability could be imposed.

In a third case, Whitcomb v. City and County of Denver, 732 P. 2d 749 (Colo. App. 1986), the court concluded that the way the police investigated and responded to a 911 emergency call did not make the agency liable for what the officer did or failed to do. In that case, the plaintiff called for police assistance using the 911 emergency number after she ran out of gas while driving in a high-crime area of Denver. The police responded to the call but refused to take her to a gas station, explaining that neither they nor the nearby open gas stations had gas cans. The police asked whether there was anyone she could call. The plaintiff replied that her sister was a possibility, but she refused to call her because it was too late in the evening. The officers offered to call a tow truck, but the plaintiff refused the offer because of limited funds. The officers then declined further assistance and left her. The plaintiff later obtained a ride to a gas station but found that no gas can was available. At the gas station, two men offered to help her, and so she got into their car. She was later assaulted by the two men. A suit was filed alleging that the officers had a duty to provide the plaintiff with adequate assistance to ensure her safety, something the police failed to do. On appeal, the Colorado Court of Appeals held that (1) police officers have no special relationship with stranded motorists when they respond to a call and determined that there is no real emergency or hazard, and (2) police officers enjoy qualified immunity, meaning they are immune from liability if they acted in good faith.

## B. The Exception: Cases Where Liability Was Imposed

In one case, De Long v. County of Erie, 457 N.E. 2d 717 (N.Y. 1983), the New York Court of Appeals held that the city and county, which jointly operated a 911 system, were equally liable for negligence in responding to a burglary call.[20] In that case, the plaintiff, who lived in Kenmore Village, adjacent to the city of Buffalo, called 911 asking the police to "please come, 319 Victoria right away" because a burglar was trying to break into the house. The house was only 1,300 feet from the police department. The person receiving the call, however, erroneously reported

the address as "219 Victoria" and mistakenly assumed that the call originated in Buffalo, because he knew there was a Victoria Avenue in that
city. Officers from the Buffalo Police Department responded to the call
but reported there was no such address and that the highest number on
Buffalo's Victoria Avenue was 195. A few minutes later, the dispatcher
told the officers at the scene to disregard the call. The plaintiff was later
seen running from her house, bleeding profusely. She later died and a suit
for damages was brought by the family. On appeal, the New York Court of
Appeals imposed liability, holding as follows:

1.  The establishment of a 911 emergency number created a special re-
    lationship sufficient to hold the city and county liable for negli-
    gently directing the police cars to the wrong location and taking no
    further action when no such address was found.
2.  The evidence was sufficient to support the conclusion that neither
    the city nor the county exercised ordinary care in handling the vic-
    tim's call and therefore both should share the responsibility for the
    foreseeable consequences.

In a second case, Trimper v. Headapohl, 412 N.W. 2d 731 (Mich. App.
1987), the police were held liable for negligent response to a 911 emergency call for assistance by a third party. In that case, plaintiff was walk-
ing home from a neighborhood tavern one bitterly cold night. He was
deeply intoxicated and suffered a slip and fall as a result of which he had
severe injuries, including multiple fractures to his leg and frostbite. A
neighbor heard the plaintiff moaning and saw him crawling on the sidewalk. The neighbor called 911 and told the dispatcher about the injured
man on the sidewalk. Officers from the Detroit Police Department responded and went to the scene, but rather than bringing the plaintiff to a
hospital or calling for an ambulance, the officers took the plaintiff to the
building where he had rented a room and left him in the vestibule. He
was later taken by somebody to a hospital, where he was hospitalized for
seventeen days for treatment of his injuries.

In finding the officers potentially liable, the court said that the officers were performing a ministerial act for which there was no immunity. Liability in this case emanated from a violation by the officers of the
provisions of the Detroit Police Department Procedures, Vol. III, Section
17.2 of which states, "Officers encountering a person who is incapacitated due to alcohol, and has his mental and physical functioning too impaired that he poses an immediate or substantial danger to his own health
and safety to the public, *shall take the person into protective custody and
ensure that he is conveyed to a designated service facility*" [italics added].

The Michigan Court of Appeals held that the above procedure was
not followed by the officers when responding to the call; hence a negli-

gence action could proceed. Department procedures, as indicated above, mandated a course of action for police officers to follow in these types of cases—which the officers failed to do. Such procedures, having been prescribed by the department, made that type of response by the police ministerial (meaning mandatory) instead of discretionary (meaning optional), and therefore the police had a duty to respond in accordance with prescribed department procedures. Failure to adhere to the guidelines meant negligence in the performance of duty. The court added, however, that while the plaintiff was entitled to maintain a state tort negligence action against the officers for failure to properly perform a ministerial act, a Section 1983 action against the police officers or the city of Detroit would not succeed, because such negligence did not amount to a violation of a constitutional right.

In a third case, City of Kotzebue v. McLean, 702 P. 2d 1309 (Alaska 1985), the Alaska Supreme Court held that a city owed a duty of reasonable care to protect potential victims of a caller who identified himself and his location and then informed the police that he was going to kill a friend. In that case, a police officer received a call at the Kotzebue police station fifteen minutes prior to a stabbing. The caller said that he was "somewhere between the Golden Whale and the Nulukvik Hotel" and that he was going to kill a friend of his. The officer later testified that he could not identify the "friend" who was to be killed but that he knew the caller—a certain Howarth, who had identified himself when making the call. The officer also testified that he knew exactly where Howarth was calling from, the two hotels being 200–300 feet apart and within a few minutes of the police station.

The officer did not immediately respond to Howarth's life-threatening call; instead he decided to finish processing a juvenile complaint report on a minor whom he had just arrested. The officer could have responded immediately had he decided to do so, because there were other available officers at that time, but he did not. Twelve minutes elapsed between the time of Howarth's call and the time the officer responded to the call. When the officer arrived at the Nulukvik Hotel, the "friend" was found wounded and lying on the floor of the bar. A lawsuit was later brought against the city for the officer's failure to respond to the life-threatening call. A jury found for the plaintiff and assessed damages at $180,000 for the officer's negligent failure to prevent the stabbing. On appeal, the Alaska Supreme Court upheld the verdict, saying that the city of Kotzebue owed a duty of reasonable care to protect potential victims of a caller who identified himself and his location and informed the police about his plan to kill a friend. Failure to respond promptly under these circumstances constituted negligence for which liability could be imposed.

In summary, the general rule, based on court decisions, is that the police cannot be held liable for negligent failure to respond to calls. The only exception would be where a special relationship exists between the police and the caller. The problem with this exception, however, is that the concept of a special relationship, in the context of 911 calls, is difficult to define. Some cases say that a special relationship exists when a statute, court decision, or a departmental policy (as in *Trimper* above) mandates a particular course of action by the police. There are instances, however, when gross negligence (as in *Kotzebue*, where the police took twelve minutes to respond to a life-threatening call) or the mere establishment of a 911 emergency number (as in *De Long*) was held to create a special relationship sufficient to establish liability. If the cases discussed above indicate a course of action, it is that police officers must follow departmental policy properly and avoid negligence in the performance of responsibilities.

## V. ARE THE POLICE LIABLE IN TRAFFIC AND ACCIDENT CASES? GENERALLY NO, BUT EXCEPTIONS EXIST

This topic is divided into three subtopics for purposes of discussion: (1) the duty to warn and protect other motorists, (2) the duty to render assistance, and (3) the duty to secure accident scenes. In all three instances, the general rule is that, because of the public duty doctrine, there is no liability on the part of the police officers, but there are exceptions.

### A. The Duty to Warn and Protect Other Motorists[21]

States and municipalities have a duty to use reasonable care in maintaining roads for the safety of the public. The general rule is that there is no liability for failure to protect motorists, but liability might attach in cases where a police officer or agency has actual or presumed knowledge of a potentially dangerous condition but fails to take reasonable action to correct the condition or remove the danger.

The general rule of no liability is illustrated in a California case, Westbrooks v. State, 219 Cal. Rptr. 674 (Cal. App. 1985). In that case, a violent rainstorm washed away a bridge located on a well-travelled portion of the roadway. State and county police were notified and responded to the call. Before notification, fire department officials in the area placed flares at the site to warn motorists of the hazard. State police officers diverted traffic on one side of the bridge, and a sheriff's department official diverted traffic on the other side. While traffic was thus being directed, two vehicles went by the sheriff's post. The officers were able to stop the first vehicle, but the second driver ignored the flares and the officers' physical attempt to stop the vehicle. The vehicle reached the spot where the bridge had been and plummeted into the water below, killing the driver.

The widow and sons of the traffic accident victim brought suit, claiming that the officers breached a duty to warn motorists of existing road hazards. The California Appellate Court held that "as a general rule, persons, including employees of public entities, have no duty to come to the aid of others unless there is a special relationship between them which gives rise to a duty to act." The judgment of the trial court, which held the county liable, was reversed and remanded.

In contrast, liability resulting from failure to warn in traffic cases is illustrated in the case of Naylor v. Louisiana Department of Public Highways, 423 So. 2d 674 (La.App. 1982). In that case, state troopers were called to the scene of a single-car accident. The accident was caused by an oil spill on a dangerous portion of the roadway. The troopers asked the Department of Transportation to cover the spill with sand and then ignited flares to warn oncoming motorists of the danger. After securing the scene, the officers returned to their normal patrol activities. Several hours later, the oil absorbed the sand and the flares expired. One trooper, who had returned to the scene, ignited additional flares and called for more sand. Remaining near the accident scene, the trooper parked his vehicle and activated his emergency lights. The flares went out and the trooper failed to replace them. Within a few minutes, an unsuspecting motorcyclist approached the oil slick. He lost control of the motorcycle, went over an embankment, struck a tree, and suffered severe brain damage. A wrongful death action was brought against the Department of Transportation and the state police for negligent failure to warn.

On appeal, the Louisiana Court of Appeals held that the state police had a duty to provide advance warning to drivers of existing highway dangers and that such duty was breached when the officers failed to "replace flares prior to the accident" and position their vehicle so as not to alert motorists of the danger. The court affirmed an award of $4,036,535.00 to the plaintiff.

The Westbrooks and Naylor cases, discussed above, show that there are two approaches to police liability for failure to warn motorists of traffic dangers. First, a duty to warn can arise when a municipality or a police agency creates a danger to the public. Second, a duty to warn can arise if the municipality or police agency has knowledge of a dangerous situation but does not take precautionary measures to prevent injury or damage. Under this concept of duty, many courts have held that police officers must take precautionary measures to prevent and avoid dangerous situations on public roadways even when the officers or the municipality did not create the danger or peril.

In contrast to this approach, some courts maintain that a police officer's conduct in maintaining the safety of public roadways is distinguishable from police protection cases. These courts apply ordinary tort principles rather than the *public duty* versus *special duty* rule used in police protection cases. Under this approach, plaintiffs in traffic cases are required to show the elements normally associated with liability based on negligence, namely, duty, breach of that duty, proximate cause, and damage. The approach assumes the existence of a duty to warn unsuspecting motorists of the hazardous behavior of other drivers. Where a police officer fails to warn oncoming traffic of a hazard and injury results, negligence may be found.

## B. The Duty to Render Assistance[22]

The general rule is that police officers are not liable for failure to provide aid or assistance to endangered or injured individuals absent a special duty do to so. This is illustrated in a California case, Rose v. County of Plumas, 199 Cal. Rptr. 842 (1984). In that case, the court held that officers called to a bar to deal with a disturbance had no obligation to offer assistance or provide medical care to some people there who were injured but who were not under police custody. The court said that the officers had not caused the injuries, neither did they encourage the injured persons to rely on their help. The court conceded that the California Penal Code provides for the mandatory training of officers in first aid, but that requirement alone did not impose a duty on the part of the officers to provide aid. On the other hand, if the officers voluntarily undertook to aid the victims or if they induced the victims to rely on their aid, then failure to provide such aid would have led to liability.

A special duty, from which liability can arise, may be created in two general ways. First, by a statute specifically providing that police officers render aid and save lives at accident scenes. In the presence of such a statute, the duty of officers to render aid becomes mandatory. Whether or not the statute requiring a police officer to help is mandatory is for the courts to decide. Second, unique circumstances may create a special duty to rescue persons in distress for which failure to perform that duty can then constitute negligence. While variations exist, the following four instances may create a special duty based on unique circumstances.

**a)** *Once an officer begins to rescue someone, a special relationship may be established.* The officer must then complete the rescue in a nonnegligent fashion even though there was no duty to rescue in the first place. A sufficient showing of negligence is made where the officer fails to take reasonable care not to increase the risk of harm. Similarly, liability may be imposed if harm is suffered because of the injured person's reliance on the officer's undertaking.

**b)** *Failure to take simple actions to reduce the risk of harm to an incapacitated individual may lead to liability.* For example, the failure of a police officer to summon or render medical aid or to transport an injured person from the scene of an accident has been considered a breach of duty by some courts. These courts have traditionally recognized a greater duty to persons who are incapable of assisting themselves due to intoxication, injury, or unconsciousness.

**c)** *Liability may be found where an officer impedes medical aid or another person's attempt at assistance.* This breach of duty may be either express or implied. An officer's presence at the scene of an accident can create a situation where others will not assist because of the officer's presence. Courts reason that the public views police officers as trained experts. Would-be rescuers might, therefore, decline to render assistance. Compounding the problem is the fact that police officers often direct other drivers away from the scene of an accident, reducing the possibility that others will render aid. If any of these situations arises, a special relationship and a breach of duty may be found.

These three possibilities are illustrated in the case of Ramundo v. Town of Guiderland, 475 N.Y.S 2d 752 (N.Y. Albany County 1984). In that case, a driver was injured in a traffic accident. Police officers were summoned, and upon arrival they found the plaintiff lying unconscious with a hot exhaust system on his face. The officers failed to correct the situation and as a result the plaintiff received serious facial burns.

Civil suit was brought against the officers and the municipality. The plaintiff argued that when the police officers arrived at the scene, they then voluntarily assumed a duty of assistance to the plaintiff and that the officers breached that duty by failing to act to prevent the plaintiff's facial burns. The New York Supreme Court applied the public duty versus special duty doctrine, noting that while police officers have no duty to provide assistance or protection to the general public, when a special relationship exists, liability may be found. The court reasoned that the presence of the officers at the scene of the accident acted as a deterrent to others who may have come forth to aid the injured party, since the public views police officers as trained to deal with these situations. Accordingly, the plaintiff's cause of action against the municipality and the police was affirmed.

**d)** *A special duty may be found where a member of the public is led to rely on a promise of the police to help but no such help is given.* This is illustrated in the case of Hartley v. Floyed, 512 So. 2d 1022

(Fla. App. 1987). In that case, a wife called the sheriff's office to report that her husband had not come back from a two-day fishing trip. He was expected in the afternoon, but it was well past midnight and he was not back. A deputy sheriff assured the wife that he would have someone check the boat ramp to see whether or not her husband's truck and trailer were still there. No such check was made, but the deputy lied to the woman and told her forty minutes later that the truck was not there. The wife was told this again twice when she called back five and seven hours later. The boat had in fact capsized and its occupants spent sixty hours in the water by using life preservers. The husband drowned less than half an hour before a helicopter found and rescued the boat's four other occupants. A lawsuit was brought and the court found the sheriff and his deputy liable, because although the deputy's decision whether or not to comply with the request by the wife was discretionary—for which no liability could be imposed—once he agreed to help, a special duty was then created and failure to give help as promised constituted actionable negligence.

## C. The Duty to Secure Accident Scenes[23]

Police officers owe a duty of protection to the general public following their arrival at the scene of an accident. But here again, the general rule is that there is no police liability unless a special duty exists between the police and the individual. A special duty may be found in a variety of situations, such as when the officer has knowledge of the impending danger, the danger is obvious, a traffic hazard existed at the time, the officer is in direct and immediate control, and the officer has ample opportunity to correct the situation but fails to do so.

An illustrative case is Johnson v. Larson, 441 So. 2d 5 (La. Ct. App. 1983). In that case the appellate court found no liability because of the absence of a special relationship. The facts were that Johnson was driving his vehicle down an interstate when he overtook a disabled vehicle in the right lane. The driver of the disabled vehicle flagged Johnson down. Both vehicles pulled off the travel portion of the roadway, and Johnson attempted to repair the disabled vehicle. A few minutes later, two deputy sheriffs arrived at the scene and inquired as to the motorist's trouble. The deputies remained at the scene and then left after determining that no assistance was required. Shortly thereafter, another driver rear-ended one of the parked vehicles. As a result of the collision, Johnson received serious injuries.

Johnson brought action against the two deputies, alleging that the officers could have taken precautionary measures to ensure his safety. The trial court ruled that the officers had no duty to protect the plaintiff from the type of injury he sustained. On appeal, the trial court's decision was affirmed, the appellate court saying that no special relationship had been established and therefore liability could not be imposed. The court said that the danger was not obvious, the traffic hazard did not exist at the time the officers left, the officers were not in direct and immediate control of the situation, and there was no ample opportunity to correct the situation.

A similar result of no liability was achieved in Long v. Soderquist, 467 N.E. 2d 1153 (Ill. App. 2nd Dist. 1984). In this case, a motorist struck a guardrail. The road conditions at the time of the accident were icy, and the driver's vehicle slid off the road. Another motorist saw the accident and stopped to assist the injured party. Shortly thereafter, a deputy sheriff arrived at the accident scene. After inquiring as to the subject's physical condition, the officer observed another traffic accident. Instructing the traffic accident victim and the would-be rescuer to remain in their respective vehicles, the officer went to investigate the second accident. The officer then left the scene without taking adequate measures to protect the parked vehicles. A few moments later a third vehicle struck the parked vehicles.

The driver of the third vehicle brought civil suit against the officer and argued that the officer was negligent in failing to do the following: light flares, direct other vehicles away from the accident scene, remove the parked vehicles, warn other motorists of the hazard, and call for assistance. Applying the public duty doctrine, the Illinois Appellate Court held that although a municipality is generally not liable for failure to provide police protection or service, this rule does not apply where the police have assumed a special duty to a person that elevates his status to something more than that of a member of the general public. In this case, the court concluded that the plaintiff failed to establish a special relationship, because he was not under the immediate control of the police; hence no liability could be imposed.

## SUMMARY

The nature of police work exposes police officers constantly to possible lawsuits from the public for failure to protect from injury and harm. Liability for failure to protect is best classified into liability under state tort law and liability under Section 1983. Under state tort law, the general rule is that there is no liability on the part of police officers for failure to protect. This is because of the public duty doctrine, which holds that government functions are owed to the general public and not to specific individuals; therefore, police officers who breach a general duty while acting within the scope of their official capacity are not liable for injury or harm to particular individuals that may have been caused by a third party. The public duty doctrine admits of one major and multifaceted exception: the exception of special relationship. This exception holds that if a duty is owed to a particular person rather than to the general public, then a police officer or agency that breaches that duty can be held liable for damages. The problem, however, is that the term *special relationship* admits of various meanings, depending on state law, court decisions, or agency regulations. Under Section 1983, the leading case on liability of government officials for failure to protect is *DeShaney v. Winnebago County Department of Social Services*, which holds that the Fourteenth Amendment right to due process does not impose an affirmative duty on the state to protect individuals who are not in state custody from harm by private persons.

The general rule is that the police are not liable for negligent failure to arrest drunk drivers. In some states, however, liability is now being imposed by the courts based on the special relationship doctrine. Although only a few states thus far have imposed liability, it is probable, given the impetus of the victims' rights movement, that other states might follow suit and carve out exceptions that make police officers liable for failure to arrest drunk drivers.

In cases involving negligent use of motor vehicles cases, the general rule is that the police are not liable for negligent use, but there are notable exceptions. Under state tort law, no liability exists unless a special duty has been created. The terms *special duty* and *special relationship* are used by many courts synonymously. A special duty may be created by law, court decisions, and departmental policy. There is no liability under Section 1983 for negligent use of motor vehicles unless what happened amounts to a violation of a constitutional right.

The general rule is that the police are not liable for negligent failure to respond to calls, including 911 calls. Again, the exception is when a special relationship exists between the police and the caller. When such a special relationship exists is determined by the courts on a case-by-case basis.

Regarding police liability for negligence in traffic and accident cases, the general rule is that, because police officers are shielded by the public duty doctrine, there is no liability on the part of the officers, but there are exceptions. Three subtopics come under the general topic of negligence in traffic and accident cases: (1) the duty to warn and protect other motorists, (2) the duty to render assistance, and (3) the duty to secure accident scenes. The general rule in cases involving failure to warn and protect other motorists is that there is no liability expect where a police officer or agency has actual or presumed knowledge of a potentially dangerous condition, but fails to take reasonable action to correct or remove the danger. Regarding the duty to render assistance, the general rule is that police officers are not liable except if a special duty exists. Such a special duty may be created by law or by unique circumstances. On the duty to secure accident scenes, the general rule, as in all negligence cases, is that there is no police liability unless a special duty exists.

## NOTES

1. A number of cases in this chapter first came to the attention of the author through the *Legal Defense Manual*, published by the Americans for Effective Law Enforcement. Of particular help were the following issues: Brief No. 88–2 (1988), Brief No. 86–4 (1986), Brief No. 85–3 (1985), Brief No. 85–2 (1985), and Brief No. 81–2 (1981). Each of these issues deals with various areas of negligence. These updates have been particularly useful in researching this chapter. Those interested in a more extensive discussion of the topics covered in this chapter are referred to the above issues of the *Legal Defense Manual*.
2. See V. E. Kappeler and R. V. del Carmen, "Police Civil Liability for Failure to Arrest Drunk Drivers," *The Police Chief*, October 1988, at 102.
3. See the *Legal Defense Manual*, Americans for Effective Law Enforcement, Brief No. 88–2, at 15.
4. *Ibid.*
5. As discussed in the *Legal Defense Manual*, Brief No. 85–2, at 5.
6. *Ibid.*
7. A good source of cases on negligent failure to protect and the special relationship doctrine are the various monthly issues of the *Liability Reporter*, published by the Americans for Effective Law Enforcement. This publication has an annual index of police cases classified according to topics. A number of cases discussed in this chapter first came to the attention of the author through this publication.
8. See Kappeler and del Carmen, "Police Civil Liability," at 103–104, for the cases discussed in this section of the chapter.
9. Taken from the *Liability Reporter*, January 1987, No. 169, at 11.
10. See D. L. Schofield, "Legal Issues of Pursuit Driving," *FBI Law Enforcement Bulletin*, May 1988, at 23–30. This is an excellent and comprehensive article on the various legal issues involved in the use by the police of motor vehicles to apprehend suspects.
11. *Ibid.*, at 24.
12. *Ibid.*
13. This section is taken from a manuscript by V. E. Kappeler, J. Vaughn, and R. V. del Carmen, prepared for submission to *The Police Chief*, titled "The Civil Liabilities of Emergency Vehicle Operation."
14. Schofield, "Legal Issues of Pursuit Driving," at 24.
15. *Ibid.*, at 25.
16. *Ibid.*, at 26.
17. *Ibid.*, at 30.
18. *Ibid.*, at 25.

19. *Ibid.*
20. For a good discussion of *DeLong v. County of Erie* and *Trezzi v. City of Detroit,* see B. A. Maas, "'911' Emergency Assistance Call Systems: Should Local Governments Be Liable for Negligent Failure to Respond?" *George Mason University Law Review,* Fall 1985, at 112–119.
21. This section is taken from a manuscript by V. E. Kappeler and R. V. del Carmen, prepared for submission to *The Police Chief,* titled "Police Civil Liability for Negligent Service at Accident Scenes."
22. *Ibid.*
23. *Ibid.*

CASE BRIEF ⎯⎯⎯⎯⎯⎯⎯⎯⎯⎯⎯⎯⎯⎯⎯⎯⎯⎯⎯⎯⎯⎯⎯⎯⎯⎯⎯⎯⎯⎯⎯

### DESHANEY V. WINNEBAGO COUNTY DEPARTMENT OF SOCIAL SERVICES
### 57 U.S.L.W. 4218 (1989)

#### FACTS

Joshua DeShaney, a four-year-old, was beaten and permanently injured by his father, to whose custody he was awarded after a divorce. The county department of social services and several social workers received several complaints that the child was being abused by his father. Over a period of time, they took various steps to protect the boy, but they did not remove him from his father's custody. Subsequently, the child was beaten by the father so severely that he suffered permanent brain damage and was rendered severely retarded. He is expected to spend the rest of his life confined in an institution. The father was tried and convicted of child abuse. The mother, acting for and as guardian of the child, later sued the officials of the county department of social services under Section 1983, charging that county officials violated the child's constitutional right to due process by failing to intervene to protect him against his father's violence. The district court decided for the county; the court of appeals affirmed.

#### ISSUE

May a county department of social services and its officials be held liable under Section 1983 for failure to protect a child from severe beating by the father? *No, with exceptions.*

#### SUPREME COURT DECISION

The Fourteenth Amendment due process clause does not impose an affirmative duty on the state to protect individuals who are not in state custody from harm by private persons. The county social services agency and the officers who failed to protect the child from severe beatings by the father did not violate the child's due process rights and could not be held civilly liable even though they had knowledge of such abuse and had continuing contact with the family.

## CASE SIGNIFICANCE

This is an important case, because for the first time the Court addressed the issue of the civil liability of public officials for failure to protect a member of the public from harm or injury inflicted by a third person (not a government official). The Court decided that there is no constitutional right on the part of the public to be protected from such harm, and therefore failure to protect does not result in civil damages against the state and its officers.

The court admitted that there are instances when the state has an obligation to protect certain individuals from harm inflicted by third parties. It specifically mentioned incarcerated prisoners and committed mental patients as entitled to an affirmative protection from the state. The reason for this is that "when the State takes a person into its custody and holds him there against his will, the Constitution imposes upon it a corresponding duty to assume some responsibility for his safety and general well-being." Such was not the case in *DeShaney*, because the child was neither a prisoner nor a committed mental patient and was therefore not under the institutional custody of the state.

Although *DeShaney* involved county social services officials and not police officers, the principle enunciated by the Court should apply equally to law enforcement. The Court's discussion focused on the existence of a constitutional right under the due process clause, not on the type of agency involved. Unless the Court modifies the *DeShaney* decision, liability under Section 1983 for failure to protect will no longer be much of a police concern. Rejoicing should be tempered, however, by a statement in the Court's opinion to the effect that liability may well exist under state tort law. Police officers therefore need to shift their gaze to their own state statutory and case laws to determine if such failure to protect might lead to liability under state tort.

# 12

## LIABILITY FOR JAIL MANAGEMENT

### INTRODUCTION

Police officers and law enforcement personnel need to be familiar with liability pitfalls in jail management. This is because they are often involved in operating jail lock-ups or, in the case of sheriffs, are ultimately responsible for jail operation and management. There used to be a time when jail personnel did not have to worry about being sued. Those days are gone forever. The "hands off" judicial doctrine, where the courts refused to try cases filed against jail personnel, has given way to a willingness on the part of courts to try cases brought by inmates against jail personnel and impose liability when warranted.

There is hardly a state prison system or a jail in a major county or city that is not currently involved in a lawsuit. As of 1987, thirty-six states, the District of Columbia, Puerto Rico, and the Virgin Islands were under court orders due to violations of the rights of prisoners. In addition, there were legal challenges pending in five other states, and there were challenges pending in six states in which there were already existing court orders dealing with one or more institutions.[1] There are no nationwide figures available on jail litigation, but it is safe to say that most, if not all, major jails in the country have had various kinds of legal problems.

A national survey of jails sponsored by the Bureau of Justice Statistics showed that in 1987 the following (ranked according to frequency from highest to lowest) were the most frequent subjects of jail litigation:[2]

1. crowded living units
2. recreational facilities
3. medical facilities or services

4. visitation practices or policies

5. disciplinary procedures or policies

6. food service (quantity or quality)

7. administrative segregation procedures or policies

8. staffing patterns

9. grievance procedures or policies

10. education or training programs

11. fire hazards

12. counseling programs

## I. RIGHTS OF PRISONERS

### A. Jails versus Prisons

Jails and prisons differ in a number of ways. First, jails are administered and financed by local governments (cities or counties), while prisons are managed and funded by the states. Second, jails are the responsibility of sheriffs in counties or chiefs of police in cities; by contrast, prisons are administered by the governor's office or by a prison board. Third, jails contain both pretrial detainees and convicted prisoners, while prisons do not house persons who have not been convicted. Fourth, jails usually incarcerate misdemeanants or minor offenders, while prisons house serious offenders whose sentences can run for long periods of time.

Despite these differences, the rights of prisoners in jails and prisons are often considered by the courts to be virtually the same. In the first United States Supreme Court decision involving the rights of pretrial detainees, the Court ruled that such practices as housing two inmates in a room designed for one, conducting inmate body searches after visits, and forbidding the receipt of most hardbound books except those coming from publishers could all be justified as "reasonably related" to the goals of security and smooth jail administration. The Court cautioned, however, that the due process clause of the Constitution requires that pretrial detainees "be subjected to only those 'restrictions and privations' which inhere in their confinement itself or which are justified by compelling necessities of jail administration." Bell v. Wolfish, 441 U.S. 520 (1979).

This chapter will discuss civil liability in the context of both jail and prison litigation. This is because most cases on civil liability brought by inmates involve prisons, not jails, despite the fact that jails in general are in worse condition than prisons. There are a number of reasons for this. One is that prison litigation can drag on for a long time; hence prisoners who are in jail for only a short time may find it more convenient to endure conditions rather than to embark on a legal challenge they cannot complete while in jail. A second reason may be that the more serious and perhaps more litiguous offenders are found in prisons. They have developed expertise as jailhouse lawyers and may be unwilling to put up with conditions with which they are uncomfortable. They might therefore be more likely to sue.

## B. Old Philosophy versus New Philosophy

Jail and prison law cases must be understood in the context of the "old" and the "new" philosophies used by the courts when deciding prison cases. The old philosophy (prevalent until about the midsixties) was aptly summarized by an early court decision, which said,

> The prisoner has, as a consequence of his crime, not only forfeited his liberty, but all his personal rights except those which the law in its humanity accord to him. He is, for the time being, the *slave of the state.*" Ruffin v. Commonwealth, 62 Va. 790 (1871) (italics added)

Under the old philosophy, prisoners were indeed virtual slaves of the state and hardly had any rights except the most basic ones—such as the right to life and food. This meant that jail administrators had wide discretion in the administration of jails and could do just about anything without intervention from the courts.

All that has changed dramatically. The old philosophy has given way to the new philosophy, which is best summarized as follows:

> Prisoners retain all the rights of free citizens except those on which restriction is necessary to assure their orderly confinement or to provide reasonable protection for the rights and physical safety of all members of the prison community.[3]

Under the new philosophy, three governmental interests may justify the adoption of prison rules that limit prisoners' rights: (1) the preservation of internal order and discipline, (2) the maintenance of institutional security against escape, and (3) the rehabilitation of prisoners.[4] This means that jail rules and regulations must be justified by jail personnel based on any or all of the above three factors. What this entails is a balancing of inmates' rights and the governmental interest involved on a case-by-case basis, the final determination being made by the courts. Under the new philosophy, the question jail administrators should ask when promulgating a rule that limits the rights of inmates is, Can this rule be justified by any of the three interests mentioned above?

The new philosophy signifies a drastic 180-degree turn in the attitude of the courts and explains why the discretion enjoyed before by jail officials has been sharply limited. Whereas in the past prisoners were virtual slaves of the state, now prisoners are presumed to enjoy the same rights as people in the "free world," subject only to the three exceptions mentioned above. Jail administrators have the burden of establishing that jail or prison regulations (which inevitably limit the rights and freedoms of prisoners) fall under any or all of the exceptions. If there is no justification for the regulation, such is deemed invalid. The new philosophy makes it harder for jail officials to make arbitrary decisions or enforce groundless rules.

## C. Cases Inmates Usually File

Like other plaintiffs who file cases against the police, jail inmates usually file two types of cases against jail administrators or agencies: state tort cases and civil rights (Section 1983) cases. A third source of redress (not often used) are provisions of state constitutions or specific state laws that provide redress for certain violations. For example, state law may prohibit requiring inmates to work without some form of compensation and may impose specific sanctions for violations of such law by jail administrators.

The usual allegation by inmates under state tort law is negligence by jail personnel. The negligence claimed is of various kinds, including negligent failure to protect, negligent classification, and negligent failure to treat. The type of negligence needed to establish liability under state tort law varies from one state to another. Some states require mere negligence, others preclude liability unless gross negligence or deliberate indifference is proved by the plaintiff. By contrast, civil liability for negligence under Section 1983 requires deliberate indifference—a much higher and harder level of proof to establish.

As discussed in Chapter 4 of this text, Section 1983 cases have two requirements: (1) that the officer must have acted under color of law, and (2) that there must be a violation of a constitutional right or of a right given by federal law. As the basis for Section 1983 cases, jail and prison inmates usually allege violations of rights under the following amendments:

FIRST AMENDMENT

Freedom of Religion

Freedom of Speech

Freedom of the Press

Freedom of Assembly

Freedom to Petition the Government for Redress of Grievances

FOURTH AMENDMENT

Right against Unreasonable Searches and Seizures

EIGHTH AMENDMENT

## Prohibition against Cruel and Unusual Punishment

FOURTEENTH AMENDMENT

## Right to Due Process
## Right to Equal Protection of the Law

RIGHT TO PRIVACY

The right to privacy is an acknowledged constitutional right that is not specified in the Constitution. It is considered a basic constitutional right because it is implicitly contained in the various amendments, particularly the Fourth Amendment against unreasonable searches and seizures.

Jail and prison law is a relatively new subcategory of law when compared with such established fields as constitutional law, criminal procedure, and criminal law. Although the United States Supreme Court over the past twenty years or so has decided prison cases involving the various constitutional rights listed above, some rights have yet to be clearly established, while others are being refined in subsequent decisions. Although there is now an extensive body of case law that defines the rights of inmates, numerous lawsuits are still slowly making their way to the Supreme Court; hence vagueness and uncertainty persist. To aggravate the problem, lower court decisions on the constitutional rights of inmates are sometimes inconsistent. Unless addressed and reconciled by a higher court, these inconsistencies persist, and therefore inmate rights may vary from one state to another.

### D. Standard Courts Use to Decide Cases Involving Constitutional Rights

What standard do the courts use to determine whether or not a prison regulation violates an inmate's constitutional right? For a long time there was no definite judicial standard applicable to all cases. That has changed. In Turner v. Safley, 41 CrL 3239 (1987), the Supreme Court set the following standard: "A prison regulation that impinges on inmates' constitutional rights *is valid if it is reasonably related to legitimate penological interests*" [emphasis added]. The Court then added that the following four factors are to be considered when determining whether the regulation is reasonable or not:

1. whether there is a *valid, rational connection* between the regulation and the legitimate governmental interest put forward to justify it

2. whether there are *alternative means* of exercising the right that remain open to prisoners

3. the *impact* accommodation of the asserted right will have on guards and other inmates and on the allocation of prison resources generally

4. the existence of *ready alternatives* to the regulation

These factors are subjective and their interpretation is left to the judge or jury on a case-by-case basis. For instance, the term "valid, rational connection" is hard to define. Given their subjectiveness, decisions of lower courts may vary from one jurisdiction to another. The above tests are to be used only if the right alleged to be violated is a constitutional right. By implication, if the right violated is a right given by statute or by agency policy, the above tests should not apply.

## II. SPECIFIC CIVIL LIABILITY ISSUES

The rest of this chapter discusses some specific liability issues in jail and prison litigation. The discussion is not meant to be comprehensive or exhaustive; instead it provides an overview of civil liability issues and seeks to familiarize jail personnel with the major cases decided by the United States Supreme Court on the issue of inmate rights.

### A. Overcrowding

Jail overcrowding is not in itself unconstitutional, but it may constitute cruel and unusual punishment if the "totality of conditions" is bad. The difficult legal problem is to determine when that point of unconstitutionality is reached. The courts have not come up with a clear formula for determining this. Simply because a jail facility provides less square footage than required by correctional experts and standards does not necessarily mean that it violates the constitutional requirement. Court decisions have held that the opinions of experts do not establish a constitutional minimum and that they merely present goals. More important than footage per inmate is the effect of overcrowding on the total facility. Court decisions have repeatedly said that the totality of conditions must be taken into account when determining when conditions are so bad as to amount to cruel and unusual punishment. Conditions that are "restrictive and even harsh" are not unconstitutional unless they violate "contemporary standards of decency." When that level is reached is decided on a case-by-case basis.

The factors courts take into account to determine whether conditions amount to cruel and unusual punishment include adequacy of staff, adequacy of cell space, quality of sanitation, quality of medical services, quality of recreational facilities, existence of work programs, quality of inmate diet, and the amount of time inmates spend in their cells during waking hours. While none of these factors individually may be way below standard, a combination may lead to a finding of unconstitutionality based on the cruel and unusual punishment clause.

One effect of overcrowding is inmate double-celling, an issue addressed by the Supreme Court in Rhodes v. Chapman, 452 U.S. 337 (1981). The Court concluded that double-celling as such is not unconstitutional but that conditions may be such that it can amount to cruel and unusual punishment. In this case, however, the district court found that the Southern Ohio Correctional Facility, a federal maximum-security institution built in the early 1970s, was "unquestionably a top-flight, first-class facility." The institution had gymnasiums, workshops, school rooms, "day rooms," two chapels, a hospital ward, a commissary, a barber shop, a library, a recreation field, a visitation area, and a garden. Each cell measured approximately sixty-three square feet and had hot and cold running water, a cabinet, a shelf, and a radio. Given these conditions, the Court concluded that although inmates were double-celled, that alone did not deprive them of any constitutional right. Were the conditions different—although the Court did not say how much different—the Court would perhaps have come to the opposite conclusion. The Court added that "the Constitution does not mandate comfortable prisons" and that conditions that are restrictive and even harsh are "part of the penalty that criminal offenders pay for their offenses against society."

Jail administrators must carefully monitor jail conditions so that overcrowding does not reach an unconstitutional level. Recent figures show that jails in big counties and cities are overcrowded and that the national picture is likely to worsen. There is need for a proactive approach to the jail problem. This involves planning for the future so that jail capacity is not grossly exceeded by the projected jail population. This means bringing the problem to the attention of the proper local authorities and working closely with political decision makers for long-term solutions. If decision makers do not react favorably, the good faith effort of jail administrators will have been demonstrated and hopefully will be considered with favor by the court when determining possible civil liability.

## B.  Use of Force

Force may be defined as any unwanted touching directed at another person. It may involve the direct laying on of hands or the setting into motion of something that touches another person, such as the throwing of a stone or the firing of a gun. Excessive use of force is punishable under state tort law, the civil rights act, and the state penal code. Discussion of the proper use of force in jail must be divided into two categories: the use of nondeadly force and the use of deadly force.

*Nondeadly force* is force that, when used, is not likely to result in death or serious bodily injury. The general rule is that jail personnel may use only as much nondeadly force as is reasonable and necessary under the circumstances. This means using only that amount of force that is necessary to get the job done legitimately. This amount varies according to circumstances and may be determined by such factors as the size and strength of the officer as compared with the inmate, the inmate's history of violent behavior, possible alternatives, and the availability of help. For example, if the disturbance in a jail cell is minor, massive violent force to control that disturbance cannot be used. On the other hand, a massive jail riot that involves dangerous prisoners calls for a higher level of non-deadly force. If sued, an officer must be prepared to justify the amount of force used in light of the prevailing circumstances when the force was used.

The opposite of reasonable force is punitive force, meaning force that is used to punish. The line between reasonable force and punitive force is often difficult to draw. If an officer uses nondeadly force because he or she is convinced that such amount of force is justified to bring a sit-uation under control, chances are that such amount of force is reasonable —and would be considered reasonable to a third person as determined by a judge or jury. On the other hand, if the amount of force used punishes rather than controls, such force is unreasonable. The question a correc-tional officer should ask in these situations is, Am I using this amount of nondeadly force because I honestly feel this is needed to bring the situa-tion under control or because I want to punish this inmate or arrestee? Using only as much force as is needed to control is reasonable; using force to punish is unreasonable and exposes the officer to civil liability.

The use of *deadly force* is governed strictly by agency policy, state law, or the United States Constitution. If a particular jail has a policy on the use of deadly force, that policy must be followed strictly, regardless of what state law might provide. For example, if departmental policy pro-hibits the use of deadly force to prevent the escape of a detainee, such policy must be followed even if state law allows the use of force in these cases. This is because the more limited policy promulgated by the depart-ment governs the behavior of its own officers despite a more permissive state law. Most jails and prisons have policies stating that deadly force can be used only in specified instances. For example, if jail policy pro-vides that deadly force can be used only in four specific instances (such as in self-defense, defense of another person, preventing escape, and con-trolling a jail riot) that policy must be followed strictly. Any deviation from that policy exposes the officer to civil liability, regardless of what state law provides. The best advice for an officer is to know agency policy on the deadly use of force and to follow that policy strictly. If an agency, however, has no such policy, state law on the use of deadly force must be followed.

Some jails have manuals or handbooks governing the use of non-deadly and deadly force. If the rules are followed, chances are that there will be no civil liability, because the employee will likely have acted in good faith. Jails should have a well-drafted policy on the use of nondeadly and deadly force if civil liability is to be minimized. It is in an agency's best interest to be clear about when force can be used by its officers.

Whitley v. Albers, 106 S.Ct. 1078 (1986), is the leading Supreme Court case on the use of deadly force in prison. In that case, the Court held that using deadly force in good faith to suppress a prison disturbance does not violate the constitutional rights of inmates. The case involved a disturbance where inmates took over a cellblock, set up barricades, smashed furniture, and took an officer hostage. The inmates threatened to kill the officer and told prison authorities that an inmate had been killed. Negotiations followed, but prison officials later decided to use deadly force to subdue the disturbance. In the ensuing assault, officers fired several shots, one of which hit the plaintiff (who was not one of the rioters), causing serious damage to the plaintiff's knee. He brought a lawsuit, claiming that the use of deadly force in this case was excessive. Rejecting the claim, the Court said that the use of deadly force by prison officials here was reasonable. There was no violation of a constitutional right, because the use of deadly force was not "wanton." In analyzing cases involving use of force in a jail or prison setting, the Whitley case suggested using four tests:

1. The need test. This asks whether there was a need for the use of force under the circumstances.

2. The proportionality test. This asks whether the force used was proportional to the need.

3. The injury test. This asks whether an injury did in fact occur.

4. The legitimate purpose test. This asks whether the force was used for a legitimate purpose or to inflict punishment.

Note, however, that the application of these tests is limited to instances when deadly force is used in a *riot situation*. The tests do not apply to all cases when deadly force is used in jails or prisons.

It is not clear whether the "objective reasonableness" standard used by the Court in the recent case of Graham v. Conner, 45 Crl. 3033 (1989), applies to the use of force in jails and prisons. That case says that a claim that law enforcement officers used constitutionally excessive force in subjecting a free citizen to arrest, an investigative stop, or another "sei- zure" of his or her person must be determined in light of the facts and circumstances confronting the officers rather than with 20/20 hindsight by the judge or jury. Under this test, malice or motivation becomes irrelevant in determining liability; rather the test is whether or not the amount of force used was objectively reasonable. In view of the use by the Court of the term "free citizen" in the *Graham* decision, the better conclusion would be that *Graham* applies to police and not to prison cases.

### C. Search and Seizure

The Fourth Amendment right against unreasonable search and seizure applies to prisoners in limited fashion. For instance, the Supreme Court has decided that an inmate has no constitutional protection from cell searches. This means that an inmate's cell can be searched at any time without a court-issued warrant, provided there is justification for such search. The Court added, however, that the Eighth Amendment prohibition against cruel and unusual punishment could provide an inmate a way to challenge harassment tactics by prison guards. Hudson v. Palmer, 35 CrL 3230 (1984). Therefore, jail personnel can search inmate cells at any time, but such searches must not amount to harassment.

Two questions must be asked by an officer in jail searches: (1) Does the inmate have a reasonable expectation of privacy in the area or part of the body to be searched? (2) Is the search reasonable? In one case, Bell v. Wolfish, 441 U.S. 520 (1979), the Court said that the reasonableness of a particular search is to be determined by taking the following considerations into account:

1. the *scope* of the intrusion
2. the *manner* in which the search is conducted
3. the *justification* for initiating the search
4. the *place* where the search is conducted

The liberal rule on cell searches does not extend to strip or body cavity searches. This is because strip or cavity searches are more intrusive. Lower courts have held that strip and body cavity searches may be done after inmate exposure to a significant opportunity to receive contraband, including the following instances:

- upon return from an unsupervised visit
- when the inmate is suspected of smuggling prohibited items or contraband
- after contact visits

- after work release
- after court appearances

Strip or body cavity searches must be conducted properly and should not be humiliating to the inmate. A cavity search is invalid if there is no justification for it or if it is not conducted properly.

There is need for clear guidelines when booking arrested persons as to when strip or body cavity searches may be conducted. Body or cavity searches on all inmates cannot be conducted routinely. In general, persons who are arrested for minor misdemeanors, who are placed in a holding area and not mixed with the general jail population, and who will be released in a few hours probably cannot be strip searched. The only exception is if there is reasonable belief that a particular inmate is concealing a weapon or contraband.[5] In fact, some states, such as California, have made it a criminal misdemeanor for officers to conduct a strip search when booking certain arrested persons who are not to be mixed with the general jail population. Inmates being admitted to the general population may, however, be strip searched.

A pat-down or frisk search may be routinely conducted on inmates. This means inspecting a fully clothed inmate using the hands, and it could include having the inmate remove objects from his or her pocket and could also include using a metal detector. These types of searches are allowed because they are less intrusive and are necessary for jail personnel safety and protection.

Searches of visitors to jail may be conducted if two conditions are met: (1) There must be notice that such searches will be made, and (2) for each search, there must be particularized justification based on reasonable suspicion. Notification may be done in several ways, but the simplest is to post signs at all entrances stating, "All persons entering and leaving these grounds are subject to routine search of their person, property, or packages." A particularized justification for a search can be established if there is reasonable suspicion that a particular jail visitor may be trying to bring in contraband or prohibited items. Frisk searches of visitors' belongings, however, can routinely be performed unless prohibited by state law or agency rules.[6]

A different form of inmate search is urine testing. The Supreme Court has said that urine testing is indeed a form of search and seizure, but no challenge to warrantless testing in a jail or prison setting has ever succeeded. This is because inmates have minimal search and seizure protection and the evidence obtained is used in disciplinary proceedings instead of in criminal trials. Moreover, such tests are easily justified as rationally related to prison security and the orderly management of the institution.

The Court has not issued any definitive guidelines as to how and when the various kinds of jail searches may be conducted. It is therefore important for jail personnel to adhere to agency rules and be familiar with court decisions in their jurisdiction, because there are wide variations in allowable procedures from one jurisdiction to another. If there are no written procedures, such must be formulated.

### D. Discipline

In the past, inmates could be disciplined by jail or prison authorities in any manner without giving them any rights. This is no longer the case. In Wolff v. McDonnell, 418 U.S. 539 (1974), the Court said that in prison disciplinary cases, inmates are entitled to the following due process rights:

1. Advance written notice of the charges against the inmate must be given at least twenty-four hours before appearance before the prison disciplinary board.

2. There must be a "written statement by the factfinders as to the evidence relied upon and reasons" for the disciplinary action.

3. The inmate should be allowed to call witnesses and present documentary evidence in his or her defense providing there is no undue hazard to institutional safety or correctional goals.

4. A counsel substitute (either a fellow inmate, if permitted, or staff) is to be provided where the inmate is illiterate or where the complexity of the issues makes it unlikely that the inmate will be able to collect and present the evidence for an adequate comprehension of the case.

5. The prison disciplinary board must be impartial.

The five due process rights listed above are not as rigid as they appear. For example, how the "advance written notice of the charges" is to be given is generally left to the discretion of prison authorities. The same is true with the requirement of a "written statement by the factfinders as to the evidence relied upon." The requirement that the inmate "should be allowed to call witnesses and present documentary evidence" is subject to the provision that "there is no undue hazard to institutional safety or correctional goals," as determined by the disciplinary board. A "counsel substitute" is not a lawyer but a fellow inmate or a staff member and is to be provided only where the inmate is illiterate or where the complexity of the issues makes it unlikely that the inmate will be able to collect and present the evidence for an adequate comprehension of the case, as determined by the disciplinary board. The requirement that the prison disciplinary board must be "impartial" is satisfied as long as the officer who wrote the report is not a member of the disciplinary board. In a great majority of jails and prisons, members of the disciplinary board are employees of the system. Nonetheless, that complies with the requirement of impartiality. In short, inmates have "watered down" due process rights.

*Wolff v. McDonnell* states that inmates are *not* entitled to the following rights in disciplinary cases:

1. the right to confrontation and cross-examination, such being left to the discretion of the disciplinary board

2. the constitutional right to retained or appointed counsel

The five rights in *Wolff v. McDonnell* do not apply to all prison disciplinary cases. They apply only to cases of "serious misconduct," meaning cases which result in solitary confinement or the taking away of "good time" credit. The requirements have been extended to cases where a prisoner is taken out of the general population and placed in a more restrictive environment. In practice, however, many jail and prison authorities extend the rights given in *Wolff v. McDonnell* to practically all disciplinary cases because of agency policy or because they are mandated by court order. The due process rights given in *Wolff v. McDonnell* are required by the United States Constitution. In addition, state law, agency policy, or court order may give inmates more rights than those enumerated above.

Ideally, a jail should have clearly written procedures that guide jail personnel when writing disciplinary reports, provide for membership on the disciplinary board, and specify how hearings are to be conducted.

In addition to *Wolff v. McDonnell*, the following are cases decided by the Supreme Court on inmate discipline.

**1. *Baxter v. Palmigiano, 425 U.S. 308 (1976).*** *Baxter* affirmed the decision in *Wolff v. McDonnell* and held that inmates do not have the right to either retained or appointed counsel in disciplinary hearings that are not part of a criminal prosecution, nor are they entitled to confront or cross-examine witnesses. It further held that an inmate's decision to invoke the Fifth Amendment and remain silent at a disciplinary proceeding may be given adverse evidentiary significance. This means that, unlike in criminal cases where an accused's silence is not be be taken against him or her in any way, silence at a disciplinary hearing may be given some weight as an indication of guilt.

**2. *Ponte v. Real, 37 CrL 3051 (1985).*** If disciplinary officials refuse to call witnesses for an inmate at a disciplinary hearing and such refusal is challenged, they must at some point explain their refusal. But the reasons need not be written or made part of the administrative record of the hearing. Instead, the disciplinary officials may explain their decision at the hearing or they may decide to explain later in court if the prisoner alleges that the denial of witnesses deprived him or her of a "liberty" interest.

**3. *Cleavinger v. Saxner, 106 S.Ct. 496 (1985).*** Members of a prison disciplinary board do not enjoy absolute immunity and therefore may be held liable for what they do. They enjoy only qualified immunity, meaning that they are immune from liability only if they acted in good faith.

### E. Segregation (Disciplinary and Administrative)

Segregation may be classified as either *disciplinary* or *administrative*. As the term implies, disciplinary segregation is the transfer of an inmate to a more restrictive confinement for the purpose of punishment because of a violation of jail rules. By contrast, administrative segregation involves the transfer of an inmate to a type of housing separate from the general population to protect that inmate or others and/or to promote and maintain order in the institution. In sum, disciplinary segregation is used to punish while administrative segregation is used to prevent future problems.

Solitary confinement is not in itself cruel and unusual punishment and may therefore be used to punish inmates. Conditions, however, may be so bad as to amount to cruel and unusual punishment. It is hard to say when that level is reached, since this is decided by the judge or jury on a case-by-case basis.

In general, solitary confinement conditions have improved tremendously because of court intervention in civil rights cases. Providing only one liquid meal a day, allowing no legal materials, allowing no clothes, providing a completely bare prison cell, or confining for weeks without review are no longer allowed by the courts.

The legal requirements for punitive segregation are more strict than for administrative confinement. *Wolff v. McDonnell*, discussed above, states that five due process rights must be given inmates if the punishment to be imposed involves solitary confinement. By contrast, the Supreme Court has said that formal hearings like those required in *Wolff v. McDonnell* are not necessary for placing inmates in administrative segregation. All that is needed is an informal nonadversary evidentiary review. This is true both for decisions that an inmate represents a security threat to the institution and for decisions to confine an inmate pending completion of an investigation into misconduct against him. An inmate must merely receive some notice and an opportunity to present his or her view to prison officials. Hewitt v. Helm, 459 U.S. 460 (1983).

The distinction between punitive segregation and administrative segregation is sometimes unclear, and in some cases administrative segregation is used by jail personnel as a pretext to impose punishment. This must be avoided, because it distorts the purpose of administrative segregation and exposes jail officials to possible civil liability for bypassing the constitutional rights given to inmates in punitive segregation cases.

### F. Protection

A recent United States Supreme Court case holds that the state has an obligation to protect individuals who are under state custody or control. DeShaney v. Winnebago County Department of Social Services, 57 U.S.L.W. 4218 (1989). In that case, which is discussed in Chapter 11, the Court said that "when the State takes a person into its custody and holds him there against his will, the Constitution imposes upon it a corresponding duty to assume some responsibility for his safety and general well-being." Jail and prison inmates are clearly persons held in custody against their will.

Possible harm to inmates can come from three sources: the staff, other inmates, and themselves. It goes without saying that inmates must be protected from harm inflicted by jail personnel. The unjustified use of force or any other form of staff violence on inmates can result in civil liability against the officer—and even against the agency if it is established that the incident is linked to what the supervisors or the agency failed to do. Injury inflicted by other inmates may also result in civil liability in instances where such injuries could have been prevented.

Although there are no authoritative cases on this issue, jail and prison authorities are best advised to provide protective housing for homosexuals and others with different sexual practices. There is also an obligation to prevent suicidal inmates from harming themselves. This is especially important in jails, because, as one source states, nearly 50 percent of all inmate deaths in jails are suicides, as opposed to about 10 percent in prisons.[7]

Liability for failure to protect inmates may arise from simple negligence under state tort law or from deliberate indifference or gross negligence under Section 1983. In Section 1983 cases, failure to protect may constitute a violation of an inmate's right not to be deprived of life, liberty, or property without due process of law. Jail administrators must make sure that inmates are safe from jail personnel, other inmates, and themselves. Absolute safety is not required in prison. What is required is the absence of negligence (under state tort law) or deliberate indifference (under Section 1983) that leads to inmate injury or harm.

### G. Medical Care

Medical care is a necessity in jails and prisons. Institutions have a legal obligation under state tort law and Section 1983 to provide adequate treatment for the medical needs of inmates. There is no constitutional right to medical services as such in the Constitution, but the absence or inadequacy of medical care is usually taken by the courts to constitute cruel and unusual punishment in violation of the Eighth Amendment.

The leading case on prison medical care is Estelle v. Gamble, 429 U.S. 465 (1976). That case held that "deliberate indifference to the serious medical needs" of an inmate constitutes cruel and unusual punishment and violates the Eighth Amendment. In that case, however, the evidence showed that the prisoner was seen by the medical personnel seventeen times in a three-month period for a back injury. The medical staff failed to make a proper diagnosis, but this at most constituted medical malpractice, not cruel and unusual punishment. What "deliberate indifference to the serious medical needs" of inmates means is decided by the courts on a case-by-case basis. The Court, in Estelle v. Gamble, said that "deliberate indifference to serious medical needs of prisoners constitutes the 'necessary and wanton infliction of pain.'" It then added that there is deliberate indifference whether the indifference is manifested (1) by prison doctors in their response to a prisoner's needs, (2) by prison guards in intentionally denying or delaying access to medical care, or (3) by prison guards who intentionally interfere with the treatment once prescribed.

While the standard courts use in Section 1983 cases to impose liability is "deliberate indifference to the serious medical needs" of inmates, the standard used in state tort cases is much lower, in that liability may ensue under state law if failure to deliver the proper medical service constitutes mere negligence. Therefore, a lawsuit that will not succeed under Section 1983 may nonetheless succeed under state tort law.

Medical care has been interpreted by the courts to include mental health and dental care. Jails and prisons therefore have an obligation to provide inmates with or allow them access to mental and dental health professionals. On a related issue, the Court, in Vitek v. Jones, 445 U.S. 480 (1980), held that states must provide the following safeguards before transferring unwilling prisoners to mental hospitals:

1. written notice to the prisoner warning of the transfer
2. a full hearing
3. a chance for the prisoner to present witnesses at the hearing and, when feasible, to cross-examine witnesses called by the state
4. an independent decision maker to preside over the hearing
5. a written statement to the prisoner citing the evidence and the reasons for the transfer
6. an explanation to the prisoner of all his or her procedural rights

Jails and prisons are often faced with the problem of having to treat with antipsychotic medication and against their will inmates who may be dangerous to themselves and others. The Court concluded, in Washington v. Harper, 46 CrL 2105 (1990), that such treatment is constitutional under the following conditions: (1) The inmate is dangerous to him- or herself or to others, and (2) the treatment is in his or her medical interest. The Court further held that the forced-treatment procedure used by the state of Washington was valid. This procedure provided an adversarial hearing before a prison official and mental health professionals not involved in the inmate's ongoing treatment. The procedure did not give inmates the right to a lawyer, nor did it require adherence to the rules of evidence or a hearing before a judge. The Court, therefore, requires a hearing prior to such forced medication, but full due process rights (including the right to counsel) need not be given.

Although it is difficult to know what level of care a court will require for a particular jail, adherence to written standards for health care published by professional organizations, such as the American Medical Association, the American Correctional Association, or the American Psychiatric Association, will likely be looked upon with favor by the courts. These standards do not have any binding legal effect, but courts usually use them in the absence of judicial precedents in that jurisdiction.

A current medical problem in prisons is AIDS. Litigation concerning AIDS may come from any of the following:

1.  *The inmate with AIDS.* An inmate who has AIDS might bring a lawsuit if (a) the inmate is segregated or isolated because of AIDS, (b) the jail or prison institutes mandatory AIDS testing for high-risk inmates, (c) the inmate desires a particular kind of treatment to alleviate the effect of AIDS, or (d) the test results are indiscriminately disclosed.

2.  *Other inmates.* Other inmates might bring a lawsuit seeking (a) the segregation of AIDS carriers to protect the rest of the inmate population, and (b) a discontinuance of required testing of all prison inmates.

3.  *Jail personnel.* Jail personnel might bring a lawsuit seeking (a) the identification and isolation of inmates who have AIDS, and (b) better and safe working conditions in the prison.

AIDS legal issues are largely governed by state law. Most states now have laws addressing the various legal aspects of the AIDS problem. These laws vary greatly from state to state; some laws are comprehensive, others are limited. Comprehensive laws cover all facets of the AIDS issue —from testing, to treatment, to release or nonrelease of AIDS information. Other laws are limited to certain aspects of the AIDS issue, such as the treatment of AIDS carriers. Given the variations in laws from state to state, it will be risky and misleading to give specific advice here. State AIDS laws are often complex and change from year to year as needs and medical developments occur. Jail personnel must be familiar with their own state law on AIDS and follow closely the provisions thereof. In the absence of state law, it is best for any jail to have policies regarding the handling of AIDS cases by jail personnel, especially policies on housing and the release of information.

Case law in various states indicates that various courses of action may be taken by jail personnel to minimize exposure to liability in medical care cases. Foremost among these is making sure that proper medical care is available, preferably a level of care that comports with standards set by professional organizations. Next is the presence of written policies that guide jail personnel in the delivery of immediate medical services in emergency cases and in their interaction with the medical staff. In addition, jail personnel should be properly trained, particularly in the handling of emergency cases. Finally, care must be exercised in the handling of medical records, particularly those involving AIDS patients. Confidentiality must be preserved and records must be available only to authorized individuals.

Inmates have a right to medical treatment; they also have a right to refuse treatment as long as they are competent adults. The courts have stated, however, that in the following instances even competent adult inmates may be forced to receive treatment: (1) The health or general welfare of other inmates or the staff is threatened (as when an inmate has a highly contagious venereal disease), (2) there is a life-threatening situation (as when an inmate will likely die unless treatment is given), and (3) according to the medical staff's professional judgment, there is an emergency situation (as when an inmate is bleeding profusely and needs a blood transfusion).

### H.  Access to Courts and Lawyers

Prisoners have a constitutional right to access to court. This means that jail and prison authorities are required to assist inmates in the preparation and filing of legal papers by providing adequate law libraries for the use of prisoners or legal assistance from persons trained in the law. Bounds v. Smith, 430 U.S. 817 (1977). The Supreme Court listed the following as possible alternative ways of complying with the duty to provide access to the courts:

1.  training inmates as paralegal assistants to work under a lawyer's supervision

2.  using paraprofessionals and law students as volunteers or in formal legal programs

3. organizing volunteer attorneys through bar associations or other groups
4. hiring lawyers on a part-time consultant basis
5. using full-time staff attorneys in a new prison legal assistance organization or as part of the public defender or legal services office.

The Court further held that indigent inmates must be provided at state expense with (1) writing materials to draft legal documents, (2) notarial services to authenticate them, and (3) postage to mail them. It is hard to say how far this obligation goes. One court upheld as valid a system where the state supplied stamps for three letters per week, with additional postage being taken from the inmate's account. Gaines v. Lane, 790 F.2d 1299 (7th Cir. 1986). In most instances, what is needed for meaningful access is decided by the court on a case-by-case basis.

Courts seldom state what approach complies with the constitutional requirement of meaningful access. The above listing is merely suggestive, and not inclusive. For example, simply providing paid full-time lawyers may not be adequate in systems with huge prison populations and where there are only a few lawyers. Providing a law library may not suffice either, because some inmates may be illiterate. Assistance from "persons trained in the law" may be needed to supplement a law library. This does not necessarily mean providing a lawyer. Providing a law clerk is sufficient as long as the law clerk is "trained and skilled in the law." Hooks v. Wainwright, 775 F.2d 2433 (11th Cir. 1985).

Unless prison authorities provide a "reasonable alternative" for helping illiterate or poorly educated prisoners gain meaningful access to the courts, they cannot prohibit educated or knowledgeable inmates (known as "jailhouse lawyers") from helping other inmates who need legal assistance. To prohibit such assistance is to deny access to the courts to those prisoners who could not prepare the documents themselves. Johnson v. Avery, 393 U.S. 483 (1969). Given limited resources, most jails suffer from an inadequate library. In some jails, a law book delivery system (from available law libraries, public or private, in the community) is used in lieu of or supplementary to a jail library. This arrangement seldom suffices as a means of court access or justifies a prohibition against legal help from jailhouse lawyers. In reality, it is hard for jails or prisons to prohibit jailhouse lawyers from helping other inmates, because the Court has not defined with certainty what a reasonable alternative may be.

### I. Visitation

Visitation lawsuits can come from two sources: (1) attorneys, religious ministers, and court officials, and (2) family members and friends. Visits by attorneys, religious ministers, and court officials cannot be prohibited completely, because such prohibition violates an inmates's constitutional right to access to court and freedom of religion. Visiting hours, however, can be regulated in the interest of prison order and security. It is best for jail administrators to agree with practicing lawyers in that jurisdiction as to the visiting hours that both sides may consider reasonable.

The United States Supreme Court has decided the issue of whether inmates have a constitutional right to visitation by family members and friends. Lower courts, however, have decided the issue with inconsistent results. It is easier for jail officials to limit the visitation privileges of family and friends than it is to regulate visits by attorneys, religious ministers, and court officials, since these latter can also claim constitutional rights under the First Amendment.

The Court has held that a nonpunitive ban on "contact visits" for pretrial detainees, based on legitimate fears for institutional security, does not violate the Fourteenth Amendment provision on due process. Block v. Rutherford, 104 S.Ct. 3227 (1984). Whether inmates have a right to conjugal visits has not been decided by the Court. Rights not given by the Constitution may, however, be given to inmates by state law or agency rules, such as the right to contact and the right to conjugal visits.

### J. First Amendment Rights

Amendment I to the United States Constitution states,

Congress shall make no law respecting an establishment of religion, or prohibiting the free exercise thereof; or abridging the freedom of speech, or of the press; or the right of the people peaceably to assemble, and to petition the Government for a redress of grievances.

**1. *Freedom of Religion.*** The First Amendment provides that "Congress shall make no law respecting an establishment of religion, or prohibiting the free exercise thereof." The wording implies there are two parts to the freedom of religion: "establishment" and "free exercise." The establishment clause prohibits the government from aiding religion, an issue that is seldom raised in inmate litigation. The free exercise clause, however, is often invoked by inmates and has been the subject of constant court battles.

Free exercise of religion means (1) that an inmate must be allowed to do what his or her religion says should be done, and (2) that an inmate must not be forced to do anything against his or her religious beliefs. As an example of item (1) above, if a Roman Catholic inmate wants to attend church service inside prison on Sundays, the inmate must be allowed to do that. As an example of item (2) above, if a Black Muslim inmate claims that because the jail food typically includes pork, he or she is forced to eat pork in violation of religious beliefs, some way must be found to accommodate that inmate's dietary needs. In both kinds of cases, the exercise of religious freedom by an inmate may be limited by prison authorities if the limitation is "reasonably related to legitimate penological interest."

An issue is whether or not an inmate's religious belief or religion is fake or bona fide. This is a difficult problem that must ultimately be resolved by the court after determining whether (1) the inmate is sincere in that religious belief, or (2) the claimed religion is in fact a religion.

In a recent significant case, the Supreme Court upheld as constitutional certain policies adopted by New Jersey corrections officials that effectively prevented Muslim inmates assigned to outside work crews from attending the weekly religious service of their religion. The Court said that these policies were valid because they were "reasonably related to legitimate penological interests." O'Lone v. Estate of Shabazz, 107 S.Ct. 2400 (1987). The effect of this decision is to make it easier for jail and prison officials to pass rules and regulations that deprive inmates even of their most basic rights, such as the freedom of religion. In the past, courts upheld such regulations only if a "strong compelling state interest" was involved. Although both terms are difficult to define with precision, it is clear that the new test is easier for administrators to meet and makes it correspondingly harder for inmates to overturn disliked policies.

In an earlier case, the Court held that the state cannot impermissibly discriminate against inmates of the Buddhist religion. This does not mean that the Buddhist sect, no matter how small, is entitled to identical facilities or personnel as the other more dominant religious groups that have more members in prisons. It is sufficient that reasonable opportunities to worship be afforded by the jail or prison management to inmates of smaller religious sects.

**2. *Freedom of the Press.*** This First Amendment right has many facets that have been litigated in prison cases. Legal challenge can come from two sources: (1) the inmate whose right has been suppressed, and (2) representatives of the press who feel that their access to an inmate has been curtailed. For example, a disturbance takes place in a jail and a group of inmates want access to the press to ventilate their grievances. Should such a request be granted? On the other hand, reporters and TV personnel might want to interview the leader of the inmate group. Must such a request be allowed?

On the right of access by the media, the Court has held that prison regulations prohibiting face-to-face interviews do not violate the prisoners' First Amendment rights if other methods of communication with the news media are available to them, including using the postal service and communicating indirectly through family members, friends, attorneys, clergy, and others who are allowed to visit inmates. Pell v. Procunier, 417 U.S. 817 (1974). Also, the media has no more right than the public at large to access to jails and other government institutions, and such institutions need not grant the press extra privileges. Houchins v. KQED, 438 U.S. 1 (1978).

**3. The Right of Inmates to Receive Mail.** The rule is that mail coming from lawyers and the court can be inspected for contraband but cannot be censored or read. The Supreme Court has said that prison authorities may constitutionally "require that mail from an attorney to a prisoner be identified as such and that his name and address appear on the communication and—as a protection against contraband—that the authorities may open such mail in the inmate's presence. The Court further said that "a lawyer desiring to correspond with a prisoner may also be required first to identify himself and his client to the prison officials to ensure that letters marked 'privileged' are actually from members of the bar." Wolff v. McDonnell, 418 U.S. 539 (1974). Mail sent by inmates to lawyers or the court cannot be censored or read by jail officials. One court has held that prisoners have a constitutional right to send sealed letters to public officials and agencies. Davidson v. Skully, 694 F.2d 50 (2nd Cir. 1982).

As for incoming mail, the Supreme Court has said that prison officials may reject incoming publications if those publications are "reasonably" found to be detrimental to prison security. At issue in the case was a comprehensive set of regulations governing incoming nonlegal mail in federal prisons. The Court's decision came despite the absence of evidence linking such publications with any detrimental or untoward acts performed by prisoners. In sum, the decision gave wide-ranging discretion to prison officials regarding the content of printed material sent to inmates. Thornburgh v. Abbott, 109 S.Ct. 1874 (1989).

Under current case law it is difficult for prison authorities to withhold publications addressed to inmates on grounds of obscenity or pornography. This is because obscenity and pornography are difficult to define and are judged on the basis of "community standards." Proving that a certain publication is pornographic is a difficult task for prison authorities and therefore censorship on that ground is hard to justify.

The so-called "publishers only" rule used in some jurisdictions has been upheld by the Court. This rule provides that only printed materials from publishers will be accepted for delivery to inmates. About printed matter packages in general, the Court said that it is "obvious that such packages are handy devices for the smuggling of contraband." The Court then stated that there was no basis for concluding that the jail officials in this case had indulged in an exaggerated response to the serious problem of smuggling prohibited items or that this restriction was irrational. Bell v. Wolfish, 441 U.S. 520 (1979).

**4. *The Right of Inmates to Send Mail.*** Mail sent by inmates to other people (other than to lawyers and the court) may be censored subject to the following rules:

1. Such censorship must further the governmental interest of security, order, or rehabilitation.

2. Such censorship must be no greater than is necessary for the protection of the governmental interest involved.

3. Such censorship or the withholding of a letter must be subject to due process protection. This means that the inmate needs to be notified of the censorship or rejection and that there must be a reasonable opportunity for the author of the letter to protest the decision to someone other than the person who made the decision. Procunier v. Martinez, 416 U.S. 396 (1974).

The above rules, taken together, are generally less strict than for incoming nonlegal mail, because mail *from* inmates causes less security risks than mail *to* inmates.

In a recent case, Missouri prison authorities prohibited correspondence between inmates except where the authorities considered such correspondence to be in the best interest of those involved. This had the effect of prohibiting inmate-to-inmate correspondence and was therefore challenged as a violation of First Amendment rights. The Supreme Court ruled that the regulation was constitutional because it was reasonably related to legitimate security interests. The Court said that inmate-to-inmate communication could contain escape plans as well as arrangements for inmate violence. The activities of inmate gangs would also be helped if inmates were allowed to communicate freely. Turner v. Safley, 41 CrL 3239 (1987).

Taken together, *Martinez* and *Turner* entail that mail sent by inmates to someone on the outside can be censored only if the censorship is based on narrowly drawn regulations that further security, order, or rehabilitation. By contrast, inmate-to-inmate letters may be censored if the censorship is "reasonably related to legitimate penological interests, with a good deal of deference being given to prison officials who make the censorship decisions."[8] It is therefore easier to censor mail sent by one inmate to another inmate than it is to censor mail sent by an inmate to somebody on the outside.

## III.  WHAT CAN BE DONE TO MINIMIZE LIABILITY?

The following suggestions are given to help jail personnel minimize liability arising from cases filed by inmates:

1. Have a written agency manual, handbook, or set of guidelines. Have

it carefully reviewed by a lawyer who knows jail and prison law.

2. Know the provisions of your agency manual and state law and follow them carefully.

3. Document your activities, particularly your efforts to improve prison conditions. Keep good records.

4. Act within the scope of your duties and in good faith.

5. Act in a professional manner, using reason instead of emotion, particularly in crisis situations.

6. Avoid undue personal involvement with inmates.

7. Confer with and get approval from your supervisor if you have doubts about what you are doing.

8. If you are an administrator, use a proactive approach to jail administration. This means identifying and anticipating problems and actively working with other officials to address these problems.

9. Through the help of your legal adviser, be informed of the latest court decisions (state and federal) on the rights of inmates.

10. Seek legal advice whenever legal problems arise.

Michael J. Dale, a noted correctional law expert, gives the following advice as to the types of programs jails must have in order to minimize liability:[9]

1. Provide what you're required to by state law, regulation, or department policy.

2. Provide adequate food, ventilation, living space, access to counsel or to a law library, medical care, and visitation (unless a blanket prohibition can be proven on security grounds).

3. Provide reasonable access to religion and reasonable mail procedures (prohibit only those materials for which a legitimate security reason or basis exists).

4. Provide a work release program that is fair and nondiscriminatory.

5. Provide as much recreation (indoor and outdoor) as is feasible. Avoid using overcrowding as a basis for denial of recreation. Withdraw the right to recreation for security reasons fairly and in compliance with due process.

## SUMMARY

Lawsuits have become a common occupational hazard in jail and prison management. The "hands off" judicial doctrine has given way to a willingness to try cases, with no sign of abatement. As a result, there is hardly a state prison system or jail in a major county or city in the United States that is not currently involved in a lawsuit.

Although jails and prisons are different in a number of ways, the rights of prisoners in jails and prisons are generally considered by the courts to be similar. Most civil liability cases brought by inmates involve prisons, not jails, but court decisions apply to both prisons and jails.

Under the old philosophy of prisoners' rights, prisoners were virtual slaves of the state. This meant that prisoners had only a few rights and jail administrators had tremendous discretion and could count on non-intervention by the courts. All that has changed dramatically. According to the new philosophy, "prisoners retain all the rights of free citizens except those on which restriction is necessary to assure their orderly confinement or to provide reasonable protection for the rights and physical safety of all members of the prison community."

Inmates usually file either state tort or Section 1983 cases against jail personnel. These cases seek injunctive relief and/or damages and cover such issues as overcrowding, use of force, search and seizure, discipline, segregation, protection, medical care, access to courts and lawyers, visitation, and First Amendment rights. The court has held that "a prison regulation is valid if it is reasonably related to legitimate penological interests." This gives jail personnel more discretion in running their institutions.

A number of practices can be instituted by jail personnel to minimize litigation from inmates, including having a carefully reviewed written manual and following its provisions carefully, acting within the scope of duty, and following state law and court decisions.

## NOTES

1. *Corrections Digest* 18, no. 6, at 1.
2. *BJS Bulletin: Jail Inmates* (Bureau of Justice Statistics, 1987), at 2.
3. American Bar Association Joint Committee on the Legal Status of Prisoners, "Standards Relating to the Legal Status of Criminals" (Tentative Draft 1977), *American Criminal Law Review* 14, at 377.
4. *Ibid.*
5. "Legal Issues for Institutional Personnel" (National Institute of Corrections, 1988, unpublished manual), at XI-14.
6. *Ibid.*, at XI-24.
7. F. Cohen, *Sourcebook on the Mentally Disordered Offender* (National Institute of Corrections, 1985), at 67, as quoted in W. C. Collins, *Correctional Law 1986*, at 95.
8. W. C. Collins, *Correctional Law 1987*, at 40.
9. Michael J. Dale, "Jail Inmate Programs: A Brief Look at the Case Law" (unpublished manuscript).

# CASE BRIEFS

## BELL v. WOLFISH
### 441 U.S. 520 (1979)

### FACTS

Pretrial detainees at the New York Metropolitan Correctional Center filed a lawsuit alleging violations of constitutional rights. The center had opened less than four months before and had been described as "the architectural embodiment of the best and most progressive penological planning" and "unquestionably a top flight, first class facility." Nonetheless, inmates filed action alleging violations of statutory and constitutional rights arising from overcrowded conditions, undue lengths of confinement, improper searches, inadequate recreational facilities, lack of educational and employment opportunities, insufficient staff, and restrictions on the purchase and receipt of personal items and books.

### ISSUE

Did the conditions and practices in the New York Metropolitan Correctional Center violate the constitutional rights of detainees? *No.*

### SUPREME COURT DECISION

1. "Double bunking" did not deprive the pretrial detainees of liberty without due process of law.
2. The "publisher only" rule did not violate inmates' First Amendment rights.
3. The policy on body cavity searches of pretrial detainees after contact visits did not violate their Fourth Amendment right.
4. The rule permitting searches of pretrial detainees' quarters in their absence did not violate their Fourth Amendment right.

### CASE SIGNIFICANCE

This is one of the few cases decided by the Court on the rights of pretrial detainees. In essence, the Court rejected the concept of presumption of innocence for pretrial detainees in favor of the need for jail authorities to run the institution in a secure and orderly manner. The Court said, however, that confinement conditions will constitute a violation of due process if (1) the detainees are subjected to "genuine privation and hardships over an extended period of time" or (2) if detainees are subjected to conditions that are "not reasonably related to a legitimate goal." These two conditions, however, are not much different from those that would also make unconstitutional the confinement of those already convicted. In effect, the Court gave the go-ahead signal for jail officials to run jails the way prisons are run, despite the fact that jails hold both convicts and pretrial detainees. This case implies that although jails and prisons are different in a number of ways, they are treated by the Court, at least in regard to inmates' rights, as though they were the same. This is because the problems of institutional order and security are similar whether an institution houses pretrial detainees or not.

## TURNER v. SAFLEY
### 41 CrL 3239 (1989)

### FACTS

Inmates brought a class action challenging two regulations of the Missouri Division of Corrections. These regulations (1) permitted correspondence between immediate family members who were inmates at different institutions and between inmates concerning legal matters but allowed other inmate correspondence only if each inmate's classification/treatment team deemed it in the best interest of the parties (this had the effect of prohibiting inmate-to-inmate correspondence), and (2) permitted an inmate to marry only with the prison superintendent's permission, which could be given only when there were "compelling" reasons. Testimony indicated that generally only a pregnancy or the birth of an illegitimate child was considered compelling.

### ISSUE

Did these two regulations violate the constitutional rights of inmates at the Missouri Division of Corrections? *No, in the case of the correspondence regulation, and Yes, in the case of the marriage regulation.*

### SUPREME COURT DECISION

A prison regulation that impinges on a constitutional right of inmates is valid if it is reasonably related to legitimate penological interests. The factors to be considered in making the reasonableness determination include these:

1. whether there is a valid, rational connection between the regulation and the legitimate governmental interest put forward to justify it

2. whether there are alternative means of exercising the right that remain open to prisoners

3. the impact accommodation of the asserted right will have on guards and other inmates and on the allocation of prison resources generally

4. whether ready alternatives to the regulation exist

The Missouri prison regulation that bars most inmate-to-inmate mail correspondence was held to be reasonably related to legitimate security interests and was held not to unconstitutionally abridge prisoners' First Amendment rights. The Missouri prison regulation that prohibited inmates from marrying except with the permission of the prison superintendent and for "compelling reasons" amounted to an exaggerated response to rehabilitation and security concerns and therefore infringed prisoners' constitutional right to marry.

## CASE SIGNIFICANCE

This case makes it easier for jail and prison authorities to impose regulations that impinge on inmates' constitutional rights, because all they have to prove is that a regulation is "reasonably related to the legitimate penological interests," meaning prison security, rehabilitation, or the orderly running of the institution. This latest Court decision dispels some of the confusion as to the standard that is to be used by courts when balancing inmates' rights and prison authority. In previous cases, the Court said that a "compelling state interest" was necessary if a prison regulation violates a First Amendment right such as the freedom to send and receive mail. The compelling state interest test has now been set aside in favor of a "reasonable relatedness" test, which is easier for jail officials to meet. The decision indicates that the reasonable relatedness standard is to be applied every time a constitutional right is alleged to have been violated. The Court also laid out four factors to be considered when determining reasonableness, hence giving lower courts better guidance when deciding cases. Note that the reasonable relatedness test applies only to Section 1983 cases, in which constitutional rights are alleged to have been violated. It does not apply to cases under state tort law, which are decided on a standard set by the law of the state.

## WOLFF v. MCDONNELL
### 418 U.S. 539 (1974)

## FACTS

Inmates at a Nebraska prison filed a complaint for damages and injunction under Section 1983 in which they alleged that (1) the Nebraska prison disciplinary proceedings violated due process, (2) the inmate legal assistance program did not meet constitutional standards, and (3) the regulations governing inmate mail were unconstitutionally restrictive.

Under Nebraska's disciplinary proceedings, forfeiture or withholding of good time credits or confinement in a disciplinary cell was used as a punishment for serious misconduct. To establish misconduct, a preliminary conference was held with the chief corrections supervisor and the charging party. At this conference, the prisoner was orally informed of the charge, and its merits were preliminarily discussed. Then a conduct report was prepared, and a hearing was held before the prison's disciplinary body, which was composed of three prison officials. At this hearing, the inmate could ask questions of the charging party.

## ISSUE

Did the Nebraska disciplinary proceedings, legal assistance program, and mail regulations violate inmates' constitutional rights?

## SUPREME COURT DECISION

In prison disciplinary proceedings that can result in loss of good time credits or punitive segregation for serious misconduct, the inmate must be given the following due process rights.

1.  Advance written notice of charges must be given to the inmate no less than twenty-four hours prior to his or her appearance before the committee.

2.  There must be "a written statement by the factfinders as to the evidence relied on and reasons for the disciplinary action."

3.  The inmate should be allowed to call witnesses and present documentary evidence in his or her defense if permitting this will not jeopardize institutional safety or correctional goals.

4.  A counsel substitute (either a fellow inmate or staff) must be allowed if the inmate is illiterate or if the complexity of the issues makes it unlikely that the inmate will be able to collect and present the evidence for an adequate comprehension of the case.

5.  The prison disciplinary board must be impartial.

The state may constitutionally require that mail from an attorney to a prisoner be identified as such, that the attorney's name and address appear on the communication, and, as a protection against contraband, that the authorities be allowed to open such mail in the inmate's presence. A lawyer desiring to correspond with a prisoner may also first be required to identify him- or herself and his or her client to the prison officials to ensure that letters marked "privileged" are actually from members of the bar.

The Court referred the legal assistance program issue to the lower court and therefore did not decide it.

## CASE SIGNIFICANCE

This is an important case, because for the first time the Court acknowledged that inmates are entitled to due process rights during prison disciplinary proceedings. These due process rights are not the same as those enjoyed by nonprisoners, but the Court said that a prisoner "is not wholly stripped of constitutional protections" and that disciplinary proceedings must "be governed by a mutual accommodation between institutional needs and generally applicable constitutional requirements." The Court did not give inmates all the rights they sought. Specifically, the Court said that an inmate has no constitutional right to confrontation and cross-examination (which are left to the discretion of prison officials, or to retained or appointed counsel. The rights given in this case do not apply to all disciplinary cases but only to instances involving serious violations, meaning violations that can result in forfeiture of good time credits or punitive segregation. They do not apply to minor offenses, although jail and prison administrators are likely to respect the above rights in all disciplinary cases anyway, either because of agency rules or court mandate.

# 13

# GOVERNMENT AGENCIES AS DEFENDANTS

## INTRODUCTION

Plaintiffs in civil liability cases use the "shotgun" approach when filing lawsuits. This means that a plaintiff will name as defendants any and all who might have anything to do with the alleged violation of rights. This includes the erring officer, the police department, the city, the county, and whichever government unit is the officer's employer. The inclusion of the employing government agency as defendant is usually based on the "deep pockets" theory and the assumption that the agency could have done something to prevent the injury. The assumption is that police officers act for the department and that what they do reflects departmental policy and practice.

Government agencies may be sued and held liable under state tort law or Section 1983. In a typical Section 1983 action against a city or agency, the plaintiff makes the following allegations:

1. that there is or was a *policy* promulgated by a city or agency policy-maker
2. that the policy caused the *injury* to the plaintiff
3. that the injury constituted a *violation* of the plaintiff's *constitutional rights*

## I. IMMUNITY OF GOVERNMENT AGENCIES FROM LAWSUITS

States and state agencies generally cannot be sued under Section 1983, because they enjoy sovereign immunity, unless waived, under the Eleventh Amendment to the Constitution. That provision states, "The Judicial power of the United States shall not be construed to extend to any suit in law or equity, commenced or prosecuted against one of the United States by Citizens of another State, or by Citizens or Subjects of any Foreign state." This does not imply that state officials are immune from liability. Sovereign immunity extends only to the state itself and its agencies; state officials, like local officials, may be sued and held liable for what they do in their personal capacity. In a recent case, the Supreme Court held that state officials cannot be sued in their official capacity under Section 1983, because such lawsuit is in effect a lawsuit against the state.

Although states are generally immune from liability under Section 1983, that protection has largely been waived in state tort cases—either by law or court decisions. Generally, states and state agencies may be sued under state tort for what their officers do. Such waiver is usually found in state tort acts, the specifics of which vary from state to state. The federal government has a Federal Tort Claims Act that waives immunity in many cases involving federal employees. That waiver of immunity is more extensive than the waiver many states have in their state tort acts.

Local agencies used to enjoy sovereign immunity in Section 1983 cases, but in 1978 the Supreme Court decided that local agencies could be held liable under Section 1983 for what their employees do, thus depriving local governments of the sovereign immunity defense. Monell v. Department of Social Services, 436 U.S. 658 (1978). This change is partly responsible for the increase in the number of liability cases against local police departments, because now plaintiffs know that if the officer is too poor to pay, the agency may be held liable—if the violation can be attributed in some way to the agency. Some courts have held that although the agency is not civilly responsible for every act of a supervisor, the higher the supervisor's rank, the greater the chances of agency liability. For example, an agency is less liable for the decision of a police sergeant than it is for decisions and policies promulgated by a police chief.

## II. LIABILITY FOR OFFICIAL POLICY

The Court held in Monell that municipal liability may be imposed for conduct that "implements or executes a policy statement, ordinance, regulation, or decision officially adopted and promulgated by municipal officers" or if such conduct results from "custom" even though such custom has not received formal approval through official decision-making channels. In short, agency or municipal liability ensues if the violation stems from "official policy." What, then, is official policy? The answer is far from clear, not least because it has been the subject of several court decisions that are difficult to reconcile.

At the risk of oversimplification, but in the interest of clarity, a working definition may be used, a definition given by the Fifth Circuit Court of Appeals in the case of Bennett v. City of Slidell, 735 F.2d 861 (5th Cir. 1984). In that case the court said,

> Official policy is:
> 1. A *policy statement, ordinance, regulation, or decision* that is officially adopted and promulgated by the municipality's lawmaking officers or by an official to whom the lawmakers have delegated policy-making authority; or
> 2. A *persistent, widespread practice* of city officials or employees, which, although not authorized by officially adopted and promulgated policy, is so common and well settled as to constitute a custom that fairly represents municipal policy. Actual or constructive knowledge of such custom must be attributable to the governing body of the municipality or to an official to whom that body had delegated policy-making authority.

Two points should be noted. First, for a policy to be official, it must be officially adopted and promulgated by the municipality's lawmaking officers or by an official to whom lawmakers have delegated policymaking authority. It may be in the form of a law, written regulations, directives, or policy statements by high executive officials. Grandstaff v. City of Borger, 767 F.2d 161 (5th Cir. 1985). Not every police supervisor falls in the category of policymaker, although the police chief probably would. In a recent case, the United States Supreme Court said that the determination of which officials have final policymaking authority is a question of state and local law and not a question of fact for a judge or jury to decide. City of St. Louis v. Praprotnik, 56 U.S.L.W. 4201 (1988).

The second point is that a custom, although unwritten, may constitute official policy. By definition, a custom is not something that has been officially adopted or promulgated by policymakers, but it may be so common and well settled that it can be said to represent official policy. This is a matter to be proved during trial.

## III.  CASES ILLUSTRATING THE MEANING OF "OFFICIAL POLICY"

The Fifth Circuit said that "a municipality is liable under Section 1983 for a deprivation of rights protected by the Constitution or federal laws that is inflicted pursuant to official policy." It then added that "actions of officers or employees of a municipality do not render the municipality liable under Section 1983 unless they execute official policy as above defined." A few cases will help clarify the above definition.

In one case, the Second Circuit Court of Appeals affirmed a jury verdict against a city whose police officers used excessive force in arresting the plaintiff. Fiacco v. City of Rensselaer, 783 F. 2d 319 (2nd Cir. 1986). In that case, the court found that the city was "knowingly and deliberately indifferent to the possibility that its police officers were wont to use excessive force and that this indifference was demonstrated by the failure of the City defendants to exercise reasonable care in investigating claims of police brutality in order to supervise the officers in the proper use of force." Evidence was introduced during the trial that the policy of nonsupervision of police officers amounted to deliberate indifference to their use of force. Such evidence included proof of the city's failure to adopt measures to deal with complaints of police brutality or even to reasonably investigate such complaints. The policy implications of *Fiacco* for police departments are clear: Each department must have a policy of active supervision of subordinates and must promptly investigate complaints of police brutality.

In Webster v. City of Houston, 735 F.2d 838 (1984), the use by the police of "throw down" guns created municipal liability, because it was established during the trial that the practice was common knowledge among supervisors in the city. One incident, however, does not a custom make. In *Webster*, the court said,

> If actions of employees are . . . to prove a custom [such actions] must have occurred for so long or so frequently that [they] warrant . . . the attribution to the governing body of knowledge that the objectionable conduct is the expected practice of city employees [so that] the governing body [is charged] with actual or constructive knowledge of such actions of subordinates.

However, in a different case, also involving the city of Houston, the Fifth Circuit Court of Appeals held that there was not sufficient evidence of a widespread custom to impose liability. Hamilton v. Rodgers, 791 F.2d 439 (5th Cir. 1986). In that case, the city of Houston was sued in connection with the alleged racial harassment of the plaintiff, an employee of the Houston Fire Department. The court found that the plaintiff's co-workers created an atmosphere of racist bigotry and that the plaintiff's supervisors contributed to that atmosphere. There was not enough evidence, however, to establish that high-ranking officers either knew or constructively knew of the persistent racist problem; hence the agency could not be held liable.

In another case, the First Circuit Court of Appeals upheld a jury verdict against a city for its failure to train its police adequately, leading to the use of excessive force against the plaintiff by two police officers. Wierstak v. Heffernan, 789 F.2d 968 (1st Cir. 1986). The court said,

> There was evidence that the City of Worcester failed to properly train its officers about policies on the use of firearms, high-speed chases, and road

blocks. There was evidence that the City failed to instruct its officers on the amount of force that should be used in making an arrest and on the need to inspect injured prisoners as required [by state law]. . . . The testimony further showed that the City never conducted any sort of investigation into the circumstances of the plaintiff's arrest nor his claims of brutality. . . .

The Wierstak decision points to the importance of proper training and the need for investigation of complaints about the conduct of the police. Inaction in either of these areas leads to agency liability.

In another case, the Eighth Circuit Court of Appeals imposed liability on a city based on custom. Harris v. City of Pagedale, 821 F.2d 499 (8th Cir. 1987). In Harris, an arrestee who had been sexually assaulted by a police officer brought a civil rights action against the city and the officer. The plaintiff established that the city failed to take any remedial action with regard to physical and sexual abuse by police officers, such failure amounting to deliberate indifference rather than mere negligence. The plaintiff presented evidence that there were a number of incidents of sexual misconduct by various officers, especially the officer who arrested the plaintiff, and that city officials in positions of authority had been repeatedly notified of the offensive acts but did nothing. The court held that (1) the plaintiff had established that there existed in the city a custom of failing to investigate or act on citizen complaints of physical and sexual misconduct by officers; (2) the evidence supported a determination that the board of aldermen, its members, and the chief of police had final authority to establish a custom of deliberate indifference to a known pattern of misconduct; and (3) the plaintiff had established that the custom proximately caused the sexual assault. Liability was therefore imposed on the city.

## IV. NO CLEAR DEFINITION OF OFFICIAL POLICY

It must be stressed that the term "official policy" has been given various meanings by different courts and that the definition given by the Fifth Circuit in Bennett is not necessarily the definition used in other courts. Whatever definition is used, it should include some of the elements in the Fifth Circuit definition, including the concept of a policy officially promulgated by decision makers and the concept of custom. Unless the United States Supreme Court gives the final word, the meaning of "official policy" will continue to be tentative and changing, with variations from one court to another.

Does written policy constitute official policy? Courts say yes. One court, for instance, has decided that a county policy established in the sheriff's handbook requiring indiscriminate strip searching of all pretrial detainees led to municipal liability. John Does 1–100 v. Boyd, 613 F. Supp.

1514 (D. Minn. 1985). Agencies need to be careful when writing manuals and make sure that the policies therein do not violate constitutional rights or rights given by federal or state law.

This discussion of agency liability makes clear that liability ensues only if the injury could be attributed to "official policy," however that term is construed. That single standard, in the opinion of many courts, does away with prior decisions that based liability on such considerations as a finding of "deliberate indifference" or "gross negligence." The only question to be asked under the single standard of liability is, Was the injury caused by official policy? If it was, then municipal liability is imposed; if not, municipal liability is rejected, even if "deliberate indifference" or "gross negligence" is involved in the act.

## V. WHO IS AN OFFICIAL POLICYMAKER FOR WHOSE ACTIONS A CITY MIGHT BE HELD LIABLE?

The crucial question in determining municipal liability (as distinguished from the liability of an individual police officer) for what employees do is this: Who is an official policymaker? The answer: the final policymaking authority, as determined by state law.

Certainly, not every city employee falls in this category. The issue was decided, although not clearly, by the Supreme Court in the City of St. Louis v. Praprotnik, 56 U.S.L.W. 4201 (1988). In that case, a management-level employee (an architect) in one of the city agencies in St. Louis successfully appealed a temporary suspension by his supervisor to the Civil Service Commission. Two years later, however, the employee was transferred to a clerical position in another city agency. The following year, he was laid off by the supervisor. The employee sued, claiming that his dismissal was in retaliation for his successful appeal and that the layoff was in violation of his First Amendment right and the right to due process.

The jury found the city of St. Louis liable. The court of appeals affirmed the jury's verdict, saying that the employee's layoff was brought about by an unconstitutional city policy. Applying a test under which a "policymaker" was determined to be one whose employment decisions are final in the sense that they are not subjected to de novo review by higher ranking officials, the court of appeals concluded that the city of St. Louis could be held liable for adverse personnel decisions made by the supervisor who laid off the employee.

On appeal, the United States Supreme Court reversed the decision. In a 7–1 vote, the Court threw out a $15,000 award against the city of St. Louis, saying that generally only the highest ranking city officials can commit constitutional violations that make the city liable. In the case of St. Louis, such high-ranking status is limited to the mayor, the aldermen, and the Civil Service Commission. Said the Court,

> The identification of officials having "final policy-making authority" is a question of state [including local] law, rather than a question of fact for the jury. Here, it appears that petitioner's City Charter gives the authority to set employment policy to the mayor and aldermen, who are empowered to enact ordinances, and to the Commission, whose function is to hear employees' appeals. Petitioner [the City of St. Louis] cannot be held liable unless respondent proved the existence of an unconstitutional policy promulgated by officials having such authority.

The Court then added that the mayor and aldermen did not enact an ordinance permitting retaliatory transfers or layoffs. Nor had the Civil Service Commission indicated that such actions were permissible. The layoff was a decision made by the agency supervisor, who, under state law, was not an official policymaker. The action, therefore, was not the result of an official policy for which the city of St. Louis could be held liable. The supervisor could be held liable for the action, but not the agency.

*Praprotnik* is important because the decision makes it more difficult for plaintiffs to win lawsuits against a city government based on allegations that low-ranking officials violated their rights. Moreover, it says that a city cannot be sued successfully based on claims that high-ranking officials failed to override a subordinate's decision that violated somebody's rights. Instead, it must be established that the violation was due to official policy and custom rather than to a mere failure to override a subordinate's decision. The case also says that the determination of which officials have final policymaking authority is a question of state and local law rather than a question of fact for the jury to decide.

## VI.  SHERIFFS AND CONSTABLES

The sheriff is the law enforcement arm of a county, usually under state law, and therefore a sheriff is considered an official policymaker. A policy of inadequate training of deputies or the ratification of unconstitutional conduct by the sheriff is attributable to the county, and hence liability attaches. Marchese v. Lucas, 758 F.2d 181 (6th Cir. 1985). On the other hand, a constable is not a policymaking official of a county, since he has no control over his selection, training, or performance of duty. Unlike a judge or sheriff, a constable has no choice of objectives and means; hence what a constable does or promulgates cannot be construed as official policy. Rhode v. Denson, 776 F.2d 107 (5th Cir. 1985).

## VII. AGENCY LIABILITY ONLY

There are instances when an officer or a supervisor may not be held liable for damages but the agency or municipality may be. An example would be where police officers act in accordance with agency rules they believe to be constitutional but which the courts later declare to be unconstitutional. For example, an agency policy might authorize indefinite detention of suspects without charges or hearing. Such a policy is violative of a suspect's constitutional rights, but an officer may have no way of knowing that. Since the suspect may in fact suffer a deprivation of rights under the policy, liability will have to be paid by the agency that drafted and promulgated the rule and should have known better. It is therefore important that agency rules and policies be properly reviewed by knowledgeable lawyers to ensure they are valid.

## VIII. IS THE GOOD FAITH DEFENSE AVAILABLE TO AN AGENCY? NO

In Owen v. City of Independence, 445 U.S. 622 (1980), the Supreme Court said that a municipality sued under Section 1983 cannot invoke the good faith defense, which is available to its officers and employees, if its policies are violative of constitutional rights. In that case, a police chief was dismissed by the city manager and the city council for certain misdoings while in office. The police chief was not given any type of hearing or due process, because the city charter under which the city manager and city council acted did not provide him with any rights prior to dismissal. The Court held that the city manager and the members of the city council acted in good faith, because they were authorized by the provisions of the city charter, but that the city itself could not invoke the good faith defense; hence the city could be liable. The justification for this decision was that the plaintiff had suffered injury and that such injury was compensable, but it was unfair to impose liability on the officers, who were merely carrying out agency policy. The agency that drafted the policy and promulgated it must therefore bear the responsibility for the injury and the financial loss. Said the Court,

> The innocent individual who is harmed by an abuse of governmental authority is assured that he will be compensated for his injury. The offending official, so long as he conducts himself in good faith, may go about his business secure in the knowledge that a qualified immunity will protect him from personal liability for damages that are more appropriately chargeable to the populace as a whole. And the public will be forced to bear only the

costs of injury inflicted by the "execution of a government's policy or custom, whether made by its lawmakers or by those whose edicts or acts may
fairly be said to represent official policy." Owen v. City of Independence,
Missouri, 445 U.S. 622 (1980)


## IX. MUST AN AGENCY BE INCLUDED IN A LAWSUIT TO BE LIABLE? NO

The Supreme Court, in 1985, ruled that a money judgment against a public officer "in his official capacity" imposes a liability upon the agency
that employs him regardless of whether the agency was named as a defendant in the suit. As a result of this decision, Section 1983 lawsuits filed
against police executives must now be regarded as actions against the
municipality, even if the municipality is not included expressly as a defendant. Brandon v. Holt, 469 U.S. 464 (1985). In this case, the plaintiff alleged that although the director of the police department had no actual
awareness of the police officer's violent behavior, because of administrative policies he should have known. The Court added that although the
director could be shielded by qualified immunity, the city could be held
liable.

   Also in 1985, the Court said that attorney's fees may only be
awarded against a government employer in a damage action where the
government unit is itself a defendant in the case or where government officials are sued in their official capacities.

   An "official capacity" suit in all respects other than name is to be
treated as a suit against the government entity. Kentucky v. Graham, 473
U.S. 159 (1985). In effect, it is not the official who is being sued but the
agency, and therefore liability lies with the agency if damages are imposed.


## X. IS THERE MUNICIPAL LIABILITY FOR A SINGLE ACT UNDER SECTION 1983? NO, BUT AN EXCEPTION EXISTS

Will local governments be held liable under Section 1983 for failure to
train or supervise based on the single act of misconduct of a police officer? The answer is no, but there is an important exception. Oklahoma
City v. Tuttle, 471 U.S. 808 (1985). In *Tuttle*, action was brought for the
fatal shooting by a police officer of a suspect who had no weapon and did
not threaten the officer. The suspect's survivors sued the police officer
and the city based on negligent failure to train and negligent supervision.
There was sufficient evidence during the trial to support a finding of an

official policy or custom of gross negligence, but such finding was based mainly on the single incident in question. Was this single incident sufficient to hold the agency liable? The Supreme Court gave a qualified answer. Said the Court, "Proof of a single incident of unconstitutional activity is not sufficient to impose liability. . . unless it was caused by an existing unconstitutional municipal policy, which policy can be attributed to a municipal policymaker."

That statement is significant, because it rejects liability based on a single incident but allows an important exception: if the incident was caused by an existing, unconstitutional municipal policy that can be attributed to a municipal policymaker. That exception was used by the Court to impose liability in the case of Pembauer v. City of Cincinnati, 475 U.S. 469 (1986). In *Pembauer*, the county prosecutor made official policy —and thereby exposed his municipal employer to liability—by instructing law enforcement officers to make a forcible entry, without search warrant, of an office in order to serve capiases (a form of warrant issued by the judge) on persons thought to be there. The case was brought by an Ohio physician after law enforcement officers, under advice from the county prosecutor, broke down the door to his office with an ax. The officers were trying to arrest two of the doctor's employees, who failed to appear before a grand jury. The Court decided that this violated the Fourth Amendment rights of the office owners and concluded that the city of Cincinnati could be held liable because the decision by the county prosecutor and the sheriff's forced entry into a doctor's office, even on a single occasion, constituted official policy or custom.

To summarize, a single act creates no municipal liability. What is needed is a persistent pattern of acts that, taken together, constitute a custom. A single act may, however, create municipal liability if the act was caused by an existing unconstitutional municipal policy that can be attributed to a municipal policymaker.

## XI. CAN CITIES BE HELD LIABLE UNDER SECTION 1983 FOR FAILURE TO TRAIN THE POLICE? YES, IF THE FAILURE AMOUNTS TO DELIBERATE INDIFFERENCE

In 1989, after years of uncertainty, the United States Supreme Court finally resolved the issue of whether cities or municipalities can be held liable for not properly training their police officers. In City of Canton v. Harris, the Court said that failure to train can be the basis of liability under Section 1983 for cities or municipalities if such failure to train amounts to deliberate indifference. City of Canton v. Harris, 57 U.S.L.W. 4263 (1989).

In *Harris*, plaintiff Geraldine Harris was arrested by police officers and brought to the police station in a police wagon. Upon arrival at the station, Harris was found sitting on the floor of the wagon. When asked if she needed medical attention, Harris responded with an incoherent remark. While being processed, Mrs. Harris slumped to the floor twice. Eventually she was released and taken by an ambulance, provided by her family, to a nearby hospital, where she was diagnosed as suffering from several emotional ailments. She was hospitalized for one week and later received outpatient treatment for a year. Mrs. Harris brought a Section 1983 suit against the city and its officials, claiming that they violated her constitutional right to due process.

Evidence was presented during the jury trial indicating that, pursuant to a city regulation, shift commanders in the Canton Police Department were authorized to determine, in their sole discretion, whether a detainee required medical care. Testimony was also presented stating that the shift commanders were not provided with any special training (beyond first aid training) that would help them make a determination as to when to ask for medical care for an injured detainee. The district court decided for Mrs. Harris on the medical claim; the Sixth Circuit Court of Appeals affirmed that decision. The case was appealed to the United States Supreme Court.

The Court gave a categorical answer: Yes, failure to train can be the basis of liability under Section 1983. Ruling 9–0, the Court held that cities and municipalities may be held liable for damages if the failure to train is based on "deliberate indifference" to the rights of those with whom the police come into contact. While the nine justices agreed that deliberate indifference should be the standard for liability, they did not define with precision (probably because such terms defy precise definition) what "deliberate indifference" means. The Court came closest to defining that term when it stated that "it may happen that in light of the duties assigned to specific officers or employees the need for more or different training is so obvious, and the inadequacy so likely to result in violation of constitutional rights, that the policymakers of the city can reasonably be said to have been deliberately indifferent to the need."

The Court then set what may be considered as additional requisites for liability based on deliberate indifference:

1.  The focus must be on the adequacy of the training program in relation to the tasks the particular officer must perform.
2.  The fact that a particular officer may be unsatisfactorily trained will not alone result in city liability, because the officer's shortcoming may have resulted from factors other than a faulty training program.
3.  It is not sufficient for liability to prove that an injury or accident could have been avoided if the officer had better or more training.

4. The identified deficiency in a city's training program must be closely related to the ultimate injury.

The *Harris* decision brings good news and bad news to potential plaintiffs. The good news is that for the first time the Supreme Court has ruled that cities and municipalities may be liable for lack of adequate training of the police. The bad news is that most plaintiffs will find it difficult to meet the tough legal standard of deliberate indifference set by the Court as the criterion for liability.

In *Harris*, the city of Canton argued that a municipality can be found liable under Section 1983 only if the policy in question is in itself unconstitutional. Had that argument prevailed, the city would not have been liable, because the Court itself admitted that "there can be little doubt that on its face the city's policy regarding medical treatment for detainees is constitutional." The Court, however, rejected this argument, holding instead that a city may be liable even if the city's policy is constitutional if the lack of training amounts to deliberate indifference. The basis for liability in *Harris* was not the policy itself but the lack of implementation of that policy.

It is also important to note that in *Harris*, the Court concluded that the "evidence in the record does not meet the standard of Section 1983," and it therefore remanded the case to the trial court to afford Mrs. Harris an opportunity to prove her case under the deliberate indifference standard set by the Court.

## SUMMARY

Plaintiffs use the shotgun approach in civil liability cases, meaning that a plaintiff will usually include as defendants any and all who might have anything to do with the alleged violation—including the department and the county or city. Prior to 1978, counties and cities were immune from Section 1983 lawsuits because of sovereign immunity. That immunity was stripped away in the Monell case, although the doctrine of sovereign immunity still applies to states. In state tort cases, sovereign immunity has been waived in most states through legislation or court decisions; hence most states can be sued under state tort law.

The Court held in *Monell* that municipal liability may be imposed for conduct that "implements or executes a policy statement, ordinance, regulation, or decision officially adopted and promulgated by municipal officers." The meaning of "official policy" varies from court to court but is usually taken to include official policy statements or persistent widespread practice that is so common and well settled as to constitute a custom that fairly represents official policy. Unless the United States

Supreme Court gives the final word, the meaning of "official policy" will continue to vary according to jurisdiction.

There are instances when an officer or supervisor may not be held liable for damages but the agency or municipality may be. Such would be the case if an officer acts on the basis of an official policy that is later declared to be unconstitutional. The officer can invoke the good faith defense, but the agency that drafted the policy may be held liable, because the responsibility for the unconstitutional policy lies with the agency. A money judgment against a public officer in his or her official capacity imposes liability upon the agency regardless of whether the agency was named as defendant in the suit.

Local governments will not be held liable for a single act of misconduct of a police officer. The only exception is where the incident was caused by an existing unconstitutional municipal policy that can be attributed to a municipal policymaker. The Supreme Court has also decided that cities and municipalities may be liable under Section 1983 if failure to train amounts to deliberate indifference.


## CASE BRIEFS

### CITY OF CANTON v. HARRIS
### 57 U.S.L.W. 4283 (1989)


#### FACTS

Geraldine Harris was arrested by police officers in Canton, Ohio, and brought to the police station in a police wagon. Upon arrival at the station, Harris was found sitting on the floor of the wagon. When asked if she needed medical attention, she responded with an incoherent remark. She slumped to the floor twice at the station while being processed. Eventually the police left Mrs. Harris lying on the floor to prevent her from falling again. Later Harris was released and taken by an ambulance to a nearby hospital, where she was diagnosed as suffering from several emotional ailments. She was hospitalized for one week and subsequently received outpatient treatment for one year. Mrs. Harris brought a Section 1983 suit against the city and its officials, claiming a violation of her constitutional right to due process.

During the jury trial, evidence was presented indicating that, pursuant to a city regulation, shift commanders in the Canton Police Department were authorized to determine, in their sole discretion, whether a detainee required medical care. In addition, testimony also stated that the shift commanders were not provided with any special training (beyond first-aid training) that would help them make a determination as to when to ask for medical care for an injured detainee. The district court decided for Mrs. Harris on the medical claim; the Court of Appeals for the Sixth Circuit affirmed the medical liability part of the district court decision. The case was appealed to the United States Supreme Court.

### ISSUE

Can a city or municipality ever be held liable under Section 1983 for constitutional violations resulting from its failure to train municipal employees? Yes.

### SUPREME COURT DECISION

Failure to train can be the basis of liability under Section 1983 for cities or municipalities if such failure to train amounts to deliberate indifference toward those with whom the police come into contact.

### CASE SIGNIFICANCE

This case settles an issue that the courts have been dealing with for a long time—whether or not a city or municipality can be held liable under Section 1983 for negligent failure to train. The Court has answered that question in the affirmative, but only under limited circumstances—when the failure to train amounts to deliberate indifference. What "deliberate indifference" means has not been defined with precision by the Court in this case or in other cases. Ultimately the meaning is determined by the courts on a case-by-case basis. In this particular case, the Court concluded that "the evidence in the record does not meet the standard of Section 1983," but the Court remanded the case to the trial court to afford Mrs. Harris an opportunity to prove her case under the deliberate indifference standard.

The closest that the Court came in this case to defining what "deliberate indifference" means is when it said that "it may happen that in light of the duties assigned to specific officers or employees the need for more or different training is so obvious, and the inadequacy so likely to result in the violation of constitutional rights, that the policymakers of the city can reasonably be said to have been deliberately indifferent to the need." It added that in resolving the issue of city liability, "the focus must be on adequacy of the training program in relation to the tasks the particular officers must perform." The fact that a particular officer may be unsatisfactorily trained will not alone result in city liability, because the officer's shortcomings may have resulted from factors other than a faulty training program. Neither is it sufficient for liability to prove that an injury or accident "could have been avoided if an officer had had better or more training, sufficient to equip him to avoid the particular injury-causing conduct." Finally, the identified deficiency in a city's training program must be closely related to the ultimate injury for the city to be liable.

In sum, a city or municipality may now be held liable for negligent failure to train but only if such failure amounts to deliberate indifference.

## GRANDSTAFF ET AL. v. CITY OF BORGER, TEXAS, ET AL.
### 767 F.2d 161 (1985)

### FACTS

The city of Borger police mistook James Grandstaff for a fugitive and killed him. Grandstaff in attempting to assist the police, was fired upon from two sides and was killed by a shot to the back from a high-powered rifle. No punitive actions were taken by the police chief subsequent to the incident. The plaintiffs sued the officers and the city, seeking damages under Section 1983 and state tort. They claimed that the officers were malicious and reckless in their use of deadly force, that the City was grossly negligent in failing to properly train its officers, and that there was a custom of abuse throughout the police force. The district court awarded $1,420,000, together with attorney's fees and expenses, to the estate and family of Grandstaff from four of the police officers and the city. The defendants appealed.

### ISSUE

May police officers, police chiefs, and cities be held liable for the police use of deadly force? Yes.

### COURT OF APPEALS DECISION

The court of appeals held (1) that the officers were liable under Texas law and under Section 1983 for the death of Grandstaff, which was caused by police use of deadly force; (2) that the city enjoyed governmental immunity from state tort claim for wrongful death; (3) that the city was liable under Section 1983 for a policy attributable to the city police chief that caused the victim's death.

### CASE SIGNIFICANCE

The court in this case held that the city was liable for what the officers did because of a policy by the city's policymaker that caused the plaintiff to be subjected to the deprivation of constitutional rights. The police chief was considered a policymaker, and hence his policies were considered policies of the city. The court also said that where the police officers know at the time they act that their use of deadly force in conscious disregard of the rights and safety of others will meet with the approval of the city policymakers, then a link is established between the injury caused and the adoption of the policy. In this case, the court also set a standard for the type of negligence that creates liability by stating "that officers consciously disregarded substantial risk to innocent persons and that their use of deadly force was maliciously, wantonly, or oppressively done, so that the officers deprived victim of life without due process of law."

## OWEN v. CITY OF INDEPENDENCE, MO.
### 445 U.S. 622 (1980)

### FACTS

The City Council of Independence, Missouri, decided that reports of an investigation of the police department be released to the news media and turned over to the prosecutor for presentation to the grand jury and that the city manager take appropriate action against the persons involved in the wrongful activities. Acting on this, the city manager dismissed the chief of police. No reason was given for the dismissal. The chief of police received only a written notice stating that the dismissal was made in accordance with a specified provision of the city charter. The chief of police filed a Section 1983 lawsuit against the city manager and members of the city council, alleging that he was discharged without notice of reasons and without a hearing and thereby in violation of his constitutional rights to procedural and substantive due process. The district court decided for the city manager and council members.

### ISSUE

Are municipalities and municipal officials entitled to the good faith defense if a right is violated while the officials are following the provisions of a city policy or custom? No.

### SUPREME COURT DECISION

A municipality has no immunity from liability under Section 1983 flowing from violations of an individual's constitutional rights and may not assert the good faith defense that is available to its officers.

### CASE SIGNIFICANCE

Owen makes clear that the municipality may be liable if a person's constitutional rights are violated (in this case, the right to due process prior to dismissal) by public officials who are acting in accordance with agency policy as contained in the city charter. Because they were acting in accordance with the provisions of the city charter, the city manager and members of the city counsel enjoyed a good faith defense, but the city did not. The implication is that municipalities must make sure that their policies do not violate individual rights. The fact that something is official policy does not mean that it is automatically valid. The Court said that individual blameworthiness is no longer the acid test of liability, substituting in its place the principle of "equitable loss-spreading," in addition to fault, as a fact in distributing the costs of official misconduct.

# 14

# LIABILITIES OF
# POLICE SUPERVISORS
# FOR WHAT SUBORDINATES DO

## INTRODUCTION

This chapter defines the term *supervisor* as *any public officer who has another person working under him or her and for whose performance the officer has supervisory responsibility.* This definition is broad and includes police sergeants, lieutenants, captains, police chiefs, sheriffs, and commission members, not just the heads of offices and agencies.

Civil lawsuits against police officers used to be filed only against the officers themselves. That has changed. The current tendency among plaintiffs is to sue the officer and anybody else who allegedly had anything to do with the act, such as the immediate supervisor, the police chief, the agency, and the members of the city council. This strategy is based on the "deep pockets" theory: While the officer may have a "shallow pocket" (his or her resources are limited), the supervisor and department have a "deep pocket" (the supervisor or police chief is paid better and the government unit can always impose taxes to raise revenue).

EXAMPLE: A police officer, while on patrol, shoots and kills a suspect. The victim's family will sue under federal civil rights and/or state tort law and include as defendants the following: the officer, the immediate supervisor, the police chief, and the city. The allegation could be that the officer is liable because he or she pulled the trigger; the supervisor or police chief is liable because of a failure to properly train, direct, supervise, or assign; and the city or agency is liable because of a custom or policy

---

This chapter is an updated and revised version of the article "Legal Liabilities and Responsibilities of Corrections Agency Supervisors," by R. V. del Carmen, *Federal Probation*, September 1984, at 52.

that contributed to the act. If some defendants are not at fault, the court will determine that during the trial based on the evidence presented. In other words, the plaintiff will include anyone and everyone who may have had something to do with the violation and let the judge or jury sort things out.

## I. REASONS FOR INCLUDING SUPERVISORS IN A LAWSUIT

There are advantages to including supervisors and departments in a liability lawsuit. First, lower-level officers may not have the financial resources to satisfy a judgment, nor are they in a position to prevent similar future violations by other officers. Second, the chances of financial recovery are enhanced if supervisory personnel are included in the lawsuit. The higher the position of the employee, the closer the plaintiff gets to the deep pockets of the county or state agency. Third, inclusion of the supervisor and agency may create inconsistencies in the legal strategy of the defense, thereby strengthening plaintiff's claim against one or more of the defendants.

EXAMPLE: P, an officer, is sued for the wrongful death of a suspect. The lawsuit includes P's immediate supervisor, the police chief, and the city. P's act may have been so outrageous that the supervisor and the city do not want to defend or align with him, hence depriving P of agency resources and creating a perception of fault on his part.

If a supervisor leaves the job, will the lawsuit continue? This has not been answered by the United States Supreme Court, but the Ninth Circuit Court of Appeals has said that in an action against police officials for promulgating a policy that allegedly gave rise to the use of excessive force during an arrest, it was improper to dismiss from the action those officials who had since left their positions and to substitute new employees. The proper individual defendants are those who were in office before or at the time of the incident and who may have adopted a plan or policy authorizing or approving the alleged unconstitutional conduct. Heller v. Bushey, 759 F.2d 1371 (9th Cir. 1985). Therefore, a supervisor who leaves the job may still be liable and is in fact the proper person to be held liable, not his or her successor.

A supervisor may be sued in his or her individual capacity. When a supervisor is sued in an individual capacity, the plaintiff implies that only the supervisor, not the agency, is responsible for what happened. Most plaintiffs prefer to sue the supervisor in his or her official capacity because of the deep pockets theory. In general, a supervisor cannot be held personally liable if the violation was not random or unauthorized but rather resulted from agency or state policy. James v. Smith, 784 F.2d 149

(2d Cir. 1986). If a supervisor is held liable in an official capacity, liability is generally paid by the agency. Conversely, if the agency was not at all at fault or in any way involved in what a supervisor did, then liability belongs to the supervisor alone.

## II. RESPONDEAT SUPERIOR DOES NOT APPLY TO PUBLIC EMPLOYMENT

Supervisors in the private sector are often sued based on the legal theory of *respondeat superior*, which literally means "let the master answer." Under this doctrine, the master is responsible for lack of care by the servant toward those to whom the master owes a duty to use care. Liability attaches if the failure of the servant to use such care occurred in the course of employment. This common-law doctrine does not, however, apply to public employment, because public officials, police supervisors, for example, are not the "masters" of their subordinates; instead they are employees who, like their subordinates, serve a common master: the government agency.

Although the respondeat superior doctrine does not apply to public employment, it does apply to sheriffs. This is because, under traditional practice and common law, deputies serve at the discretion of the sheriff and therefore act in the sheriff's name and on his or her behalf. The only exception is when state law modifies this traditional relationship.[1] In some states, such as Mississippi, state law specifically provides for the liability of sheriffs for acts of their deputies. In most countries or local governments, sheriffs are elected directly by the public and are answerable directly to the voters rather than to a council, a board, or an elected official. This is not the case with police chiefs, who obtain their position by appointment.

## III. STATE OFFICERS CANNOT BE SUED IN THEIR OFFICIAL CAPACITY UNDER SECTION 1983: THE WILL v. MICHIGAN CASE

In a 1989 case, the Supreme Court said that "neither a state nor its officials acting in their official capacities are persons under 42 U.S.C. 1983 and therefore cannot be sued for damages for depriving a citizen of constitutional or statutory rights while acting under color of law." Will v. Michigan, 45 Crl 3087 (1989). In that case, a law enforcement officer filed a Section 1983 suit in Michigan, alleging that the Department of State Police and the Director of State Police, acting in his official capacity, denied the officer promotion for an improper reason. The Court said, based on the statute's language, congressional purpose, and legislative history, that "a State is not a person under Section 1983." Inasmuch as a state, because of its immunity under the Eleventh Amendment, cannot be sued, a suit against state officials in their official capacities will not succeed, because the suit is in fact a suit against the state itself. *Will* is important because, although it had long been decided that state officials, as a result of state immunity under the Eleventh Amendment, could not be sued in federal court in their official capacity under Section 1983, it is the first case wherein the Court said that such immunity extends to Section 1983 lawsuits filed in state courts.

The one exception to the *Will* rule is where state immunity has been waived, in which case a lawsuit can then proceed against the state or a state official. Such waiver may be by state law or court decision.

## IV. LIABILITY TO THE PUBLIC FOR WHAT SUBORDINATES DO

A supervisor is liable to the public for what he or she does if the supervisor

1. authorized the act, as when a police chief authorizes the arrest of a suspect without probable cause and without a warrant

2. participated in the act, as when a police chief takes part in the illegal arrest of a suspect

3. directed the act, as when a police chief directs his officers to search an apartment without probable cause and without warrant

4. ratified the act, as when a police chief later learns of an illegal act committed by a subordinate and approves of it

5. was present at the time the act was committed and could have prevented it but failed to do so, as when a police chief fails to stop the beating up of a suspect in his or her presence

In one recent case, the Second Circuit Court of Appeals ennumerated several ways in which a supervisor may be personally involved in the violation of a constitutional right and thus liable under Section 1983:

1. The supervisor directly participated in the infraction.

2. The supervisor, after learning of the violation through a report or appeal, failed to remedy the wrong.

3. The supervisor created a policy or custom under which unconstitutional practices occurred or allowed such a policy or custom to continue.

4. The supervisor was grossly negligent in managing the subordinates who caused the unlawful condition or event.

In general, supervisors may be liable in Section 1983 cases only if there is an "affirmative link" between the plaintiff's injury and the action or inaction of the supervisor. For instance, a supervisor may be liable for negligent failure to train if there is an affirmative link between the injury caused by the subordinate and the lack of training.

EXAMPLE: X, an innocent bystander, is seriously wounded because of the negligent shooting by the police of a crime suspect. X can possibly recover damages if it is proved that had the officer been properly trained, X's injury would not have been inflicted.

Supervisory liability stemming from negligence is one of the most frequently litigated areas of liability and therefore merits extended discussion. Negligence, for purposes of tort liability, may be simple or gross. *Simple negligence* generally means an absence of that degree of care and vigilance that persons of extraordinary prudence and foresight are accustomed to use. Stated differently, simple negligence is failure to exercise great care. In contrast, *gross negligence* means failure to exercise ordinary care or that care which a careless person would use under the circumstances. For example, driving 60 miles an hour on a 55-mile-an-hour highway may be simple negligence, but driving 100 miles an hour may come under the category of gross negligence. Most courts require at least gross negligence or deliberate indifference to establish supervisory liability.[2] The problem, however, is that the difference between simple negligence and gross negligence is one of degree and is not always easy to ascertain. What is simple negligence to one judge or jury might be gross negligence to another.

Current case law indicates there are seven general areas from which supervisory liability based on negligence may arise:

1. negligent failure to train
2. negligent hiring
3. negligent assignment
4. negligent failure to supervise
5. negligent failure to direct
6. negligent entrustment
7. negligent failure to investigate or discipline

These areas of supervisory liability are not mutually exclusive, meaning that they overlap. In fact, plaintiffs often allege two or more areas in the same complaint and leave it to the court or jury to determine the grounds for liability. For example, it is not unusual for a plaintiff who files a case based on police use of deadly force to allege that the supervisor should also be held liable for negligent failure to train, supervise, direct, hire, or entrust. In many cases, plaintiffs allege negligence in all seven areas in the hope that some, if not all, can be proved by the facts presented during the trial.

As stated in Chapter 2, civil liability cases may be brought under state tort law and/or Section 1983. It is clear that a lawsuit for supervisory negligence may be brought under state tort law, negligence being a category of state tort. Controversy, however, surrounds the issue of whether supervisory liability for negligence can be brought under Section 1983. Some lower courts say that liability exists, others say it does not. In a recent case, the United States Supreme Court said that inadequate police training may serve as the basis for municipal liability under Section 1983 but only if the failure to train amounts to deliberate indifference to the rights of persons with whom the police come in contact and the deficiency in the training program is closely related to the injury suffered. City of Canton v. Harris, 57 U.S.L.W. 4270 (1989). It is not clear from that decision, however, whether the term "deliberate indifference" used by the Court to impose liability refers to a form of negligence or to an act of commission.

## A. NEGLIGENT FAILURE TO TRAIN

Negligent failure to train has generated a spate of lawsuits under state tort law and Section 1983. As early as 1955, a state court entertained a tort action for monetary damages resulting from improper or negligent training. Meistinsky v. City of New York, 140 N.Y.S. 2d 212 (1955). The usual allegation in these cases is that the employee has not been instructed or trained properly by the supervisor or agency and thus lacks the skills, knowledge, or competence required of him or her in the job. The rule is that the administrative agency and the supervisor share a duty to train employees and that failure to discharge this obligation subjects the supervisor and agency to liability if it can be proved that the violation at issue was the result of failure to train or improper training. Owens v. Haas, 601 F.2d 1242 (2nd Cir. 1979).

In McAndrew v. Mularchuk, 162 A.2d 820 (N.J. 1960), an officer wounded a minor while firing a shot to scare him. The court held that liability on the part of the agency could arise because it negligently armed the officer with a service revolver without adequately training him as to its use. The court added that because firearms are dangerous and create risk to the safety of others, officers must be trained properly so as to minimize that risk. In a 1986 case, the court said that a claim that police officers were inadequately trained to verify information supplied by informants could lead to liability if gross negligence was alleged and proved. Bergquist v. County of Cochise, 806 F.2d 1364 (9th Cir. 1986). And in Leslie v. Ingraham, 786 F.2d 1533 (11th Cir. 1986), the court said that a claim that a sheriff failed to train officers in arrest procedure and property seizure could lead to liability.

In Rymer v. Davis, 754 F.2d 198 (6th Cir. 1985), the Sixth Circuit

Court of Appeals upheld a judgment of $82,000 against the police officer and $25,000 against the city for deprivation of rights arising from injuries sustained during an arrest. In this case, the police officer beat and kicked the plaintiff violently during the arrest. The arrestee was treated by an emergency medical technician, who recommended that he be taken to a hospital. The officer rejected this recommendation and instead jailed the arrestee for the night. Liability was imposed on the city because the court found the following at the time of the incident:

> [T]he City has no rules or regulations governing its police force. Nor did the City require any pre-employment training. The initial training received by the officers was on-the-job training. Although the City required the officers to complete forty hours of training each year after being hired, none of the training received by Officer Stillwell instructed him on arrest procedures or treatment of injured persons. The City's police officers used their own discretion in the arrest and treatment of persons suspected of criminal activity.

The decision is significant because it suggests the following courses of action police departments must take: (1) A preemployment training program must be in place, and (2) the training program must focus on the skills needed in policing, including arrest procedures and the treatment of injured persons.

On the other hand, not every allegation of failure to train leads to liability. For example, in Hinshaw v. Doffer, 785 F.2d 1260 (5th Cir. 1986), a police chief was exonerated from liability for failure to train or for imputed knowledge of a pattern of false arrests and use of excessive force where the following factors were present: (1) There had been scattered incidents involving dog killings by the police, (2) there had been no complaints in twenty-six years, and (3) 320 hours of officer training were required by the department, including instructions on the use of force. No liability was imposed despite three previous incidents that involved the subordinate officer. In the same case, the Fifth Circuit Court of Appeals laid out the general requirements for supervisory liability in failure-to-train-or-supervise cases as follows:

1. The police chief failed to train or supervise the officer.

2. A causal connection existed between the failure to train or supervise and the violation of plaintiff's rights.

3. The failure to train or supervise amounted to gross negligence or deliberate indifference.

In City of Canton v. Harris, 57 U.S.L.W. 4263 (1989), the United States Supreme Court held that failure to train can be held the basis of municipal liability under Section 1983. The Court held that cities and municipalities may be held liable for damages if the failure to train is based on deliberate indifference to the rights of those with whom the police come into contact. The Court then said that "it may happen that in light of the duties assigned to specific officers or employees the need for more or different training is so obvious, and the inadequacy so likely to result in violation of constitutional rights, that the policymakers of the city can reasonably be said to have been deliberately indifferent to the need." It would seem to follow that if a municipality can be held liable for failure to train based on deliberate indifference, supervisors could also likely be held liable based on the same standard.

The question supervisors often ask is, Will a single act by a subordinate suffice to make the supervisor liable for failure to train? Although there is no unanimity, most lower court cases hold that a pattern must be proved and established for liability to ensue. A single act, therefore, usually does not suffice. The exception is if the act is the result of an agency policy or custom.

Lawsuits against supervisors and agencies for failure to train come from two sources:

1. persons whose rights have been violated by officers who have not been properly trained

2. subordinates who suffer injury in the course of duty because they have not been trained properly

In one case, a police officer in West Linn, Oregon, reportedly sued the city and the police chief for over $1.2 million, alleging the absence in the department of training programs and a failure to provide psychological counseling dealing with stress. The officer had shot and wounded a robbery suspect he thought was reaching under his coat for a gun (a gun was later found on the floor of the suspect's car). The shooting was reportedly the first incident of its kind in more than twelve years. After the shooting, the officer took a leave of absence and brought the lawsuit.[3]

Training may in fact be deficient due to circumstances beyond a supervisor's control, such as lack of funds and expertise. May the supervisor be liable if no resources have been allocated to provide the desired level of training? The answer is yes, but the supervisor may be able to establish good faith. In Anderson v. City of Atlanta, 778 F.2d 678 (11th Cir. 1985), the court said that chronic understaffing, even if the cause was lack of funding, was actionable if the policy led to the prisoner's death due to inadequate medical care. Budgetary constraints generally have not been considered a valid defense by the courts, which can place a supervisor in a difficult position. With proper documentation, however, the supervisor should be able to establish good faith if he or she repeatedly calls the attention of those who hold the purse strings to the need for training.

Even if financial resources are available, unstructured training alone may not be sufficient. The nature, scope, and quality of the training program must be properly documented and its relevance to job performance identified. There is a need to document training sessions with detailed outlines to substantiate the course content. Attendance sheets are necessary for defense purposes in lawsuits brought by one's own subordinates.

To summarize, negligent failure to train has resulted in judgments against supervisors and is perhaps currently the most frequently litigated area in the field of supervisory liability. Supervisors must be aware of the need for proper training. Furthermore, this need must be brought to the attention of policymakers who may also be liable for damages if injury results.

Based on court decisions, one risk management manual suggests the following training program guidelines, which agencies will be well advised to follow:[4]

1.  The training should be job-relevant and based on a validated "task analysis" of the position.

2.  The instructors must be properly qualified.

3.  Records should be made so that it can be proved that the training took place and that it was properly conducted.

4.  The training curriculum must be correct and up to date.

5.  Actual learning should be measured and documented and follow-up training or supervisory actions should be taken if necessary.

## B. NEGLIGENT HIRING

The risk of negligent hiring liability increases the importance of proper background investigation prior to employment. Liability ensues when (1) an employee is unfit for appointment, (2) such unfitness was known to the employer or should have been known through a background investigation, and (3) the employee's act was foreseeable. In Moon v. Winfield, 383 F. Supp. 31 (N.D. Ill. 1974), the department hired a police officer despite a record of preemployment assault conviction, a negative recommendation from a previous employer, and a falsified police application. The officer later assaulted a number of individuals in separate incidents. He and the supervisor were sued and held liable. In Peters v. Bellinger, 159 N.E. 2d 528 (Ill. App. 1959), the court held a city liable for the actions of a police officer who was hired despite a felony record and who appeared to have been involved in many street brawls. Liability was based on the complete failure of the agency to conduct a background check prior to the hiring of the applicant.

A case recently decided by the Fifth Circuit sheds light on some aspects of liability for negligent hiring. Wassum v. City of Bellaire, 861 F.2d 453 (5th Cir. 1988). In Wassum, a city police officer who was raped by a fellow police officer brought a civil rights action against the officer, the police chief, and the mayor. Carol Wassum was working as a police dispatcher in the Bellaire Police Department. She began work at 7:00 A.M. and her shift was to end at 3:00 P.M. At about 2:30 P.M., Wassum allowed Officer John Casey to enter the dispatcher's office. Casey was not on duty but was scheduled to go on duty with the next shift. After entering the office, Casey sexually assaulted Wassum.

Casey had been hired by the department in 1981. Before hiring him, the department interviewed supervisors at two Houston-area police departments where Casey had worked from 1978 to 1981. Casey's application showed that he had been self-employed as a California private investigator from 1975 to 1978. The department did not verify this information, but it did do the following:

1. It conducted state and National Crime Information Center (NCIC) computer searches, which showed Casey had no criminal record.

2. It submitted Casey's fingerprints to state authorities and the FBI for criminal background checks.

3. It sent confidential questionnaires to all persons listed as references.

4. It did NCIC checks on all of Casey's references.

5. It interviewed Casey's former wife.

6. It conducted a financial check.

7. It confirmed Casey's educational background.

8. It required Casey to be certified as emotionally and psychologically fit by a licensed physician.

Wassum alleged that the department did not verify Casey's employment before 1978. If such a check had been made, it would have revealed that in 1975 Casey was detained in California for indecent exposure and that he resigned from the Costa Mesa Police Department, where he refused to submit to a polygraph test about the incident. Wassum charged that the hiring practices of the Bellaire Police Department were deficient for three reasons:

1. The department failed to verify Casey's employment background before 1978, as required by state of Texas guidelines.

2. It failed to conduct a polygraph examination of Casey prior to hiring him.

3. It failed to have Casey undergo a more extensive psychological or psychiatric examination.

The district court held Casey liable in the amount of $1 million in actual damages and $3 million in punitive damages, but the city, the mayor, and the police chief were not held liable. The court conceded that these officials were arguably negligent in their preemployment screening of Casey but concluded that they did not act with *gross negligence or deliberate indifference,* the standard of culpability needed for liability in negligent hiring cases. The failure of the city to administer a polygraph test to screen the applicant was held not to constitute gross negligence. The court said, "While polygraph tests are used with greater frequency today, there is still some question of their efficacy. Some states have prohibited the practice of requiring submission to a polygraph test as a precondition of employment."

On appeal, the Fifth Circuit affirmed the decision of the district court. Regarding the agency's failure to verify Casey's employment record back to age sixteen, as suggested by the Texas Commission on Law Enforcement Officer Standards and Education guidelines, the court concluded that such failure amounted to no more than simple negligence, adding that "failure to follow this recommended screening guideline does not render the city consciously indifferent to the safety of its citizens."

*Wassum* reiterates a principle enunciated by the Fifth Circuit in an earlier case also decided in 1988. Stokes v. Bullins, F.2d 269 (5th Cir. 1988). In *Bullins,* the plaintiff was shot by a police officer. The plaintiff subsequently sought damages against the town, alleging that it failed to establish adequate hiring practices for its officers. The town hired the officer knowing that he had been arrested a few times in nearby towns for various minor offenses. The background investigation of the officer was cursory. The hiring officer did not use the NCIC computer to look into the background of the applicant. An NCIC computer search would have revealed that the officer had been arrested fifteen times for offenses ranging from simple assault to armed robbery.

The trial court concluded that the town's failure to conduct a more complete investigation of Officer Bullins's background constituted gross negligence and conscious indifference to the public welfare. The Fifth Circuit disagreed and held that the evidence failed to establish deliberate indifference or gross negligence. The Fifth Circuit's standard for gross negligence in Section 1983 cases was expressed by the court this way: "We would require a plaintiff to establish actual knowledge of the seriously deficient character of an applicant or a persistent, widespread pattern of hiring of policemen, for instance, with a background of unjustified violence." In both *Wassum* and *Bullins,* the Fifth Circuit found that the hiring practices and procedures in the agencies did not constitute gross negligence, and therefore no liability was imposed on the supervisors or the agencies.

Despite the Fifth Circuit's rather favorable decisions (for supervisors and agencies) in *Wassum* and *Bullins,* good background investigations are a must for protection against lawsuits in negligent hiring cases. Such investigations can be undertaken in a number of ways, depending on agency resources. Regardless of the method used, background investigations must follow adequate procedures whereby unfit applicants may be identified and rejected.

## C. NEGLIGENT ASSIGNMENT

Negligent assignment is the assigning of an employee to a job without ascertaining employee competence or the keeping of an employee on a job after he or she is known to be unfit. An example would be assigning a reckless driver to drive a government motor vehicle or assigning an officer who has had a history of child molestation to run a weekend camping program for juveniles. The rule is that a supervisor has an affirmative duty not to assign a subordinate to a position for which he or she is unfit or to leave a subordinate in such a position.

In Moon v. Winfield, 393 F. Supp. 31 (N.D. Ill. 1974), a case also discussed above under negligent hiring, liability was imposed on the police superintendent for failure to suspend or transfer an errant police officer to a nonsensitive assignment after numerous disciplinary reports had been brought to the supervisor's attention. In *Moon*, the superintendent had five separate misconduct reports before him within a two-week period and also a warning that the officer had been involved in a series of acts indicating mental instability. The court held that supervisory liability ensued because the supervisor had authority to assign or suspend the officer but failed to do so. *Moon* is also a good example of a case where the plaintiffs allege several areas of supervisory negligence in their lawsuit.

Negligent assignment cases collectively say that supervisors must be aware of the weaknesses and competencies of their subordinates and must not assign them to perform tasks for which they lack skill or competence.

## D. NEGLIGENT FAILURE TO SUPERVISE

Negligent failure to supervise is the abdication of the responsibility to properly oversee employee activity. An example would be tolerating a pattern of physical abuse of suspects, racial discrimination, or pervasive deprivation of suspects' rights and privileges. In Lenard v. Argento, 699 F.2d 874 (7th Cir. 1983), the Seventh Circuit held that, at a minimum, a plaintiff must show that the supervisory official at least implicitly authorized, approved, or knowingly acquiesced in the unconstitutional conduct of the offending officers. The mere fact that the supervisor, long before attaining his position, had heard rumors that the subordinate officer had shot and injured another person while on duty was not sufficient, according to the court, to establish liability on the part of the supervisor. Chestnut v. City of Quincy, 513 F.2d 91 (5th Cir. 1975).

Tolerating unlawful activities in an agency might constitute deliberate indifference, to which liability attaches. The essential question is, Did the supervisor know of a pattern of behavior but fail to act on it? Also, in Section 1983 cases, failure to supervise leads to liability only if there is a history of widespread abuse. Brown v. Watkins, 669 F.2d 979 (5th Cir. 1982)

A related question is, What constitutes knowledge of a pattern of behavior? Some courts hold that actual knowledge is required, which may be difficult for the plaintiff to prove; others have ruled that knowledge is present if a history of violation is established and the official had direct and close supervisory control over the subordinates who committed the violations.

In one case, the Eleventh Circuit Court of Appeals decided that a supervisor can be held liable for the use of excessive force by a police officer "when a history of widespread abuse puts the responsible supervisor on notice of the need for improved training or supervision, and the official fails to take corrective action." In that case, the plaintiff alleged that the city's public safety director, who was responsible for disciplining police officers and setting departmental policy, was aware of a pattern of police use of excessive force but failed to correct the problem. Such failure resulted in the use of excessive force by a police officer against the plaintiff. Fundiller v. City of Cooper, 777 F.2d 1436 (11th Cir. 1985).

In another case, a court said, "A police chief who persistently fails to discipline or control subordinates in the face of knowledge of their propensity for improper use of force thereby creates an official custom or de facto policy actionable under Section 1983." Skevofilax v. Quigley, 586 F. Supp. 532 (D.N.J. 1984).

In Marusa v. District of Columbia, 484 F. 2d 828 (D.C. Cir. 1973), the allegations were that the defendant chief of police failed to adequately supervise an off-duty officer who shot the plaintiff. In Thomas v. Johnson, 295 F. Supp. 1025 (D.D.C. 1968), the police chief allegedly also failed to supervise an officer against whom numerous complaints had been filed, resulting in an assault, a battery, negligence, and a violation of the plaintiff's civil rights. In both cases, the courts noted possible liability for negligent failure to supervise. And in Cortes Quinones Jimenez v. Nettleship, 773 F.2d 10 (1st Cir. 1985), the court decided that overcrowding and the lack of prison guards permitted the jail to be run by gangs and that the facility had a long history of violence. The court held that some supervisors, because of lack of authority over conditions, good faith attempts to remedy the situation, or insufficient time of service to become acquainted with jail conditions, were not liable for the prisoner's death, but it also said that other supervisors could be liable.

In another case, the failure of a supervisor to act properly after an incident had taken place led to liability. Grandstaff v. City of Borger, 767 F.2d 161 (5th Cir. 1985). In Grandstaff, the police chief failed to make departmental changes or to reprimand or fire the officers involved in the shooting of an innocent man during the apprehension of a suspect. The officers opened fire on a pickup truck driven by a man who had entered the area to offer assistance after seeing police activity near his house one dark and rainy morning. The court concluded that the behavior of the police chief constituted "dangerous recklessness," saying,

> The disposition of the policymaker may be inferred from his conduct after the events of that night. Following this incompetent and catastrophic performance, there were no reprimands, no discharges, and no admissions of error. . . . If what the officers did and failed to do on August 11, 1981, was not acceptable to the police chief, changes would have been made.

Liability was imposed on the police chief because what he failed to do in effect constituted a ratification of what his employees had done.

The current law on liability for negligent failure to supervise is best summarized as follows:

> To be liable for a pattern of constitutional violations, the supervisor must have known of the pattern and failed to correct or end it. . . . Courts hold that a supervisor must be "causally linked" to the pattern by showing that he had knowledge of it and that his failure to act amounted to approval and hence tacit encouragement that the pattern continue.[5]

Another writer notes, "The importance of this principle is that supervisors cannot shut their eyes and avoid responsibility for the acts of their associates if they are in a position to take remedial action and do nothing."[6]

### E. NEGLIGENT FAILURE TO DIRECT

Negligent failure to direct is the failure to inform employees of the specific requirements and proper limits of the job to be performed. An example would be the failure on the part of a supervisor to inform an officer of the proper limits of the use of deadly force or the allowable scope of searches after arrest. In Ford v. Breier, 383 F. Supp. 505 (E.D. Wis. 1974), the court held that the supervisor's failure to establish policies and guidelines concerning the procurement of search warrants and the execution of various departmental operations made him vicariously liable for the accidental shooting death of a young girl by a police officer. In another case, Dewell v. Lawson, 489 F.2d 877 (10th Cir. 1974), the failure to direct consisted in the chief's negligence in establishing procedures for the diabetic diagnosis and treatment of jail inmates. The suspect, detained for public drunkenness, experienced a diabetic reaction that resulted in a diabetic coma, a stroke, and brain damage. The jailer did not recognize this condition and therefore failed to provide for proper medical care; the result was death. Liability was assessed for negligent failure to direct.

A good defense against charges of negligent failure to direct is a written manual of policies and procedures for departmental operations. A good manual must:

1. be accurate, be legally updated, and form the basis for agency operations in theory and practice

2. cover all the necessary and important aspects of the job an employee is to undertake

As part of the orientation to the agency, the employees must be required to read and be familiar with the manual. A signed statement by an employee to the effect that he or she has read and understood the manual may later exempt a supervisor from liability based on negligent failure to direct. Moreover, giving a written examination based on the manual strengthens the claim against liability and gives a new officer added incentive to know the provisions thoroughly.

### F. NEGLIGENT ENTRUSTMENT

Negligent entrustment is the failure of a supervisor to properly supervise or control an employee's custody, use, or supervision of equipment or facilities entrusted to him or her on the job. An example would be the failure to supervise the use of vehicles and firearms resulting in death or serious injury to a member of the public. Negligent entrustment differs from negligent assignment in that it concerns, not overall employee competence, but instead competence in the handling of hardware, equipment, or facilities, such as a gun or a motor vehicle.

In Roberts v. Williams, 356 F.2d 819 (5th Cir. 1971), an untrained but trustworthy guard was given a shotgun and the task of guarding a work crew by a convict farm superintendent. The shotgun discharged accidentally, seriously wounding an inmate. The court held the warden liable based on his negligence in permitting an untrained person to use a dangerous weapon.

In McAndrews v. Mularchuck, 162 A. 2d 820 (N.J. 1960), a periodically employed reserve patrol officer was entrusted with a firearm without adequate training. He fired a warning shot that killed a boisterous youth who was not armed. The city was held liable in a wrongful death suit. Courts have also held that supervisors have a duty to supervise errant off-duty officers where the officers had property, guns, or nightsticks belonging to a government agency.

The test of liability for negligent entrustment is deliberate indifference. The plaintiff must be able to prove that the officer was incompetent, inexperienced, or reckless and that the supervisor knew or had reason to know of the officer's incompetence. The supervisor's best defense in these cases is to show that there had been proper supervision and training concerning use and custody of equipment and that the act occurred despite adequate precautions.

## G. NEGLIGENT FAILURE TO INVESTIGATE OR DISCIPLINE

Negligent failure to investigate or discipline is the failure on the part of the supervisor to look into complaints and take proper action when needed. In one case, the court said that when it can be shown that supervisors are aware of the dangerous tendencies of an officer but do nothing to correct the problem, the supervisors retain that officer in that job at their own risk. Sims v. Adams, 537 F.2d 829 (5th Cir. 1976).

The rule is that *a supervisor has an affirmative duty to take all the necessary and proper steps to discipline and/or terminate a subordinate who is obviously unfit for service.* Unfitness can be determined either from acts of prior gross misconduct or from a series of prior acts of lesser misconduct indicating a pattern. Knowledge of fitness may be actual or presumed. In Brancon v. Chapman, LR #10509 (W.D. Tennessee, 1981), the court held a police director liable for damages to a couple who had been assaulted by a police officer. The judge said that the officer's reputation for using excessive force and as someone with mental problems was well known among the police officers in his precinct and that the director therefore ought to have known of the officer's dangerous propensities and ought to have fired him before he assaulted the plaintiffs. This unjustified inaction was held to be the cause of the injuries to the couple, for which they could be compensated.

In McCrink v. City of New York, 71 N.E. 2d 419 (Ct. App. N.Y., 1947), a police commissioner who personally interviewed an errant officer and yet retained him after a third offense of intoxication while on duty was deemed to have actual knowledge of the officer's unfitness. In contrast, presumed knowledge arises where a supervisor should have known or, by exercising reasonable diligence, could have known the unfitness of an officer. No supervisory liability arises where the prior acts of misconduct were minor or unforeseeable based on the prior conduct of the officer.

Supervisory liability may be found if the agency's disciplinary system is inadequate. In one case, the head of the police department disciplinary system was held personally liable as a supervisor because the court found the system to be so grossly deficient as to reflect a reckless and callous indifference to the rights of the citizens. Gutierrez-Rodriguez v. Cartagena, 882 F.2d 553 (1st Cir. 1989). Specifically, the court found the following procedures to be inadequate:

1. The officers investigated could refuse to testify or give a statement.

2. The complaining members of the public had to go to the police station if they were to give sworn written statements about police misconduct.

3. The agency did not have any provision for remedial training as one of the disciplinary options.

4. The withdrawal of a complaint closed the internal investigation without the agency doing anything about it.

5. The immediate supervisors of the officers were not at all involved in the disciplinary process.

This case indicates that (1) a department must have clear disciplinary procedures, and (2) these procedures must be adequate and proper, not just in terms of protecting the rights of the police officers involved but also in terms of protecting the rights of the general public.

The best defense against negligent retention is to show that proper action was taken against the employee and that the supervisor did all he or she could to prevent the damage or injury. This suggests that a supervisor must know what is going on in the department. If the supervisor's power to take strong action is limited by agency rules, civil service regulations, or state law, less drastic sanctions, such as transfer, demotion, suspension, or reprimand, may be imposed. It is important for the supervisor to establish good faith in trying to rectify an existing condition. Such good faith efforts must be documented properly.

Proper investigation of any and all complaints against subordinates is needed if a supervisor is to successfully raise a defense. Internal investigation procedures must be in place and followed in cases of complaints or incidents that require investigation. Not all investigations need to be formal or time consuming. The type of investigation required and the procedure to be followed should be defined by agency policy or the agency manual. The results of the investigation must be properly documented by the supervisor. Documentation can range from a brief entry in the personnel record of the officer to a more extensive record of the internal investigation entered in the subordinate's file.

## SUMMARY

Supervisory liability is a relatively new and developing area of law, but it has become a fertile source of civil litigation against public officials. Indications are that the number of lawsuits filed against supervisors will escalate as the courts continue to probe into direct and vicarious liabilities of higher officials and as the public becomes more aware of developing law and the advantages to be derived from the inclusion of supervisors and agencies in state and federal liability lawsuits. It is therefore important for supervisors to be knowledgeable about the nature and scope of the legal liabilities to which they may be exposed in the course of task performance.

Supervisory liability for what subordinates do arises in a variety of circumstances, but the basis is always negligence. While most courts impose supervisory liability only when the negligence is gross or amounts to deliberate indifference, state courts in state tort cases may impose liability based on a lower standard. Regardless of the standard used, the determination of negligence rests with the trier of fact, be it a judge or jury, and so the distinction may not be all that significant.

The developing case law in this field strongly suggests the need for supervisors to know the legal limits of their job and to be more aware of what goes on among, and the competencies of, subordinates in their department. An area that deserves immediate attention, because of increasing court litigation, is negligent failure to train. Problems arise for supervisors because of financial constraints occasioned by the reluctance of political decision makers to commit financial resources to training, despite a perceived need. Negligence in providing adequate training carries serious legal implications for supervisors and decision makers, and hence the provision of such training must be given proper and immediate attention.

## NOTES

1. *Legal Defense Manual*, Brief No. 87–1, at 10.
2. S. Nahmod, *Civil Rights and Civil Liberties Litigation*, 2d ed. (Shepard's McGraw-Hill, 1986), at 174.
3. See *Liability Reporter*, August 1985, at 3.
4. *Risk Management Manual for Texas Police Departments* (Texas Advisory Commission on Intergovernmental Relations, August 1986).

5. P. Hardy and J. Weeks, "Personal Liability of Public Officials under Federal Law" (1980, unpublished manuscript), at 7.
6. J. Palmer, "Civil Liability of Correctional Workers" (1980, unpublished manuscript), at 24.

## CASE BRIEFS

### RONALD HELLER v. CRAIG BUSHEY ET AL.
### 259 F.2d 1371 (9th Cir. 1985)

#### FACTS

Ronald Heller was stopped by the police on suspicion of driving while intoxicated. After unsatisfactory conduct in field sobriety tests, Heller was placed under arrest. Heller later brought suit, claiming that Officer Bushey violated his Fourth and Fourteenth Amendment rights by arresting him without reasonable cause and by the use of excessive force. Heller also filed a Section 1983 claim against various city government officials and the city, alleging that it was also liable because the officer had acted pursuant to an official policy condoning excessive force. The district court dismissed the individual government members as defendants and replaced them with the city board of police commissioners and the police department. The jury returned a verdict for the officer, and the court dismissed the action against the municipal entities. The plaintiff appealed.

#### ISSUE

Did the district court act properly in substituting the Los Angeles Board of Police Commissioners and the Los Angeles Police Department (as agencies) for the individual government defendants? No.

#### COURT DECISION

In an action against police supervisors for a policy that may give rise to police misconduct, the proper defendants are those who were in office at the time of the incident and who may have had a hand in the policymaking. The substitution of defendants by the court in this case was therefore improper.

#### CASE SIGNIFICANCE

In legal liability cases, plaintiffs often include supervisors and agencies as defendants because of their involvement in the case and because of their "deeper pockets." Supervisors, however, come and go. Should a supervisor leave office and a new supervisor be appointed in the course of the lawsuit, will the old supervisor be dismissed as a defendant and the new supervisor substituted in his or her place? This case indicates that such substitution is improper: The proper defendants are those who were in office at the time of the incident and thus may have had a hand in making the policy that led to the injury of the plaintiff. This is a sound doctrine; otherwise liability could be avoided by a supervisor through resignation from office.

## FUNDILLER v. CITY OF COOPER
### 777 F.2d 1436 (11th Cir. 1985)

### FACTS

During a drug transaction with an undercover police officer, Fundiller was shot five times without provocation. Uniformed officers arriving at the scene dragged Fundiller from the car and handcuffed him, exacerbating one of his wounds. Fundiller brought suit in United States District Court, charging that (1) he was denied his right to due process guaranteed by the Fifth and Fourteenth Amendments; (2) the city had a custom of negligently hiring, training, and supervising its police officers; (3) the city was negligent in allowing such a custom to exist; and (4) the police officers' actions constituted assault and battery. The district court ruled that there was no federal issue involved and that it had no jurisdiction in state matters. Charges were therefore dismissed.

### ISSUE

Is the use of nonlethal force by the police actionable under Section 1983, and may police supervisors and the agency be held liable for what their subordinates do? *Yes.*

### COURT DECISION

Nonlethal force may be actionable under Section 1983, and when a custom traceable to official policy is linked to the injury, the city and its officials may also be liable.

### CASE SIGNIFICANCE

This case set the standard for determining the liability of municipalities and their officials and officers for practices that have become a custom or policy. The court ruled that for a custom to be substantial enough to engender liability, it must be "created" by an individual who may be said to represent official policy and there must be a causal link between the act and the custom. The court conceded, however, that the custom does not necessarily have to be adopted by the rule-making authority to have the force of law. Additionally, the court ruled that, even though supervisors do not incur liability for employees solely based on respondeat superior, there only needs to be a causal link between the employees' acts and the acts of the supervisor for liability to be established. The court also ruled that participation in an act is not necessary for an officer to be held liable; mere presence at the scene and a failure to protect the victim suffices for liability.

## WILL v. MICHIGAN DEPARTMENT OF STATE POLICE
### 45 Crl 3087 (1989)

### FACTS

Ray Will filed a Section 1983 case, alleging that he was denied promotion in violation of his constitutional rights to a data systems analyst position in the department because his brother had been a student activist and the subject of a "red squad" file maintained by the department. Claiming that his constitutional rights were violated, he named as defendants the Michigan Department of State Police and the Director of State Police in his official capacity.

### ISSUE

May state officials, acting in their official capacity, be sued under Section 1983 in a state court? *No.*

### SUPREME COURT DECISION

Neither the state nor state officials acting in their official capacities may be sued under Section 1983. A suit against state officials in their official capacity is in fact a suit against the state itself. Therefore, it will not succeed, because a state cannot be sued under Section 1983.

### REASON

"Section 1983 provides a federal forum to remedy many deprivations of civil liberties. The Eleventh Amendment bars such suits unless the State has waived its immunity. . . . Given that a principal purpose behind the enactment of Section 1983 was to provide a federal forum for civil rights claims, and that Congress did not provide such a federal forum for civil rights claims against States, we cannot accept petitioner's argument that Congress intended nevertheless to create a cause of action against States to be brought in State courts, which are precisely the courts Congress sought to allow civil rights claimants to avoid through Section 1983."

### CASE SIGNIFICANCE

This decision has limited significance, because it applies only to state law enforcement officials and not to the local police. Public officials can be sued either in their public capacity or private capacity. If an officer is successfully sued in his or her public capacity, the agency will most likely pay, as long as the officer acted within the scope of authority. If sued in his or her personal capacity, the liability is personal with the officer and so the agency will most likely refuse to pay. Plaintiffs prefer to sue officials in their public capacity because of the "deep pockets" theory. *Will* says that state officials cannot be sued under Section 1983 in state courts in their official capacity, because the Eleventh Amendment exempts the states from liability in such lawsuits, unless liability is waived. This decision extends state immunity to state public officials when sued in state courts in their official capacity on the grounds that such lawsuits are in fact lawsuits against states. The following points, however, need to be emphasized in connection with this decision:

1. This case says that state officials cannot be sued in their official capacity in a Section 1983 suit filed in a *state court*. It has long been settled that state officials cannot be sued in their official capacity in a Section 1983 suit filed in a *federal court*.

2. Although state officials cannot now be sued in their official capacity in a Section 1983 lawsuit, they can be sued in their personal capacity, although that approach is less attractive to plaintiffs.

3. State officials can be sued in their official or personal capacity in a state tort case, because *Will* applies only to Section 1983 cases.

4. *Will* applies only to state public officials. Most law enforcement officers are municipal or county officials and therefore may be sued in their official or private capacity under Section 1983. This is because the Eleventh Amendment grants immunity only to states, not to local governments.

# 15

# LIABILITIES OF POLICE SUPERVISORS FOR WHAT THEY DO TO SUBORDINATES

## I. SOURCES OF EMPLOYEE RIGHTS

As stated in Chapter 14, supervisory liability is best classified into liability for *what subordinates do* and liability for *what supervisors do to their subordinates*. This chapter discusses liability for what supervisors do to their subordinates.

Chapter 2 summarizes the types of liability to which police officers are exposed in connection with their work. Among various possibilities, two emerge as the most likely remedies plaintiffs will use: lawsuits under state tort law and lawsuits under Section 1983. Supervisors are particularly exposed to these types of lawsuits. In addition, there are other federal and state laws that increase a supervisor's liability exposure. These laws will be discussed in this chapter.

Responsibilities arise in hiring, termination, demotion, suspension, or reassignment. There are usually two issues important in supervisor-subordinate liability cases. The first has to do with the *cause* for which an employee was terminated, demoted, suspended, or reassigned. The second issue involves the *procedure* that must be followed before an employee may be terminated, demoted, suspended, or reassigned. Both cause and procedure for supervisory action are governed by the following (ranked according to order of priority):

1. *The contract with the employee, if any exists.* In most cases, no such contract exists in public employment; hence the employee invokes other sources of rights. Most police officers do not have an individual contract with the police department. Instead they work under general provisions applicable to all other police officers.

2. *Collective bargaining agreements.* In some states, the police are unionized and disciplinary causes and procedures might be governed by a collective bargaining agreement.

3. *Agency rules, regulations, manuals, and guidelines.* In the absence of an individual contract, the employee relies on agency rules, regulations, manuals, and guidelines. In many police departments, these specify the causes for which an employee may be disciplined and the procedure to be followed. Most courts consider agency manuals or handbooks as sources of police officers' rights, and therefore the causes and procedures specified therein must be followed by the department even if they give more rights than what state law or policy allows.

4. *State law and court decisions governing employment.* In the absence of a contract or agency rules, the agency relies on state law or court decisions, even if these are not specified in the agency rules and regulations. In most departments, however, the rules and regulations incorporate applicable state law that the department is bound to follow. State law may include civil service rules applicable to government employees.

5. *Basic constitutional rights.* These include freedom of speech and the rights of association, due process, equal protection, and privacy. All employees have constitutional rights, and these rights are not necessarily waived when an employee accepts a job. There are some rights a public employer cannot force an employee to waive even if the employee signs a waiver. These are rights considered so fundamental that requiring a waiver as a condition for employment amounts to coercing a waiver, which makes it invalid. For example, a waiver of freedom of religion or speech as a condition of employment is not necessarily valid, even if the employee signs the waiver, unless a compelling reason justifies the agency's request for such waiver.

These sources of rights are not mutually exclusive and in fact supplement each other in many cases. For example, an employee contract may be supplemented by prevailing state laws in matters not covered by the contract. Moreover, basic constitutional rights prevail over individual contracts or agency regulations; therefore, unconstitutional provisions in contracts or agency guidelines may be challenged in court.

## II. LIABILITY OF SUPERVISORS UNDER SECTION 1983

Section 1983 cases are discussed more extensively in Chapter 4. They are lawsuits brought against public officials alleging violations of constitutional rights or rights given under federal law and for which monetary damages and an injunction against certain policies are sought. They may be brought against police officers or supervisors who violate constitutional or federally given rights belonging to members of the general public. In the case of supervisors, civil rights cases may be brought by subordinates whose constitutional rights have allegedly been violated by their supervisors.

The two basic requirements of a civil rights lawsuit are these: (1) The defendant must have been acting under color of law, and (2) there must have been a violation of a constitutional or federally protected right. When supervisors make decisions affecting their subordinates, those decisions come under color of law and therefore fulfill the first requirement. The more difficult question concerns the second requirement.

Many issues in a supervisor-subordinate relationship can lead to the filing of a Section 1983 case. A potential Section 1983 case arises whenever there is an alleged violation of a subordinate's constitutional rights. A supervisor must ask the question, What are the constitutional rights of my subordinates? This section reviews these constitutional rights briefly and focuses on some of the more pressing and often-litigated issues. It must be stressed, however, that the law on employee's rights is evolving and far from established. Many issues are unresolved, and court decisions even in the same jurisdiction are sometimes in conflict. It is important that reference be made to local law and court decisions regardless of what is said here. The discussion in this chapter merely provides a general framework for understanding employee rights; it is not meant to be an authoritative guide in all jurisdictions.

As a general rule, an employee may be disciplined if the supervisor can prove that what the employee did (1) impairs the employee's efficiency in the department, or (2) demonstrably affects the employee's job performance. The problem is that these two standards tend to be subjective and may be interpreted differently in various jurisdictions.

## A. First Amendment Rights

Amendment I to the United States Constitution provides that "Congress shall make no law respecting an establishment of religion, or prohibiting the free exercise thereof; or abridging the freedom of speech, or of the press; or the right of the people peaceably to assemble, and to petition the Government for a redress of grievances." This amendment is the source of the five fundamental freedoms: religion, speech, press, assembly, and petition for redress of grievances.

**1.  *Freedom of Religion.*** Questions arise as to whether an applicant may be denied employment or whether a current employee may be dismissed if religious beliefs prohibit the applicant or employee from working on a certain day. For example, may an officer be fired if religious beliefs proscribe him or her from working during Sundays or religious holidays? Most courts hold that an agency must *reasonably accommodate* the religious practices of employees if that is at all possible. Adverse action may be taken only when such practices cause undue hardship on the agency. It is easier for big police departments than for small ones to accommodate the religious practices of their officers. For example, a department with a hundred officers would find it easier to allow officers time off during religious holidays than a department with four officers. The burden of proving undue hardship rests with the agency.

**2. *Freedom of Speech and Freedom of the Press.*** Freedom of speech and of the press may cause employment-related problems. For example, may officers be disciplined for criticizing superiors or departmental policies? Courts have generally held that freedom of speech and of the press are not lost because of employment. Such freedoms, however, may be limited. The classic First Amendment standard is that no one has the freedom to yell "Fire" in a crowded theatre, because the danger from an ensuing panic overrides a person's freedom of speech.

A balance must be struck between an employee's freedom of speech and the department's right to maintain discipline and efficiency. False statements made knowingly, with recklessness, and with malice are not protected by the First Amendment.[1] For example, an off-duty police officer who was in a nightclub falsely charged that on-duty officers who were about to close the nightclub because of overcrowded conditions were harassing the club, and he also stated that the owner ought not to be harassed because he was a supporter of the police department and did not deserve the harassment. The dismissal of the officer for making these statements was upheld on the ground that such statements were unsubstantiated and were made with the knowledge by the officer that they were false. Hughes v. Whitmer, 714 F.2d 1407 (8th Cir. 1983).

Criticism regarding matters of legitimate "public concern" is protected by an employee's freedom of speech, but criticism regarding matters of "private concern" is not. In a leading case, an assistant district attorney, after receiving an unwanted transfer to a new position within the district's attorney's office, sent out a questionnaire to her coworkers asking their views on several matters concerning the district attorney's office, including whether these employees had confidence in their particular superiors and whether they felt pressured to work in political campaigns to support candidates specified by the district attorney's office. The district attorney considered this an act of insubordination and fired the employee. In a 5–4 vote, the United States Supreme Court upheld the decision to fire the employee, saying that there is a distinction between employee speech on matters of public concern and speech involving only private concern. The Court considered what the employee did to have touched on matters of private concern; hence it was unprotected by the First Amendment. Connick v. Myers, 461 U.S. 138 (1983). Although *Connick* did not involve a police officer, it did involve a public officer, and therefore it should be applicable to police cases.

Four years later, the United States Supreme Court applied the standard in *Connick* to a case involving an employee in a county constable's office. Rankin v. McPherson, 107 S. Ct. 2891 (1987). In *Rankin*, the Court, in a 5–4 vote, held that a clerical employee in the county constable's office could not be dismissed for what she said. The employee, on hearing of John Hinckley's attempt to assassinate President Reagan, said, "If they go for him again, I hope they get him." The Court decided that the employee's dismissal was a violation of her freedom of speech, saying that the comment was a matter of public concern, for it was in essence a commentary on President Reagan's policies.

Public criticism of an agency's policy on the use of deadly force is protected speech if made in a responsible manner. On the other hand, unfounded and malicious criticism of specific persons within the agency may fall outside the umbrella of protected speech. In a Third Circuit Court of Appeals case, an employee was suspended for two days when she responded to a reporter's questions about alleged disciplinary measures taken in retaliation against her and another employee. The court held that participation by a public employee in an interview sought by a news reporter on a matter of public concern is protected by freedom of speech even if the employee has a personal interest in the substance of the interview. Rode v. Dellarciprete, 845 F.2d 1195 (3d Cir. 1988). If criticism is made by officers, such criticism must be of policies rather than personalities and must be made in a responsible manner and not primarily to destroy a supervisor's or department's reputation. In *The Rights of Law Enforcement Officers*, Will Atchison enumerates the general subject matters that are likely to be protected by the First Amendment, based on decided cases:[2]

1. criticism of the performance of the chief or sheriff
2. discussion of the department's budget
3. speech about departmental procedures
4. speech about departmental morale
5. speech about union issues
6. speech about alleged discrimination
7. speech after an officer has exhausted appeals to the supervisory chain of command
8. speech made in private

9.  whistleblowing speech

The same writer also enumerates the types of speech that are not likely to be protected:[3]

1.  speech that is knowingly false
2.  statements made as an extension of a personal dispute
3.  statements arising from a personality conflict
4.  speech endorsing services related to the job
5.  profanity and name calling
6.  speech that is disruptive of morale

**3. *Freedom of Association.*** This is another source of employer-employee litigation. In police work, the issue usually focuses on the officer's right to join a labor union. The general rule is that police officers have a constitutional right to join a labor union. They do not, however, have a constitutional right to collective bargaining, but such may be allowed by state law or agency policy. The police do not have a constitutional right to resort to strikes or slowdowns, and laws prohibiting strikes by the police have been declared valid. Courts have held that the nature of police work justifies curtailment of this right that is available to other employees whose functions are not as vital to public order.

Freedom of association cannot be used to hinder a good faith effort by the department to discipline an employee. In one case, a police officer filed a civil rights suit against the department, alleging that he was demoted twice because of his support of an opposition candidate. The court rejected his claim, saying that evidence presented during the city council hearing proved that the demotions were justified as disciplinary measures and were not made in retaliation for his political activities. Black v. City of Wentzville, 686 F.Supp. 241 (E.D. MO. 1988). By contrast, in another case, two officers who claimed that they were demoted for supporting a candidate other than the mayor were awarded compensatory and punitive damages. Although the violation of a constitutional right was proved, a motion for a new trial was granted because of improper jury instruction. Bennis v. Gable, 823 F.2d 723 (3d Cir. 1987).

Mere *membership* in a political party cannot be prohibited or used as a basis for disciplinary action, but *participation* in partisan politics may be regulated because of possible conflicts of interest and potential abuse of the prerogatives of one's office. There are federal and state laws restricting the political activities of certain public officers. Those laws have generally been held to be valid as long as they are narrowly drawn and restrict activities, not membership.

## B.  Fourth Amendment Rights

Amendment IV to the United States Constitution states, "The right of the people to be secure in their persons, houses, papers, and effects, against unreasonable searches and seizures, shall not be violated, and no Warrants shall issue, but upon probable cause, supported by Oath or affirmation, and particularly describing the place to be searched, and the person or things to be seized."

A number of recent cases have been decided on the issue of employees' Fourth Amendment rights. In general, these cases say that employees do not lose their Fourth Amendment right not to be subjected to unreasonable searches and seizures by virtue of employment, but this right can be limited. Two areas call for elaboration: drug testing and searches of an employee's desk and file cabinet.

**1.  *Drug Testing.*** Two cases have been decided by the Supreme Court on drug testing public employees. Although these cases did not involve police officers, they give helpful insight into what the Court would likely allow.

In the first case, Skinner v. Railway Labor Executives' Association, 44 CrL 3189 (1989), the Court, on a 7–2 vote, held that employees do have Fourth Amendment rights but that in this instance testing wit 10ut warrant was justified because of the government interest involved. The Federal Railroad Administration had promulgated regulations requiring railroads to conduct blood and urine tests without warrant following several major train accidents. The employees challenged this rule on the grounds that it violated their Fourth Amendment rights. The Court rejected the challenge, saying that testing without warrant in this instance was justified because of the government's interest in regulating the conduct of railroad employees engaged in safety-sensitive tasks. The Court said that the government interest involved plainly justified prohibiting employees from using alcohol or drugs while on duty, adding that the interest involved presented "special needs" beyond normal law enforcement and therefore warranted departure from the usual warrant and probable cause requirements.

In a secor-d case, National Treasury Employees Union v. Von Raab, 44 CrL 3192 (1989), the Court, on a 5–4 vote, held that suspicionless drug testing was reasonable. The United States Customs Service had implemented a drug-screening program that required urinalysis tests of employees in three categories: (1) employees seeking transfer or promotion to positions having direct involvement in drug interdiction, (2) employees required to carry firearms, and (3) employees required to handle classified material. The program was challenged by the employees' union on the basis of a Fourth Amendment violation. The Court rejected the challenge, saying that the government's compelling interests in public safety and in safeguarding the borders justified employee drug testing without suspicion. The Court added that employees seeking positions in the Customs Service that required drug testing had diminished privacy rights.

These two cases do not necessarily authorize police departments to conduct random and suspicionless drug testing of police officers. That issue has yet to be resolved by the United States Supreme Court. What they say is that drug tests under the circumstances are reasonable. In *Skinner*, drug testing took place after a major train accident and was therefore for cause, while in *Von Raab* drug testing was allowed only for employees who were directly involved in drug interdiction or who were required to carry firearms or handle classified material. *Skinner* and *Von Raab* do not speak to the question of random testing or testing without cause. Lower court decisions on across-the-board drug testing of police officers are not consistent; some courts say that they are valid because of the nature of police work, while other courts say they are unconstitutional. In the absence of an authoritative decision from the United States Supreme Court, mandatory and random drug testing of police officers will have to be considered on a case-by-case basis.

While random and suspicionless drug testing of police officers may be of doubtful constitutionality, drug testing *for cause* has been consistently declared valid by the courts. What is less clear is whether "cause" means mere suspicion, reasonable suspicion, or probable cause. Lower courts have also decided that preemployment drug testing and drug testing during regular physical examinations are also valid.

**2. Search of an Employee's Desk and File Cabinet.** Do employers need a warrant or probable cause to search an employee's desk and file cabinet in his or her public office? The United States Supreme Court has said no, stating that there is no need for a government employer to have a warrant or probable cause for a search "that is appropriately initiated and reasonable in scope, and conducted either for a non-investigatory, work-related purpose or to investigate work-related misconduct." O'Connor v. Ortega, 41 CrL 3001 (1987). In this case, hospital authorities suspected mismanagement of the hospital's residency program by its chief of professional education. The doctor was placed on administrative leave and hospital authorities seized items from his desk and file cabinets, not making any distinction between his personal property and that owned by the state. The doctor brought a lawsuit under Section 1983, saying that the search violated his Fourth Amendment right because the search was conducted without a search warrant or probable cause. The Court rejected these allegations, saying that although employees have Fourth Amendment rights, employers frequently need to enter the offices and desks of employees for work-related reasons. Requiring an employer to obtain a warrant each time the need arises constitutes an undue burden. The Court added that probable cause for such search was not required, saying that "even when employees are being investigated for work-related misconduct, a governmental employer's interest in conducting efficient operations argues in favor of a lesser standard of suspicion." What is required instead is "reasonable suspicion," a lower standard than probable cause.

*Ortega* says that employees have Fourth Amendment rights but they are limited. To prevent successful challenges, a police department should adopt a policy stating that the desks, lockers, cabinets, offices, and vehicles used by the police are public property and therefore subject to inspection by authorized personnel at any time in connection with any ongoing administrative investigation. This reduces, if not eliminates, employee claims that they have a reasonable expectation of privacy with respect to these public properties.

### C. Fifth Amendment Right

Amendment V to the United States Constitution provides in part, "No person . . . shall be compelled in a criminal case to be a witness against himself, nor be deprived of life, liberty, or property, without due process of law; nor shall private property be taken for public use, without just compensation."

This amendment gives an accused the right against self-incrimination. This right, however, applies to criminal proceedings and not necessarily to administrative investigations against an employee. The general rule is that an employee may be required, on pain of disciplinary action, to answer questions asked in an administrative investigation provided that (1) the questions are directly related to the performance of official duties, and (2) the results of such questioning will not be used in a criminal proceeding.

The use of polygraph examinations has raised constitutional questions. Courts have held that the use of polygraphs for *preemployment* screening is valid and violates no constitutional rights of applicants to police positions. Its use *during employment* has been held by the courts to be valid subject to the two conditions stated in the preceding paragraph.

### D. Fourteenth Amendment Rights

Amendment XIV of the United States Constitution provides in part, "No State shall make or enforce any law which shall abridge the privileges or immunities of the citizens of the United States; nor shall any

State deprive any person of life, liberty, or property, without due process of law; nor deny to any person within its jurisdiction the equal protection of the laws." This amendment is the source of the right to *due process* and the right to *equal protection*.

**1. *Due Process.*** Due process may be *procedural* or *substantive*. Procedural due process involves questions of "fundamental fairness," while substantive due process involves matters that are outside the regulatory power of the state. Procedural due process is usually invoked in police cases where the issue is the fairness of certain disciplinary procedures. For example, must an officer be given a hearing before he or she is fired, demoted, suspended, or transferred? The answer is that these matters are usually governed by state statute, case law, or agency policy. Outright dismissal of a permanent employee required due process, because a property interest (the job being considered property) is involved. What process is due depends on the provisions of state law, agency policy, or court decisions. For example, if a hearing must be given, must the other pertinent constitutional rights (such as the right to counsel, to cross-examination, and against self-incrimination) also be respected. Probationary or provisional employees generally do not enjoy due process rights, because no property interest is involved at this stage of employment.

If the agency has procedures for disciplinary action, such procedures must be followed. Supervisors must be aware of the concept of "state-created liberty interest." What this means is that if a right is not given by the Constitution but is otherwise provided for by state law, local ordinance, or agency policy, then the individual is entitled to due process to determine if in fact the relevant provisions have been followed. For example, if departmental policy provides that an officer can be suspended only if what he or she did brings discredit to the department in the eyes of the public, then a hearing must be given to determine if in fact this cause was present. The procedures outlined by state law, local ordinance, or agency policy must be followed. Some police departments come under state civil service rules, while others do not. If civil service rules apply, they must also be followed.

In one case, the equal protection clause was used by plaintiffs to challenge the constitutionality of polygraph tests to screen police applicants. In this case, unsuccessful applicants for police and correctional officer positions challenged the requirement, saying that applicants for other public and private jobs did not have to submit to a polygraph examination. The Third Circuit Court of Appeals rejected the challenge, saying that the plaintiffs lacked the necessary property or liberty interest to make the challenge because they had not yet been hired. It noted that the burden was on the applicants to demonstrate that the use of a polygraph test (now used in approximately 50 percent of police departments throughout the country) did not produce better police departments. Anderson v. City of Philadelphia, 845 F.2d 1216 (3rd Cir. 1988). It is clear from this and other cases that the use of polygraph tests to screen applicants is valid. The use of such tests for disciplinary purposes, however, has produced mixed results. Some lower courts say that the tests can be used for administrative purposes; others prohibit their use even if allowed by departmental policy. Police departments will have to be guided by case law in particular jurisdictions.

**2. *Equal Protection.*** The right to equal protection means that all employees must be treated in the same manner unless there is a justifiable basis for treating them differently. The constitutional right to equal protection has been applied primarily to race, meaning that there can be no discrimination based on race. A supervisor who treats officers differently according to race is in clear violation of constitutional rights. Although race can never be the basis for differential treatment, other factors, such as seniority and work classification, can be. Promotion based on seniority is justifiable, and so is differential pay based on the nature of the job performed.

While discrimination based on race is prohibited under the Fourteenth Amendment right to equal protection, discrimination based on sex has not enjoyed such protection. Litigation to combat sex discrimination is better brought by the plaintiff under the provisions of Title VII of the Civil Rights Act of 1964, which clearly prohibits such discrimination.

### E. The Right to Privacy

The right to privacy is not expressly provided for in the Constitution, but the United States Supreme Court has said that it is a constitutional right derived from the amendments. The right to privacy has become a fertile source of litigation in police work.

The general rule is that what an employee does in the privacy of his or her own home is none of the department's business and therefore cannot be the basis for disciplinary action. The exception is if it demonstrably affects job performance. For example, living together without the benefit of marriage is generally no longer a valid basis for disciplinary action. The same is true of sexual behavior unless the person's sexual conduct becomes so open and notorious as to demonstrably bring discredit to the department.

Homosexuality has become a controversial topic in many police departments. The general rule is that a sufficient link must exist between homosexuality and adverse job performance to justify refusal to hire, dismissal, or disciplinary action. In one case, the court held that a homosexual junior high school teacher could not be dismissed or transferred simply because he was a homosexual. Some showing had to be made that his homosexuality was notorious. Acanfora v. Board of Education of Montgomery County, 359 F. Supp. 843 (D.Md. 1973). In another case, the court held that civil servants could not be discharged for homosexuality unless their homosexuality was rationally related to job performance. Norton v. Macy, 417 F.2d 1161 (D.C. Cir. 1969). One writer suggests that "an employer would have a very heavy burden to establish a basis for not hiring an individual who professes to be or is discovered to be a homosexual solely on the status of that person as such." The same writer says that the following must be shown for a refusal to hire based on homosexuality to be valid:

> It must be shown that there is a rational, factual nexus between the potential employee's homosexual conduct and his ability to perform his work; that conduct related to his homosexuality would adversely affect the efficiency of the department and would subject the department to public contempt; and that the refusal to provide a position to such an individual is not arbitrary and capricious.[4]

Some writers maintain, however, that refusal to hire might be justified in states where homosexual conduct is criminally punishable and where such prohibition has been upheld by the court.

While homosexuality itself may be a difficult basis for disciplinary action or employment refusal, lying about homosexuality in an application may justify an adverse action, because the basis for the disciplinary action would not be life-style but lack of honesty.

In other sexual activity cases, the general rule is that an employee's private sexual conduct is within the zone of privacy and is therefore shielded from government intrusion. Most disciplinary actions by supervisors have not been sustained, because these are areas of an employee's life over which the government has no legitimate interest. For example, living with somebody without the benefit of marriage should not be cause for departmental action. An exception occurs if the sexual activities or views of the employee are open and notorious or if such activities take place in a small town where an adverse impact on the department may be demonstrable. An example might be where an officer advocates on television that free sex be encouraged. In such a case, the supervisor might very well have an interest in investigating the employee's activities and terminating the employee. Shuman v. City of Philadelphia, 470 F. Supp. 449 (E.D. Pa. 1979).

An issue closely related to privacy is the question of whether or not police departments can regulate an employee's appearance through grooming and dress codes. Court decisions have answered this in the affirmative, provided there is justification for these regulations. The justification might be that the regulations enhance the department's public image, employee discipline, and departmental morale.

The above discussion indicates some of the difficult issues in a supervisor-subordinate relationship that can lead to the filing of a Section 1983 lawsuit. They are basically employment issues that involve possible violations of constitutional rights. The difficult task is determining what exactly are the constitutional rights of subordinates. This is an extremely complex legal problem that is still in the process of being answered by the courts. Supervisors are therefore strongly advised to seek the aid of legal counsel when making personnel decisions that implicate the constitutional rights of their subordinates.

## III. LIABILITIES OF SUPERVISORS UNDER OTHER FEDERAL LAWS

In addition to Section 1983, which is a federal law passed in 1871, there are other federal laws under which a supervisor may be held liable. Most important among these are Title VII of the Equal Employment Opportunity Act of 1964, the Age Discrimination in Employment Act, the Equal Pay Act, and the Rehabilitation Act of 1973. These laws establish the principle that job qualifications must be job related and that arbitrary job requirements are no longer valid. Only the first three laws will be discussed in this chapter, because the fourth law, the Rehabilitation Act of 1973, is not often invoked in law enforcement employment situations. It basically prohibits recipients of funds from the federal government from discriminating against handicapped persons solely on the basis of their handicap. Its direct relevance in employment situations lies mainly in that AIDS comes under the provisions of this act and that discrimination against applicants with AIDS is therefore prohibited. No court cases have come up in law enforcement on this issue, but although it may not be of significant concern as of now, it may become so in the future.

### A. Title VII of the Equal Employment Opportunity Act of 1964

#### 1. Main Provisions

In 1964, Congress passed a comprehensive law known as the Equal Employment Opportunity Act of 1964, which has had a significant impact on employment practices in the public and private sectors. Section 703(a) of that law makes it unlawful for an employer

1. to fail or refuse to hire or to discharge any individual or otherwise to discriminate against any individual with respect to his compensa-

tion, terms, conditions, or privileges of employment because of such individual's race, color, religion, sex, or national origin; or

2. to limit, segregate, or classify the employees or applicants for employment in any way which would deprive or tend to deprive any individual of employment opportunities or otherwise adversely affect his status as an employee because of such individual's race, color, religion, sex, or national origin.

For law enforcement employment purposes, Title VII of the Equal Employment Opportunity Act of 1964 is most significant. It prohibits discrimination based on five protected categories namely, race, color, religion, sex, and national origin. Discrimination is prohibited in hiring, promotion, discharge, pay, fringe benefits, and other aspects of employment. Other types of discrimination are not covered by this law, although they may be prohibited by other federal laws. For example, discrimination based on age is not protected by the Civil Rights Act of 1964 but is prohibited by another federal law: the Age Discrimination in Employment Act. The other titles of the Civil Rights Act of 1964 prohibit discrimination in education and housing and therefore will not be discussed here.

### 2. Bona Fide Occupational Qualification (BFOQ) Exceptions

A BFOQ is a bona fide occupational qualification. The Equal Employment Opportunity Act of 1964, the Age Discrimination in Employment Act, and the Equal Pay Act all have BFOQ exceptions. This means that discrimination under these laws may be allowed as long as the discrimination is based on a bona fide occupational qualification. For example, a religious denomination advertising for a new pastor may specify that the applicant must belong to that religious denomination. BFOQs have been taken by the courts to be qualifications that are "reasonably necessary" for the job and not just "preferable or desirable." For example, it may be preferable to have males as police officers, but maleness is not reasonably necessary for the job; therefore it is not a BFOQ. On the other hand, it is reasonably necessary and not just preferable that a minister of a Methodist church be Methodist.

Race or color will not be considered by the courts as a BFOQ. This means that while discrimination based on religion, sex, or national origin may be allowed if a BFOQ is established, discrimination based on race or color will not be allowed. In order for discrimination based on religion, sex, national origin, or age group to be allowed on the basis of a BFOQ, the following two questions must be answered in the affirmative by the agency: (1) Does the job require that the person performing it be of a particular sex, national origin, religion, or age group? (2) Is such requirement reasonably necessary for the job and not simply preferable or desirable?

The burden of proving a BFOQ is on the agency and not on the person challenging it. Establishing a BFOQ is a difficult task, and therefore a BFOQ defense seldom succeeds.

### 3. *Types of Prohibited Discrimination*

a) *Discrimination Based on Race.* Supervisors must be familiar with some of the basic prohibitions and case law for each of the protected categories, namely, race, color, religion, sex, and national origin.

Racial discrimination is prohibited by the Civil Rights Act of 1964, but it also violates the equal protection clause of the Fourteenth Amendment. It is therefore actionable under both laws. This type of discrimination is absolutely prohibited, meaning it cannot be justified on the basis of a BFOQ. A supervisor will not be allowed to establish in court that there was a bona fide reason for discriminating on the basis of race.

The term "race" is generic, and the Civil Rights Act of 1964 protects all races, not just blacks or Hispanics. It also prohibits discrimination against whites. Racial discrimination is prohibited both in the hiring of applicants and the treatment of employees. The prohibition includes various forms of racially oriented harassment that may create a hostile or offensive work environment for the employee.[5]

As in the case of discrimination based on sex, racial discrimination may be unintentional—yet such discrimination is nonetheless prohibited.

Discrimination may be of two types: *disparate treatment* and *disparate impact*. Disparate treatment discrimination is more open and easier to prove. An example would be an outright refusal to hire Hispanics or women. Disparate impact discrimination is subtle and more difficult to prove, because it may involve rules and practices that are, on the surface, neutral and generally acceptable. For example, specific height and weight requirements in police departments have, in the past, been acceptable. They are no longer valid, because they discriminate against Orientals and women, who are generally shorter and lighter. What is valid, however, is the requirement of proportionality, meaning that a person's weight must be proportional to his or her height.

Another possible example of disparate impact discrimination is the use of written examinations. These examinations are valid as long as they are job related. The Civil Rights Act of 1964 provides that a written test is not unlawful "provided that such test, its administration or action upon the results is not designed, intended or used to discriminate because of race, color, religion, sex, or national origin." If the written examination is unrelated to job performance, the examination is invalid. In one case, a company in North Carolina that operated a generating plant required a high school diploma or the passing of an intelligence test as a condition of employment at the plant. Black employees brought action under Title VII of the Civil Rights Act of 1964, challenging the validiy of these requirements. They alleged the requirements were not job related and had the effect of excluding blacks from promotion or qualification for the better paying jobs. The United States Supreme Court agreed, saying that the purpose of the act was the elimination of artificial, arbitrary, and unnecessary employment barriers that discriminate on the basis of race and the other protected categories. If requirements are not shown to be job related, they must be considered invalid. Griggs v. Duke Power Company, 401 U.S. 424 (1978).

In the case of police departments, written examinations are considered valid as long as they are unchallenged. If challenged by a racial group, the initial burden of proving discrimination based on test results is with the complainants. Discrimination is proved through the 80 percent rule. If discrimination is established, the burden of proving that the examination is job related shifts to the agency. The 80 percent rule provides that discrimination is established if the selection or success rate for any race, sex, or ethnic group is less than 80 percent when compared with the selection rate of the majority group.

EXAMPLE: Assume that only 60 percent of blacks who take the police examination pass, while 80 percent of whites who take the examination pass. The passing rate for blacks is only 75 percent when compared with the passing rate of whites (60 divided by 80 = 75). The test is therefore discriminatory, because 75 percent is less than 80 percent. Now assume that 70 percent of blacks pass the examination, compared with 80 percent of whites. The passing rate for blacks is 87.5 percent when compared with the passing rate of whites (70 divided by 80 = 87.5). Since this is more than 80 percent, the test is not considered discriminatory against blacks.

Two things must be noted in connection with the 80 percent rule. First, the rule applies to other forms of alleged discriminatory treatment and not just to the use of examinations. For example, it also applies to disproportinate hiring from a pool of applicants, as when 80 percent of white applicants but only 60 percent of black applicants are hired. Second, even if discrimination is found by using the 80 percent rule, the discrimination may be justified if it is based on a BFOQ. However, the burden of proving a BFOQ is on the agency once discrimination has been established.

Asking an applicant about his or her arrest record (if such exist) is generally prohibited unless there is a justifiable reason for this inquiry. Equal Employment Opportunity Commission (EEOC) rules hold that it is unlawful to refuse to hire an applicant merely because of a record of arrest, the assumption being that arrest is not equivalent to guilt. Taking into account an arrest record may be considered a form of racial discrimination, because statistics show that more racial minorities, for one reason or another, are arrested by the police.

Refusal to hire based on criminal conviction leads to legal problems. EEOC rules prescribe that "it is unlawful to discharge or refuse to employ a minority person based on a conviction record unless the particular circumstances of each case (such as the time, nature, and number of convictions and the employee's immediate past employment record) indicate that the employment of that particular person for a particular job is 'manifestly inconsistent with the safe and efficient operation of that job.' "[6] What constitutes manifest inconsistency with the safe and efficient operation of a job in law enforcement is not clear. What is clear, however, is that it is easier to invoke this criterion in law enforcement work than in other types of public jobs. No cases, however, indicate authoritative guidelines for police supervisors to use on the issue of employing applicants convicted of various types of crimes.

**b)** *Discrimination Based on Color.* Color differs from race in that two individuals may come from the same race but be of different color. For example, two applicants may both be "black," but one may be lighter than the other. Hiring the person with the lighter skin based on skin color is a form of discrimination prohibited by law.[7]

**c)** *Discrimination Based on National Origin.* The term *national origin* refers to "the country where the person was born or where such person's ancestors originated."[8] In this type of discrimination, there occurs a "denial of equal employment opportunity because of an individual's, or his or her ancestor's place of origin; or because an individual has the physical, cultural, or linguistic characteristics of a national origin group."[9] Also covered by the prohibition is discrimination based on the fact that the person "is married to or otherwise associated with persons of a certain national origin group or because the person belongs to an organization identified with or promoting a certain national origin group."[10] An example would be the refusal to hire applicants because they are Nigerian, Chinese, or Cuban or because they speak English with an accent.

Requiring American citizenship for employment is discrimination based on national origin. The general rule is that American citizenship may be required only if it is necessary for job performance. For example, the United States Supreme Court has held that citizenship is a BFOQ for the job of law enforcement officer, stating that to be effective, an officer must be familiar with the norms, mores, and practices of the group he or she is policing.

Height and weight requirements are considered discriminatory unless justified as BFOQs. Requirements that law enforcement officers be of a certain height and weight are invalid unless necessary for job performance, which would be hard for an agency to establish. Instead of specifying height and weight, law enforcement qualifications are better stated in terms of height and weight proportionality. For example, instead of requiring that an applicant be at least 5′8″ in height and 160 pounds in weight, it is better to require that "height and weight be proportional."

Discrimination based on national origin includes rules mandating the use of English in the workplace. This type of discrimination is justified if it comes under a BFOQ exception, meaning that it is a matter of business necessity, efficiency, or safety. Some states, such as California, have passed laws mandating English as the official language of the state. It remains to be seen whether or not these state laws prevail over the provisions of the Age Discrimination in Employment Act or the rules passed by the EEOC.

**d) *Discrimination Based on Religion.*** Title VII defines religion broadly to include religious observance, belief, and religious practice. The term "religious practices" includes "moral or ethical beliefs as to what is right and wrong which are sincerely held with the strength of traditional religious views." It covers religious beliefs as well as nonbelief in religion, such as atheism.

The general rule is that an employee's religious beliefs and practices must be respected and that employers are under an obligation to "reasonably accommodate" the religious practices of employees. Only when such accommodation creates an "undue hardship" on the employer would discrimination be allowed. For example, if the religious beliefs of a police officer prohibit the officer from working during Sundays, the employer must reasonably accommodate the officer's beliefs. This is easier to do if the department is big, because schedules can be adjusted more easily to meet the need. In a small department, however, such accommodation may cause undue hardship. If the police chief or sheriff can prove this, then such religious discrimination as is necessary may be allowed. The burden of proof falls on the employer.

**e) *Discrimination Based on Sex.*** Discrimination based on sex takes many forms. The most obvious is a prohibition against the employment of women. Police departments had such prohibitions in the past, but they have been abandoned as a result of the Civil Rights Act of 1964. Jails and prisons also used to employ only males, but they have also yielded to nondiscriminatory employment. However, there may be instances when, based on a BFOQ, only members of one sex may perform certain types of police work, such as cavity inspections or monitoring the giving of urine samples by prisoners.

Height and weight requirements are also sexually discriminatory. Prescribing a certain height or weight has the unintended effect of discriminating against women because they tend to be shorter and lighter than men. For example, in Dothard v. Rawlinson, 433 U.S. 321 (1977), the state of Alabama required an applicant to be 5'2" in height and 120 pounds in weight to qualify for the job of correctional counselor (prison guard). Statistics showed that this height requirement would disqualify more than one-third of all women in the United States and that the weight requirement would disqualify more than one-fourth. By contrast, the height requirement would disqualify only 1.28 percent of all men, and the weight requirement would disqualify only 2.35 percent. The United States Supreme Court concluded that these requirements, although nondiscriminatory on their face, would in fact have a discriminatory effect on women; therefore they were prohibited by the Civil Rights Act of 1964.

A third type of sex discrimination involves pregnancy. The current rule is that an employer must treat pregnancy like all other medical disabilities and provide access to benefits or health programs. This does not mean that an employer must have a health or benefit program for employees; instead, current law requires that if such program is available, pregnancy must be treated just like the other disabilities.[11] For example, firing a woman because she is pregnant or depriving her of seniority because of a pregnancy leave is illegal. Laws mandating pregnancy leaves for women employees before and after delivery are also invalid under this law. While pregnancy leaves for women are to be treated like leaves for all other disabilities, paternity leaves for men have not been authoritatively addressed by law or by the courts. Some cases maintain that giving maternity leaves to women and refusing paternity leaves to men is a form of sex discrimination. Court decisions on this issue have not provided much guidance. The few cases there are have led to inconsistent results.

A fourth type of sex discrimination is sexual harassment. Sexual harassment is defined as "unwelcome verbal or physical conduct of a sexual nature." EEOC guidelines prohibit sexual harassment in the workplace. There are generally four types of sexual harassment:

1. *Quid pro quo harassment.* This takes place when a supervisor takes adverse action against a subordinate because the subordinate refuses to submit to the sexual advances of the supervisor. For example, a police chief propositions a female police officer, who spurns the chief's advances. She is then fired from the police force or demoted in rank. This is the most widespread type of sexual harassment prohibited by EEOC guidelines.

2. *The creation of an intimidating, hostile, or offensive working environment.* This type of harassment occurs when, as a result of a supervisor's action, a subordinate feels that the working environment in the agency has become "intimidating, hostile, or offensive." For example, a sheriff propositions a female deputy. She refuses but no

adverse action is taken by the sheriff—she is not fired or demoted. Despite the absence of an adverse action, the sheriff's proposition by itself may make the working environment intimidating, hostile, or offensive for that female deputy.

3. *Special treatment given to certain employees for sexual favors.* Suppose a police chief promotes one female officer instead of another because of sexual favors granted by the former. Sexual harassment is inflicted on the person who did not get the promotion but who otherwise deserved it.

4. *Harassment by outsiders.* For example, a secretary at the reception desk gets unwanted sexual remarks from outsiders because of her physical endowments. In this case, the police supervisor has an obligation to ensure that efforts are undertaken to protect the employee from the unwelcomed remarks.

Sexual harassment may be by *superiors* or by *peers*. Harassment by superiors of the quid pro quo type automatically leads to agency liability, meaning that if a superior harasses a subordinate in this manner, the agency will automatically be liable if the harassment is established. By contrast, harassment by peers leads to liability on the part of the supervisor only if the supervisor knew or should have known about it but did nothing.

Will a single act constitute sexual harassment? The answer is yes, if the harassment is in the nature of quid pro quo. For example, if a sheriff fires a female deputy for not submitting to his sexual advances, then sexual harassment takes place. In cases where the harassment is brought about through the creation of an intimidating, hostile, or offensive working environment, there is harassment only if the single act is so severe as to automatically create that type of environment. Usually, however, this type of harassment involves repetition of the offensive behavior.

The following suggestions should minimize a supervisor's exposure to liability in sexual harassment cases:

1. The agency should have a well-written and comprehensive policy regarding sexual harassment.

2. The policy must contain procedures for the filing of complaints and provide prompt response to allegations of sexual harassment.

3. The policy must be reviewed by a knowledgeable lawyer familiar with sexual harassment guidelines and case law.

4. The policy must be disseminated among agency personnel.

5. Agency personnel must be informed of and given proper training concerning the policy.

6. All complaints must be in writing and be properly and promptly investigated.

7. All violations must be punished appropriately.

8. All investigations and disciplinary actions by the agency must be documented properly.

### 4. Enforcement and Implementation

Enforcement and implementation of Title VII of the Civil Rights Act of 1964 is left to the EEOC, a federal agency headed by a five-person board, with headquarters in Washington, D.C., and with regional offices throughout the country. The EEOC is authorized to pass guidelines implementing the provisions of the law. These guidelines are not binding on the courts but are usually given a lot of weight by judges when deciding cases. The guidelines are valid unless declared otherwise by the courts.

Over the years, the EEOC has passed numerous guidelines expanding the provisions of the law and prohibiting discrimination that involves the five protected categories but is not explicitly mentioned in the law. For example, sexual harassment by employers is not expressly mentioned in Title VII of the Civil Rights Act of 1964, but it is prohibited by EEOC regulations on the grounds that it is a form of sex discrimination. In 1979, a presidential reorganization order gave the EEOC authority to enforce not only the provisions of the Civil Rights Act of 1964 but also the provisions of the Age Discrimination in Employment Act and the Equal Pay Act. The EEOC has therefore become an umbrella organization that enforces the provisions of antidiscrimination laws.

Enforcement of the provisions of Title VII of the Civil Rights Act is different from enforcement of Section 1983. While a Section 1983 lawsuit is filed directly in federal court (although the jurisdiction may sometimes be concurrent with state court), complaints of discrimination based on the Civil Rights of 1964 are first filed with the EEOC. The commission investigates the complaint and, if the complaint is meritorious, tries to come to an amicable settlement with the agency without having to go to court. The commission is mandated by law to try to settle complaints by conference, conciliation, mediation, or persuasion. If no satisfactory settlement is reached, the commission, through the United States Attorney's Office, may then file a case in federal court. If the commission refuses to file the case, the person allegedly discriminated against may obtain a "right to sue" letter from the commission and may then pursue the remedy on his or her own.

The EEOC need not enforce the provision of the Civil Rights Act of 1964 on its own. The law itself provides for possible enforcement by state and local authorities. Several states have reenacted the provisions of Title VII of the Civil Rights Act of 1964 to prohibit the same type of discrimination at the state level. If such a law is enacted by a state, the EEOC usually adopts a "hands off" policy and allows the state to enforce the law. This has the advantage of a more intensive and immediate enforcement at the state level and frees the federal government from enforcement responsibilities, except when implementation lags or is ineffective. In return, the federal government gives money through grants to state governments to encourage the passage and implementation of antidiscrimination laws.

Most state laws prohibiting discrimination on the basis of race, color, religion, sex, and national origin are called "human rights commission laws." In addition to prohibiting discrimination based on the five protected categories, state laws usually add provisions prohibiting discrimination based on age and physical handicap. State laws typically authorize the creation of human rights commissions at the local level. This means that if a local government decides to enforce the law on its own, the local government can pass an ordinance providing for local implementation and prosecution of violations. In these cases, the state leaves the implementation and enforcement of the law to local authorities.

### 5. Remedies under Title VII of the Civil Rights Act of 1964

The Civil Rights Act of 1964 does not impose personal liability on the supervisor. The remedies imposed are usually directed against the agency. Remedies for violations include these:

- The agency may be ordered to hire, reinstate, or promote the employee who has been discriminated against.
- An injunction may be issued against the repetition or continuation of the discriminatory practice.
- The agency may be made to pay backpay or actual wages the victim of the discrimination would have earned.
- The agency may be ordered to adopt an affirmative action program for minority hiring.
- Damages may be awarded to the person discriminated against.
- Plaintiff's attorney's fees and the cost of litigation may be awarded at the expense of the agency.

By contrast, Section 1983 cases have only two forms of remedy: damages and injunction.

### 6. Similarities and Differences Between Title VII of the Civil Rights Act of 1964 and Section 1983

The similarities and differences between Title VII of the Civil Rights Act of 1964 and Section 1983 may be summarized as follows:

SIMILARITIES

1.   Both are federal laws.
2.   Both laws prohibit certain types of employment practices.
3.   Both laws involve court action to settle disputes.
4.   Both laws provide penalties for violation.


DIFFERENCES

| | SECTION 1983 | TITLE VII OF THE CIVIL RIGHTS ACT OF 1964 |
|---|---|---|
| 1. When enacted: | Became law in 1871. | Became law in 1964. |
| 2. What is prohibited: | Prohibits violations of constitutional rights, including discrimination based on race. | Prohibits discrimination based on five protected categories: race, color, religion, sex, and national origin. |
| 3. Type of violation: | Usually covers only intentional violations. | Covers both intentional and unintentional discrimination. |
| 4. Enforcement: | Enforced directly through a lawsuit filed in federal or sometimes state court. | Enforced through a complaint filed with the Equal Employment Opportunity Commission. Only if no settlement is arrived at will the EEOC file a case in court. |
| 5. Plaintiff: | Plaintiff is the person discriminated against. | Plaintiff is usually the EEOC. |
| 6. Defendant: | Defendant may be the individual officer or the agency. | Defendant is usually the agency. |
| 7. Remedies: | Remedies consist of damages, injunction, and attorney's fees. | More extensive remedies, including rehiring, backpay, and affirmative action. |

## 7. Equal Employment Opportunity versus Affirmative Action

Equal employment opportunity is what Title VII of the Civil Rights Act of 1964 is intended to achieve. Its purpose is to prohibit employment discrimination based on the five protected categories. In contrast, affirmative action requires minorities to be given employment preference based on past discrimination. (The term *minorities* usually refers to racial minorities, but it can also refer to women, who are in fact a majority.) Affirmative action is not mandated by the Civil Rights Act of 1964, although the absence of a proportional racial, ethnic, or sexual mix may sometimes prove discrimination.[12]

It is clear that the Civil Rights Act of 1964 is constitutional. There is, however, a question whether all affirmative action programs are constitutional. Most United States Supreme Court decisions have upheld affirmative action programs as necessary in view of prior acts of discrimination, but limits have been placed on some programs. In general, racial quotas for affirmative action are frowned upon by the courts, but goals or timetables have been looked upon with approval. The differences between racial quotas and goals or timetables, however, tend to be more symbolic than real, because in either case a preference is being given to a minority group.

The differences between equal employment opportunity and affirmative action may be summarized as follows:

|   | EQUAL EMPLOYMENT OPPORTUNITY | AFFIRMATIVE ACTION |
|---|---|---|
| 1. Purpose: | To prohibit discrimination in hiring, promotions, etc. | To achieve greater minority representation in the work force. |
| 2. Source of authority: | Title VII of the Civil Rights Act of 1964 | Court order or self-initiated agency policy. |
| 3. What it does: | Seeks equal employment opportunities for everybody. | Gives preferences to underrepresented groups in the work force. |
| 4. Who are covered: | Almost all public and private agencies regardless of minority representation. | Only agencies where minorities are underrepresented, including racial minorities and women. |

|  | EQUAL EMPLOYMENT OPPORTUNITY | AFFIRMATIVE ACTION |
|---|---|---|
| 5. When used: | All the time regardless of employment history. | May be initiated by the agency but may be ordered by the court when prior discrimination is shown. |
| 6. Remedy: | Complaint with the EEOC and then lawsuit. | Contempt citation if affirmative action court order is not implemented. |

## B. The Age Discrimination in Employment Act

The Age Discrimination in Employment Act (ADEA), first enacted in 1967 and later amended, protects employees aged forty and above from discrimination in hiring, firing, pay, promotions, fringe benefits, and various other aspects of employment. It protects older persons and applies to all federal, state, and local governments and also to all private employers with twenty or more workers. This law does not protect those younger than forty against age discrimination, because they are not within the protected age group. This sounds strange (why not protect those aged eighteen to thirty-nine?), yet the primary aim of the law is "to promote the employment of older persons based on their ability rather than age." Moreover, state laws often prohibit age discrimination against those as young as eighteen (the usual age of adulthood).

Taken together, the ADEA and state laws make it difficult to retire employees because of age. This should not be much of a problem in police departments, however, because Section 626 (i) of the law provides that, as of 1987, law enforcement officers and firefighters may be refused employment or may be discharged because of their age if (1) the employees are past the limit specified by state or local law, and (2) the refusal to hire or the firing is pursuant to a bona fide hiring or retirement plan.

The ADEA does not apply if the age requirement or limit is (1) a bona fide job qualification (BFOQ), (2) part of a bona fide seniority system or employee benefit plan, or (3) based on reasonable factors other than age, such as physical fitness or productivity. Responsibility for enforcement of the law lies with the EEOC, which is authorized to file lawsuits against erring employers. Violation complaints are therefore filed with the EEOC.

The ADEA originally prohibited discrimination from ages forty to sixty-five but was later amended to include age seventy. In 1987, Congress abolished the mandatory retirement age of seventy for most employees but allowed temporary exemptions for some law enforcement and firefighter positions. Despite the provisions of the ADEA, early retirement may be enforced based on a BFOQ exception. However, the public employer must prove that relative youth is reasonably necessary for the normal operation of a particular job. A BFOQ exception is used by many police agencies to require mandatory retirement at a certain age. The burden of establishing a BFOQ exception rests with the department, and such exceptions are usually judged on a case-by-case basis. Forced retirement of police officers at ages fifty, fifty-five, or sixty have produced mixed results; some courts have upheld early retirement, others have not.

### C. The Equal Pay Act of 1963

The Equal Pay Act (EPA), enacted in 1963, protects employees, men and women, against pay discrimination based on sex. Federal, state, and local government employees come under the act. The following are the main provisions of the law:

1. Sex discrimination in the payment of wages to women and men performing substantially equal work in the same establishment is prohibited.

2. Employers are prohibited from reducing wages of either sex to comply with the law.

3. Labor organizations are prohibited from causing employers to violate the law.

The EPA does not apply to differences in pay if such differences are based on factors other than sex. Examples are pay differences based on seniority, merit, or productivity. Responsibility for enforcement of the law has been given to the EEOC, which is authorized to file a lawsuit in federal court seeking back pay from the agency.

### SUMMARY

The rights of employees in a job may be based on the following: an individual contract with the employee; agency rules, regulations, manuals, and guidelines; state law and court decisions governing employment; and the United States Constitution. These sources are not mutually exclusive; in fact, they often supplement each other.

There are two general sources of supervisory liability: (1) liability under Section 1983, and (2) liability under other federal laws. The two basic requirements for liability under Section 1983 are that the supervisor must have been acting under color of law and that there must have been a violation of a constitutional or of a federally protected right. In the context of the supervisor-subordinate relationship, the following constitutional rights are the most likely sources of litigation: the First Amendment freedoms of religion, speech, press, and association; the Fourth Amendment right against unreasonable searches and seizures; the Fourteenth Amendment rights to due process and equal protection; and the right to privacy.

Supervisory liability can arise under Title VII of the Civil Rights Act of 1964, the Age Discrimination in Employment Act, and the Equal Pay Act, all of which are enforced by the Equal Employment Opportunity Commission. Title VII of the Civil Rights Act of 1964 prohibits discrimination on the basis of race, color, religion, sex, and national origin. The Age Discrimination in Employment Act proscribes discrimination against those aged forty and above, and the Equal Pay Act prohibits pay discrimination based on sex. All of these laws, however, are subject to the bona fide occupational qualification exception.

## NOTES

1. L. K. Questel, *Federal Laws Prohibiting Employment Discrimination: For State and Local Officials* (Carl Vinson Institute of Government, 1989), at 97.
2. W. Atchison, *The Rights of Law Enforcement Officers* (The Labor Relations Information Systems, 1989), at 204–212.
3. *Ibid.*, at 212–218.
4. G. J. Franscell, "Legal Protection for Those with Alternate Lifestyles?" *The Police Chief*, September 1989, at 44.
5. Questel, *Federal Laws Prohibiting Employment Discrimination*, at 33.
6. *EEO Compliance Manual* (Prentice-Hall, 1979), at 1202.
7. C. Roberson, *Staying out of Court: A Manager's Guide to Employment Law* (D.C. Heath and Company, 1985), at 64.
8. Questel, *Federal Laws Prohibiting Employment Discrimination*, at 36.
9. Roberson, *Staying out of Court*, at 64.
10. *Ibid.*
11. *Ibid*, at 35.
12. Questel, *Federal Laws Prohibiting Employment Discrimination*, at 31.

CASE BRIEFS

## O'CONNOR v. ORTEGA
### 480 U.S. 709 (1987)

### FACTS

Officials of a state hospital became concerned about the activities of Magno Ortega, a physician and psychiatrist who was an employee of the state hospital and had primary responsibility for training residents in the psychiatry program. There were allegations against Ortega about dishonesty, sexual harassment of female employees, and an inappropriate disciplinary action against a resident. While Ortega was on administrative leave and an investigation of the charges was pending, hospital officials searched his office and seized personal items from his desk and file cabinets. These were later used in administrative proceedings that resulted in Ortega's discharge. Ortega brought a Section 1983 suit, alleging that the search of his office violated constitutional protection under the Fourth Amendment.

### ISSUE

Is the warrantless search of a government employee's desk and file cabinets a violation of that employee's right under the Fourth Amendment?

### SUPREME COURT DECISION

A search of a government employee's desk and file cabinets without warrant or probable cause by a government employer, either for noninvestigatory, work-related purposes or to investigate work-related misconduct, is reasonable under the Fourth Amendment if it is justified by a work-related need or reasonable suspicion and is reasonable in scope.

### CASE SIGNIFICANCE

This case holds that although public employees are entitled to Fourth Amendment rights while at work, such rights are diminished by work-related considerations. Involved in this case was the seizure of personal items of an employee from his office desk and file cabinets and the use of such items, not in a criminal trial, but in an administrative proceeding. The problem is that, while this case says that warrantless searches of an employee's desk and file cabinets may sometimes be allowed, it fails to provide definitive guidelines for use by agency supervisors. The Court said that "what is reasonable search depends upon the context within which the search takes place, and requires balancing the employee's legitimate expectation of privacy against the government's need for supervision, control, and the efficient operation of the workplace." The Court added that "given the great variety of work environments in the public sector, the question whether an employee has a reasonable expectation of privacy must be addressed on a case-by-case basis." These statements are broad, vague, and fail to provide adequate guidance for supervisors. Given the uncertainty, searches of employees' desks and file cabinets must be done with caution. It is safe to say that places to which other employees have access may be searched without warrant. What is unanswered by this decision, however, is the legality of searches of places in an employee's office to which only the employee has access, such as a file cabinet to which only the employee has the key. This issue will have to be resolved in future cases.


## NATIONAL TREASURY EMPLOYEES UNION v. VON RAAB
### 109 S. Ct. 1384 (1989)


**FACTS**

The United States Customs Service implemented a drug-screening program requiring urinalysis tests without individualized suspicion in three job categories: (1) jobs having a direct involvement in drug interdiction, (2) jobs requiring the employee to carry firearms, and (3) jobs requiring the employee to handle classified material. The program required that an applicant for promotion or transfer be notified that selection was contingent upon successful completion of drug screening, and it set forth procedures for the collection and analysis of urine samples. The employees union filed suit, alleging that the program violated employee rights against unreasonable searches and seizures.


**ISSUE**

Is the drug testing of employees without individualized suspicion and under the circumstances provided for in the Customs Service program a violation of the employees' Fourth Amendment rights?


**SUPREME COURT DECISION**

The suspicionless drug testing program of the Customs Service for employees seeking promotion or transfer to specified positions constitutes "search" within the meaning of the Fourth Amendment, but such search is reasonable and therefore valid in light of the government's compelling interests in public safety and in safeguarding the country's borders and also in light of the diminished privacy interests of employees when seeking such positions.

## CASE SIGNIFICANCE

This case, decided by the United States Supreme Court on a 5–4 vote, is important, because it gives the "go-ahead" to test public employees for drugs in the absence of individualized suspicion. It says that public employees do enjoy Fourth Amendment rights but that such rights are diminished by virtue of public employment. It must be noted, however, that this case does not validate any and all forms of public employee drug testing. Careful attention must be given to the facts of this case, particularly the types of employees who could be subjected to drug testing. The three categories mentioned in the program covered only half of the Customs Service's 16,000 employees.

The decision of the Court came on an close vote. This case was decided together with another case involving the same issue of drug testing. In *Skinner v. Railway Labor Executives' Association*, the Court, voting 7–2, held that drug testing employees pursuant to Federal Railroad Administration regulations that require private railroads to administer blood and urine tests to railroad employees involved in certain kinds of accidents also constituted a "search" within the meaning of the Fourth Amendment but that such was valid because the "special needs" beyond normal law enforcement justified departure from the usual Fourth Amendment warrant and probable cause requirements. There is no question that drug testing police officers "for cause" is valid, as is drug testing for cause in the case of any public employee. What cause is sufficient to justify warrantless drug testing is not clear. Across-the-board and random drug tests of police officers, however, has yet to be addressed by the United States Supreme Court. Lower court rulings are mixed; some courts say it is valid, while others reject it. Court decisions in specific jurisdictions must therefore be looked into and studied.

# AMENDMENTS TO THE CONSTITUTION OFTEN USED IN LAW ENFORCEMENT

The first 10 Amendments were ratified December 15, 1791, and are known as the "Bill of Rights"

**AMENDMENT 1**

Congress shall make no law respecting an establishment of religion, or prohibiting the free exercise thereof; or abridging the freedom of speech, or of the press; or the right of the people peaceably to assemble, and to petition the Government for a redress of grievances.

**AMENDMENT 2**

A well regulated Militia, being necessary to the security of a free State, the right of the people to keep and bear Arms, shall not be infringed.

**AMENDMENT 3**

No Soldier shall, in time of peace be quartered in any house, without the consent of the Owner, nor in time of war, but in a manner to be prescribed by law.

**AMENDMENT 4**

The right of the people to be secure in their persons, houses, papers, and effects, against unreasonable searches and seizures, shall not be violated, and no Warrants shall issue, but upon probable cause, supported by Oath or affirmation, and particularly describing the place to be searched, and the persons or things to be seized.

## AMENDMENT 5

No person shall be held to answer for a capital, or otherwise infamous crime, unless on a presentment or indictment of a Grand Jury, except in cases arising in the land or naval forces, or in the Militia, when in actual service in time of War or public danger; nor shall any person be subject for the same offence to be twice put in jeopardy of life or limb; nor shall be compelled in any criminal case to be a witness against himself, nor be deprived of life, liberty, or property, without due process of law; nor shall private property be taken for public use, without just compensation.

## AMENDMENT 6

In all criminal prosecutions, the accused shall enjoy the right to a speedy and public trial, by an impartial jury of the State and district wherein the crime shall have been committed, which district shall have been previously ascertained by law, and to be informed of the nature and cause of the accusation; to be confronted with the witnesses against him; to have compulsory process for obtaining witnesses in his favor, and to have the Assistance of Counsel for his defense.

## AMENDMENT 7

In Suits of common law, where the value in controversy shall exceed twenty dollars, the right of trial by jury shall be preserved, and no fact tried by a jury, shall be otherwise re-examined in any Court of the United States, than according to the rules of the common law.

## AMENDMENT 8

Excessive bail shall not be required, nor excessive fines imposed, nor cruel and unusual punishments inflicted.

## AMENDMENT 9

The enumeration in the Constitution, of certain rights, shall not be construed to deny or disparage others retained by the people.

## AMENDMENT 10

The powers not delegated to the United States by the Constitution, nor prohibited by it to the States, are reserved to the States respectively, or to the people.

## AMENDMENT 11 (Ratified February 7, 1795)

The Judicial power of the United States shall not be construed to extend to any suit in law or equity, commenced or prosecuted against one of the United States by Citizens of another State, or by Citizens or Subjects of any Foreign State.

## AMENDMENT 14 (Ratified July 9, 1868)

Section 1. All persons born or naturalized in the United States, and subject to the jurisdiction thereof, are citizens of the United States and of the State wherein they reside. No State shall make or enforce any law which shall abridge the privileges or immunities of citizens of the United States; nor shall any State deprive any person of life, liberty, or property, without due process of law; nor deny to any person within its jurisdiction the equal protection of the laws.

# INDEX